Honest Sins
Georgian Libertinism and the Plays and Novels of
Henry Fielding

Originally cruel, manipulative, and self-serving, the Restoration rake evolved during the eighteenth century into a more cheerful sinner: the good-natured libertine. While *Tom Jones* was Henry Fielding's most complete embodiment of this new ideal, Tiffany Potter shows that the revised Georgian libertinism informs and illuminates all of Fielding's work.

Potter is the first author to make clear how English libertinism changed during the eighteenth century as the violent, hypersexualized Hobbesian libertine, typified by the Earl of Rochester, was tempered by England's cultures of sentiment and sensibility. The good-natured Georgian libertinism that emerged maintained the subversive social, religious, sexual, and philosophical tenets of the old libertinism, but misogynist brutality was replaced by freedom and autonomy for the individual, whether male or female. Libertinism encompasses issues of gender, sexuality, and literary and cultural history and thus provides a useful cultural context for a discussion of a number of critical approaches to Fielding's work, including feminism, queer theory, new historicism, and cultural studies.

The traditional view of Fielding as a warm-blooded but essentially prudent moralist is reconsidered here in light of the symbiotic relationship Potter argues existed between Fielding and this mediated libertinism. Fielding developed the discourse in his own terms, beginning with his licentious early plays and continuing with *Shamela* and *Joseph Andrews*, in which Fielding first subverts, then reforms, popular social constructs of virtue. Fielding later develops his archetypal Georgian libertine in *Tom Jones*, and continues his consideration with *Amelia*, whose virtuous heroine embodies Fielding's balance of masculinity and feminity, his controversial understanding of virtue, and the individualism, privilege, and passion of the libertine discourse in which he so prominently positioned himself.

TIFFANY POTTER teaches English at the University of Calgary.

THE UNIVERSITY OF
WINCHESTER

Martial Rose Library
Tel: 01962 827306

To be returned on or before the day marked above, subject to recall.

Honest Sins

Georgian Libertinism and the Plays and Novels of Henry Fielding

Tiffany Potter

McGill-Queen's University Press

Montreal & Kingston · London · Ithaca

© McGill-Queen's University Press 1999
ISBN 0-7735-1803-7

Legal deposit first quarter 1999
Bibliothèque nationale du Québec

Printed in Canada on acid-free paper

This book has been published with the help of a grant
from the Humanities and Social Sciences Federation of
Canada, using funds provided by the Social Sciences
and Humanities Research Council of Canada.

McGill-Queen's University Press acknowledges the financial
support of the Government of Canada through the Book
Publishing Industry Development Program for its activities.
We also acknowledge the support of the Canada Council for
the Arts for our publishing program.

Canadian Cataloguing in Publication Data

Potter, Tiffany, 1967–
    Honest sins: Georgian libertinism and the plays and novels of
    Henry Fielding
    Includes bibliographical references and index.
    ISBN 0-7735-1803-7
    1. Fielding, Henry, 1707–1754 – Criticism and
    interpretation. 2. Libertinism in literature. 3. English
    literature – 18th century – History and criticism. 4. English
    literature – 17th century – History and criticism. I. Title.

    PR3457.P68 1999   823'.5   C98-901108-9

This book was typeset by Typo Litho Composition Inc.
in 10.5/13 Garamond.

For my family

Contents

Preface   ix

1 Toward a Re-vision of Georgian Libertinism   3

2 Early Georgian Libertines: Fielding's Drama   34

3 Georgian Libertinism and the Reclamation of Virtue:
   Shamela and *Joseph Andrews*   74

4 Threads in the Carpet: *Jonathan Wild*   101

5 The Road to Archetypal Georgian Libertinism:
   Tom Jones   119

6 The Mature Faces of Libertinism: *Amelia*   145

   Conclusion   169

   Notes   173

   Bibliography   187

   Index   201

Preface

I first encountered the idea of libertinism in the study of John Wilmot, Earl of Rochester, perhaps the best known and most extreme of the Restoration rakes. In the following years, I often wondered about the apparent extinction of such a powerful discourse so shortly after the death of Charles II. Samuel Richardson's Lovelace and Belford, Henry Fielding's Tom Jones and William Booth, Oliver Goldsmith's good-natured men, and narratives considering gender and power by the likes of Delariviere Manley and Frances Sheridan seemed parts of an ongoing process of recontextualizing libertinism in forms masculine and feminine throughout the eighteenth century proper. This study addresses this recontextualization, examining Fielding's place in the process with the hope of establishing an initial canonical ground for future consideration of a broad spectrum of eighteenth-century life.

Peter Sabor and H. Grant Sampson from the beginning encouraged my pursuit of a revised understanding of Georgian libertinism, and Thomas Cleary, Isobel Grundy, John Pierce, and Robert Malcolmson gave insightful commentaries on earlier versions of the project. I could not have hoped to be a part of a more open or giving scholarly community, and I offer these people my thanks.

Portions of chapter 1 relating to the female libertine appeared in *TransAtlantic Crossings: Sexuality & Textuality in the Eighteenth Century*, and an earlier version of parts of chapter 2 related to *The Old Debauchees* appeared in *Text and Presentation* 14 (1993); thank you to editors Don Nichols and Karelisa Hartigan for permission to reprint this material.

I also gratefully acknowledge the Social Sciences and Humanities Research Council of Canada for its support of this study in the form of doctoral and post-doctoral fellowships and a travel grant for further work at Oxford University and the University of London.

Finally, I owe great thanks to my family and to my husband for unending support and patience.

May 1998

Honest Sins

1 Toward a Re-vision of Georgian Libertinism

For all that modern scholarship has attempted to establish Henry Fielding as a moralist – latitudinarian or otherwise – popular understanding of Fielding was significantly more ambiguous in the eighteenth century. He was reputedly a libertine in life, and he was assailed throughout his career by attacks on both his personal and public morality, and for the purported effects of his plays and novels on the virtue of society as a whole.

Fielding consistently refused to subject his artistic individualism to the kind of constraints imposed by the conservative element of his society, as exemplified by the voice of Samuel Johnson who asserted in 1750 that "the best Examples only should be exhibited; and that which is likely to operate so strongly, should not be mischievous or uncertain in its Effects ... It is therefore not a sufficient Vindication of a Character, that it is drawn as it appears; for many Characters ought never to be drawn ... Vice, for Vice is necessary to be shewn, should always disgust; nor should the Graces of Gaiety, or the Dignity of Courage, be so united with it, as to reconcile it to the Mind" (*Rambler* 4, 31 March 1750). Instead, Fielding recognized the ambiguous nature of humanity and the complexity that cannot be ignored if the truth of that nature is to emerge. In "To John Hayes, Esq." (1743), for example, Fielding makes clear that vice must be conflated with virtue to achieve an honest representation of humanity and society:

> See how various Men at once will seem;
> How Passions blended on each other fix,
> How Vice with Virtues, Faults with Graces mix;

How Passions opposite, as sour to sweet,
Shall in one Bosom at one Moment meet

....

So Vice and Virtue lay such equal Claim,
Your Judgment knows not when to praise or blame.

(ll.16–20, 25–6)

Such poetry, in concordance with the essays and other pieces included in his *Miscellanies*, demonstrates Fielding's moral and social beliefs and their implicit challenge to certain hegemonic social discourses.
These revelations of his understanding of society, morality, the law, and
human nature offer one key to the ambiguity that colours the primary
works. His work consistently engages eighteenth-century libertine discourse, from the plays, which appear to be dominated by libertine philosophy, to the later novels such as *Tom Jones* and *Amelia*, which are
generally read as moral tracts on prudence and virtue. The ostensibly
moral texts, however, clearly offer libertinism as a viable alternative, essential perhaps even as part of the most virtuous character; the libertine
texts make several traditionally moralistic points in alternately explicit
and subtle ways.

From the very beginning of Fielding's literary career there was tension between the moralist implications and the frequent glorification of
licentious and libertine values: contemporary response to his works was
strongly mixed, viewing them as both explicitly instructive and outrageously licentious. Twentieth-century criticism has been more decided,
however, tending to favour the view of Fielding as Christian moralist,
an understanding appropriate to some of his later work and to many aspects of his later life, but one that neglects the significance of the explicitly libertine qualities of his earlier works and their persistence in his
later writing. In fact, Fielding should not be seen primarily in isolation
as a focal point for a new generation of writers and of the genre of the
novel, but as a part of a much broader cultural tableau, in the tradition
of important libertine thinkers like Rochester, Saint-Evremond, and
Mandeville, the *carpe diem* poets, French libertines, and philosophers
such as Montaigne and Hobbes. Fielding's plays and novels reveal the
existence of a significant form of libertinism so far unrecognized by
twentieth-century readers, and Fielding himself appears to be central to
the recording and even development of Georgian libertinism, a cultural
discourse I hypothesize based on changing contemporary standards and
discussions of libertines, rakes, and the men and women of the Georgian social elite.

An evaluation of Fielding in terms of such culturally influential forces seems particularly appropriate in the context of recent work that considers Fielding and women, Fielding and gender studies, and Fielding and the development of the novel as genre, often without full consideration of the cultural space shared by these different specialized perspectives. One significant quality of this shared space is the acceptance, enunciated or tacit, of Fielding's position as energetic masculinist, even among those who attempt to redeem him from his popular shorthand position in binary opposition to the ostensibly feminist (or at least feminized) Samuel Richardson. An understanding of the presence and influence of Georgian libertine discourse makes possible a new sense not only of Fielding's good-natured men and their responses to the (im)moral dilemmas in which they are placed, but also of Fielding's women. From Shamela and Lady Booby to Sophia Western and Amelia Booth, his female characters embody social and sexual self-determination, individualistic pursuit of fulfillment of desire, and an active and intellectually engaged challenge to prescriptive constructs of femininity. For the libertine, the empowerment of the good-natured and privileged individual is all, and this is the position from which we see Fielding orient his characters as he represents the developing Georgian libertinism of his aristocratic society.

Libertinism is a philosophical and social system that incorporates much more than the simple expansion of the boundaries of sexual behaviour. Even beyond what James Turner and others have recently added to our understanding of eighteenth-century libertinism – social subversion, religious disassociation, expansive individualism, and a passionate need for originality and control of image and other – lies the almost entirely unacknowledged shift in the libertine paradigm after 1700.[1] Critics and libertine theorists tend to assume that the English libertine was culturally marginalized and eventually rendered extinct as libertinism was subsumed by the sentimentalism of the early eighteenth century. In fact, libertinism continued as a powerful cultural force long after 1700, informing the public personae and private discourse of the most privileged part of English society. Considerable evidence suggests that rather than replacing the libertine discourse, sentimentalism became a fashion and a filter through which libertinism moved. The resulting Georgian libertinism maintained the central philosophical tenets of libertinism but manifested them less aggressively, allowing the individual still to be skeptical and to pursue various freedoms, without the brutal Hobbesian domination of others so essential to the Restoration libertine.

Libertinism is discussed by both cultural historians and literary critics, but it is rarely defined, and even more rarely defined effectively.[2] One reason for this is that virtually all discussions of libertinism focus almost exclusively on the Restoration ideology of the libertine as a rake of varying intellectual complexity, and offer historical information and dramatic representations from the seventeenth century as context. Such discussions often depend upon Dale Underwood's definition of libertinism in *Etherege and the Seventeenth-Century Comedy of Manners* (1957) as a central cultural force that molds both dramatic characterization and the representation of artifice and reality:

Philosophically the libertine was an antirationalist, denying the power of man through reason to conceive reality ... Accordingly the libertine rejected the orthodox medieval and Renaissance concept of universal order and of man's place and purpose therein ... His ends were hedonistic, 'Epicurian,' and embraced the satisfaction of the senses in accordance with the reasonable dictates of Nature – that is, in this case, one's 'natural' impulses and desires ... At least three philosophic lines of thought are involved: Epicurianism, skepticism, and a type of primitivism or naturalism for which unfortunately there is no other received name. (13–14)

Even some forty years after publication, this is an excellent starting point for the consideration of libertinism, but its usefulness for the discussion of eighteenth-century culture and literature is limited by Underwood's absorption in seventeenth-century dramatic representations of the libertine. To continue the discussion of libertinism into later contexts, we must consider the limitations of Underwood's definition, prescribed as it is by the social conditions of the seventeenth century.

In "Rakes, Rogues, and the Empire of Misrule," Harold Weber attempts to supplement Underwood's definition, but his effort, like those of other critics who strive to divide the libertine into manageable segments, still does not move past Restoration ideology. His analysis of the rake and the rogue as two versions of the libertine hero – different in that the rake's rejection of society is primarily sexual and the rogue's primarily economic – does demonstrate that libertinism exists in many forms. The changing nature of the libertine becomes problematic, however, as such taxonomy is taken to extremes. Weber's later commentary on "The Rake-Hero in Wycherley and Congreve" adds a potentially confusing division of the libertine rake into the Hobbesian and the philosophical to the already dense categorizations of Robert Hume and Robert Jordan. Jordan's "extravagant rake" is characterized as a comic figure, but not a fool, who fills a carnival role. Hume then builds upon

Jordan by naming the polite rake, the vicious rake, the philosophical libertine, and the debauch (including subspecies such as the "country blockhead ... the hypocritical, wenching puritan ... and old whore-mongers" ["Myth" 38]). Hume clarifies the differences among these often overlapping categories by explaining that the distinction between vicious rake and debauch is almost entirely one of social position and power; that he also distinguishes between the debauch and the polite rake in terms of social class, however, contributes to a problematic lack of distinction among his subspecies.

Such attempts to break down the overarching paradigm of the libertine are perhaps useful in reconciling the varieties of Restoration dramatic characters with the idea of the libertine, but they are neither necessary nor particularly helpful when considering the evolution of the libertine, especially into the eighteenth century. All of the elements so discussed and divided are clearly included in the libertinism of the later period of more complex literary and historical figures, particularly in the more psychologically detailed narrative form of the novel. If one is going to break down the paradigm at all, I think the only viable way to do so is to follow Turner's approach in "Properties of Libertinism," where he divides the libertine not intrinsically, but according to the approaches of later literary critics. His sense of the "maximalist approach," which "depicts libertinism as a broad movement of sensibility, evolving towards cultured hedonism and incorporating the ideals of rakish vitality, psychological honesty and a fair-minded assumption of combative equality between the sexes," is useful in an examination of cross-period libertinism because it does not subdivide its subject into static types. However, Turner accepts neither this "maximalist" approach nor the "minimalist" approach that "imposes sharp distinctions between the genuine libertine and the more agreeable aspects of the late seventeenth-century mentality; it limits the duration, typicality, and influence of libertinism, and seeks to deny altogether its hegemony in English Restoration literature" ("Properties" 77). What Turner defines as a middle ground between these two frameworks does suit the discussion of Restoration libertinism and even eighteenth-century typological throwbacks like Richardson's Lovelace, but is too narrow for the Georgian libertine, since it omits the influence of sentimentalism and the ideal of the good-natured man in the later developments and manifestations of libertinism.

For all of the apparent cultural dominance of sentimentalism and sensibility in the eighteenth century, even so popular a discourse as sensibility could not replace a social construct as entrenched and privileged as libertinism. Libertinism continued to be engaged by writers throughout the eighteenth century, from the stage characters of George Farquhar and Richard Steele to the novels of Fielding, Richardson, Smollett and Cleland, to Hugh Kelly's *Babler* essays in 1766 and 1767 and articles in *Town and Country Magazine* on such topics as "The Generous Libertine" (September 1769), "The Female Libertine" (June 1772), and "The Married Libertine" (August 1778). Libertinism could, however, be affected by the expansion of the culture of sentiment, resulting in an embodiment of libertinism for the Georgian period informed by the sentimental ethic, but driven by the same passionate desire for culturally privileged individualism, skepticism, and challenge to the hegemonic discourses of sexuality, religion, and social order. The libertine still pursued privilege and freedom, but rejected the Hobbesian domination of others that was the central strategic device of the Restoration ideology of libertinism.

Though most discussions of sentimentalism deny any possible links between sentiment and libertinism, R.F. Brissenden's still valuable commentary on the novel of sentiment supports the understanding I propose of a symbiotic relationship between libertinism and sensibility. His brief comments on libertinism term Richardson's Pamela a libertine just as surely as Lovelace: he notes that the libertine can be sentimental in some ways and yet recognize that at least by conviction, he or she must also be "the arch enemy of all forms of sentimentality" (135–6).[3] The reformed libertine of the Georgian period thus rejects the passivity of body and thought that informs sentimentalism, opting instead for thoughts and acts occasionally subversive, but always considered. It is this active nature in particular that both distinguishes libertinism from sensibility, and establishes a degree of interdependence. Both the libertine and the sentimentalist seek sensation. The libertine experiences, indulges in, and creates sensation, and, as Barbara M. Benedict argues, the sentimentalist locates sensation in observation, separating "sexual sensation from benevolence to maintain its ideal of the aesthetic and tasteful control of response" (14). The pleasure of the culture of sensibility depends to a certain extent on the voyeuristic observation of the energy and consequences of cultural forces like libertinism, and the libertine gains both status and a source of pleasure from being observed in the acts that very often increase in pleasurability as they increase in publicity: in this symbiotic relationship the figure of the libertine is entrenched and enhanced.

A further link between these two apparently oppositional discourses is exposed in a consideration of feminine sexuality. G.J. Barker-Benfield makes much of the potentially subversive implications of a culture that so relishes sensual response, and argues that the impermeability of the

image of the woman as moral thermometer in sentimental fiction occurs as a conscious or unconscious attempt to manipulate and suppress
these implications. Markman Ellis makes a similar point as he notes,
"In the late eighteenth century, manners were widely perceived as being
recast in a more feminine mould, a process in which a destabilization of
sexual categories was implicit" (24). At a primary level, then, libertinism and sensibility promote some of the same ends: a space for an
acknowledgment of feminine desire, play in the previously assumed
emotional and intellectual responses of women and men, and a sense of
the significance of masculinized power in fostering and often manipulating these presumed-natural responses. Fielding certainly seems to acknowledge this discursive codependency as he explicitly establishes
certain qualities of sensibility in characters clearly grounded within a
powerful, if at times unarticulated, discourse of Georgian libertinism.
Barker-Benfield notes that Tom Jones is described as physically manifesting "the most apparent Marks of Sweetness and Good-nature" with
"Spirit and Sensibility in his Eyes ... joined to a most masculine Person
and Mien" (341). But Jones is much more than a sentimental hero. He
is specifically constructed as Fielding's "good-natured libertine," a man
of a passionate and frequently indulged sexual appetite and a desire to
challenge thoughtless submission to religious and cultural hegemonies;
he is a libertine aligned with a revised libertinism shaded by the coexist-
ent culture of sensibility.

Tom Jones was not at all unique, however, in his conflation of sensibility and libertinism, but was followed by other, similar representations. Twenty years later, for example, *Town and Country Magazine*'s
"The Generous Libertine" tells the story of Frank Bellenden, a Georgian libertine who, in the course of one of his frequent visits to a
brothel, meets and rescues a young woman who has been tricked away
from her parents and (almost) forced into a life of prostitution. He
takes the young Miss Colby home to his sisters who, in a comparison
between the prudish *"outrageously virtuous"* sister and the good-natured
one, devoid of *"ridiculous prejudices,"* demonstrate the hypocrisy of unconsidered and prescriptive virtue. Miss Colby is soon returned to her
parents, and Bellenden continues merrily on his way with nary a hint of
reformation or return to the moralist fold. He remains "formed by nature to be a woman's man, and extremely well fitted by a vicious education to occasion considerable mischief in the female world ... Being of
an amorous complexion, and having no idea of an honourable engagement, he made it the whole employment of his life to sport with the fair
sex upon his own terms." Like any citizen of the eighteenth century,
Bellenden has the capacity to be moved by sentiment and a weepy

story, but he is never required to surrender his libertinism in order to do
so; he is handsome, sexually vigorous, and socially privileged, as well as
both generous enough and powerful enough to prevent harm from
coming to the innocent. He shows the same good nature as his younger
sister, a quality both share with Tom Jones and other Georgian libertines. And while the tale's narrator still rejects the kind of libertine who
spreads "misery in families by giving a loose to his licentiousness," he
also notes that when a libertine carries out an act of good nature, "he
ought surely to be applauded for the generosity of his behaviour: it
would be unjust, it would be uncharitable, not to say *unchristian*, to
attempt to obscure the lustre of *that* action, by dwelling upon his dishonourable triumphs over innocence and virtue." Bellenden's uncon-
verted but still generous libertine forms another part of a significant
pattern of good-natured, possibly even sentimentalized libertines over a
substantial portion of the eighteenth century.

Considering the general lack of critical consideration of libertinism
after 1700, and recognizing the significance of other cultural forces
moving toward dominance in the new century, I wish to outline a
working definition of this new Georgian libertinism, starting from a
general definition of libertinism. Libertinism of any period is based on
the need to challenge social dogma and the assumptions of the hegemonic group. This in itself is interesting, since, of course, most of those
we would now classify historically as libertines were male, upper-class
members of that group. Still, they felt themselves limited and even op-
pressed by the boundaries of acceptable behaviour and thought as outlined by Parliament and the majority of public opinion, and so they led
a movement designed to procure freedom for certain aristocratic individuals to think and act according to their own judgment, regardless of
convention or social constructs of morality. This striving toward individualism is a second major quality of any libertinism. And these two
characteristics of the libertine together create subsidiary qualifications:
the distrust of and reaction against traditional religious doctrine, the
pursuit of freedom of sexuality, and the subsequently necessary increase
in the sexual independence and general empowerment of women
(within various limits, depending on the period and the individual tolerance of the libertine sub-hegemony). These elements, in turn, are related to the libertine fascination with disguise (manifested in masks and
masquerades as well as more explicitly appropriated identities), which,
in addition to providing a source of amusement, allowed both men and
women to act without being held publicly accountable. Finally, any
misbehaviour which did have to be acknowledged was justified by the
Restoration libertine's valorization of the Hobbesian view of humanity,

by the privileging of the Natural over the artificial limitations constructed by society, and by the anti-rationalism which dictated that moralism is dependent on the very reason and rationality of humanity in which libertines chose not to believe.

Such a broad definition of the transhistorical nature of libertinism is not, I believe, difficult to accept, since all of these elements have been acknowledged by scholars, though no single discussion seems to have encompassed all of them. Most of these criteria have been applied at some point to Restoration libertinism, but have not been developed adequately past the era of Congreve. The Georgian incarnation of libertinism thus stands awaiting critical consideration as a preface to taking its appropriate position as a heretofore neglected, but highly influential cultural discourse of the eighteenth century.

The Georgian libertinism that I believe emerges after the turn of the century is more moderate. It is typified by a movement away from extremes and polarization of behaviour and toward a continuum of social challenge that accepts the central tenets of Restoration libertinism but eliminates the cruelty and aggressive egocentrism of the Restoration comedy and satire that have so often served as definitive sources. There remains the public challenging of the cultural assumptions of the hegemonic order, and a striving toward individualism, self-determination, and controlling power. Distrust of traditional religious doctrine continues, of course, but less in the extreme form of atheism than in the recognition of the dangers of blind faith, and what might be termed selective faith, subscribing to the parts of religion that serve the desires of the individual, but rejecting those that interfere with self-satisfaction or threaten punishment. In the Georgian construction of libertinism, the pursuit of freedom of sexuality surrenders much of its previously extravagant masculinism, resulting in greater levels of autonomy and empowerment for women both in the private sphere and in public representations of feminine desire in early fiction. The libertine fascination with disguise and deceit also continues, particularly within the forum of the masquerade, allowing both men and women periods of escape from the enclosure of gendered regulation. The Georgian libertine still privileges the Natural over artificial constructs of social acceptability, but with the proviso that no other individual be injured in the pursuit of pleasure.

The life and writings of Saint-Evremond are one historical example of the new incarnation of libertinism. Saint-Evremond enunciates many ideals typical of the libertines around him, but with less aggressive assumptions of appropriate response than are usual to the Restoration. He demonstrates the flaws of unthinking acceptance of social assumptions as he explains why the Restoration understanding of the philosophy of Epicurus differed from that of the ancients. "It's very easy to give the reason; we do not act like them, we make no *enquiry*, we do not *sift* matters, we adhere only to what is *told* us, without instructing our selves in the *nature* of things ... we retain our errors, because they are authoriz'd by those of *others*" (64). He also acknowledges outright the libertine argument that one should not abstain from "the *Gifts* of *Heav'n* ... we ought to use 'em, provided we use 'em *according* to *nature*" (75). Among all of this desire for naturalism and pursuit of pleasure, however, as Quentin Hope points out, the assumption that "certain limits should be observed under any circumstances is an essential part of his code, whether it is applied to standards of social behaviour or literary expression" (22).

This Epicurian moderation amid the pursuit of naturalized pleasure, conscientious consideration, and subversion of widely accepted social and intellectual limitations prefigures some of the central qualities of Georgian libertinism; the two were also connected in the public perception in other, broader ways. Much like the common modern perception of the disappearance of libertinism, most of the multiple understandings of Epicurianism faced an apparent decline in popularity after the late seventeenth century. Epicurianism began in popular mythology as a representation of licentious Bacchanalia, and by the Restoration was seen by many as desirable, with freedom from fear, pain, and anxiety as major elements. It was also popularly known, however, for its denial of the immortality of the soul, its demystifying approach to religion, and its contempt for legal and intellectual authority. Libertinism and Epicurianism suffered from the same common, if not fully justified equation with atheism, and this equation contributed to both the declining acceptability of Epicurianism and the paradigmatic shifts that allowed libertinism to survive in its revised Georgian form.[4] Thus pursuits traditionally associated with Epicurianism – love of food and wine, and the non-malevolent pursuit of pleasure – need not be assumed to have declined along with the presumed-atheistic discourse termed Epicurianism in the eighteenth century. Many of these elements survived well into the eighteenth century proper as Epicurianism continued to be almost completely reinvented to suit the needs of a series of different groups: an easy manipulation considering the fragmentary nature of the extant part of Epicurus's voluminous writings, and one that is clear in the absorption of many Epicurian traits into the libertine discourses of both the Restoration and Georgian periods.

Examples of this absorption can be found in the writings of both Fielding and Philip Dormer Stanhope, Lord Chesterfield, as well as less recognized writers. Such voices refer repeatedly to the shifts in the contemporary discourse of libertinism in ways that echo the moderate philosophical, rather than popular, elements of Epicurianism. Lord Chesterfield wrote to his son in 1750,

> I mean to allow you whatever is necessary, not only for the figure, but for the pleasures of a gentleman, and not to supply the profusion of a rake ... Having mentioned the word Rake, I must say a word or two more on that subject, because young people too frequently, and often fatally, are apt to mistake that character for a man of pleasure; whereas, there are not in the world two characters more different. A rake is a composition of all the lowest, most ignoble, degrading, and shameful vices ... A man of pleasure, though not always so scrupulous as he should be, and as one day he will wish he had been, refines at least his pleasures by taste, accompanies them with decency, and enjoys them with dignity. Few men can be a man of pleasure, every man may be a rake. (2: 82–3)

Chesterfield has earlier defined pleasures as "the elegant pleasures of a rational being, and not the brutal ones of a swine. I mean *la bonne chère*, short of gluttony; wine, infinitely short of drunkenness; play, without the least gaming; and gallantry, without debauchery" (1: 350). The elements of power, appetite, alcohol, sex, and privilege are still present and definitive, but the extremes in their usage once held to be normative have been left behind.

A public, fictionalized representation of these same mediated libertine and Epicurian values appeared a decade after Chesterfield's private observation. In *The Rake of Taste, or The Elegant Debauchee* (1760), the titular rake narrates an account of a coach trip to Bath. The characters include Obadiah Broadbrim, a "jolly quaker of forty-five years; who, having professed a religion (if it may be called one) for the meer purposes of worldly gain (a character by no means uncommon) had fully answer'd his original purposes" (5). Instead of rendering Obadiah reprehensible for his abuse of the Church and ridiculous for his religious connections, or adopting an atheistic stance above such ecclesiastical conflicts, the rakish narrator ultimately praises him for taking from religion what seems most appropriate and will serve him best, a particularly lighthearted instance of a common Georgian libertine position. The four travellers seek sensual pleasure and indulge appetites for Shandean wit, food, and alcohol, and then pair off for a passionate and consequence-free night at an inn on the road. The next day our narrator decides to marry his bedmate, an heiress of "wit and good nature" (35), even though he recognizes that she has long before this night "gone thro' the mysteries of initiation" (4). He declares himself "a convert to love and virtue." The very notion of a worthy and traditionally prescriptive virtue beyond good nature and generosity (sexual and otherwise) is rendered immediately, delightfully problematic, though, both as we remember from the title that he never surrenders his claim to be a "rake" and "debauchee," and as he describes his bride with affectionate irony: "The charms of my Polly shone forth … a woman of as much virtue, as she had beauty and good sense." Cultural constructions of feminine virtue have here been deconstructed by events, with the values of generosity, naturalness, and passion superseding the quality of virginity so consistently equated with virtue throughout the eighteenth century. Their nocturnal tumble is now termed "the natural consequence of warm passions" (91), and the couple goes on to live a life according to natural desires and this revisionist virtue. Unconcerned with conventional behaviour and thought, they "possess fortune sufficient to chear and bless the poor around us, and they have our generous assistance" (93), and remain firm friends with the religiously unorthodox Obadiah and the sexually energetic Honoria.

Both the rake's tale and Chesterfield's comments complement Fielding's 1743 definition of a central aspect of this new Georgian libertinism. "Good-nature" was linked explicitly to libertinism in Fielding's works through the characterization of Tom Jones as the "good-natured libertine": "Good-nature is that benevolent and amiable Temper of Mind, which disposes us to feel the Misfortunes, and enjoy the Happiness of others; and consequently, pushes us on to promote the latter and prevent the former; and that without any abstract Contemplation on the Beauty of Virtue, and without the Allurements or Terrors of Religion" (*Miscellanies* I 158). As is evident upon evaluation of his plays and novels as well as his non-fictional writing, Fielding approves of actively pursuing one's own happiness as long as no other individual is intentionally led into misfortune.

This element of individualized pursuit of pleasure seems frequently to lead to the libertine assumption that life is worth living only on one's own terms, but libertines are not anarchistic in this belief since they accept the necessity of laws to govern the lower classes. They claim a privilege that not only permits but actually compels them to defy social norms and laws in order to prove the validity of the broader system that grants them status. As Turner puts it, "Libertines may be seen as secular antinomians, not simply above the law, but deeply in need of the law to guarantee their privileges and to fuel their emotional rebellion. They confirm in the very act of infraction" ("Properties" 81). It is this paradoxical quality that separates the libertine from the merely ill-behaved: while those of less privileged birth might well be derided or even jailed for blasphemy, illicit sexuality, or public subversiveness, both libertines and the society above which they position themselves know that the libertine is virtually always above such consequences. The essential quality of libertinism is difference; distinct from all others, the libertine embraces social privilege as the means to entrench further the capacity to subvert the cultural assumptions empowering that difference.

Sir Richard Blackmore's preface to *Prince Arthur* (1695) certainly recognizes the connection between privilege and libertinism: "The *Man of Sense*, and the *Fine* Gentleman in the *Comedy*, who as the chiefest Person propos'd to the Esteem and Imitation of the Audience, is enrich'd with all the Sense and Wit the Poet can bestow; this *Extraordinary Person* you will find to be a *Derider* of Religion, a great *Admirer* of *Lucretius*, not so much for his *Learning*, as his *Irreligion*, a Person wholly *Idle*, dissolv'd in Luxury, abandon'd to his Pleasures, a great Debaucher of Women, profuse and extravagant in his Expences, and in short, this *Finish'd Gentleman* will appear a *Finish'd Libertine*." In "The Second Part of the History of the London Clubs" (1746), Ned Ward demonstrates that these assumptions of privileged order continued into the Georgian period for libertines such as those belonging to the Society of Dilettanti: "Thus Libertines, to Vice resign'd, / Avers'd to be by Laws Confin'd / Disdaining Virtue's sober Rules, / Are only fit to Govern Fools." Significantly, Ward notes the privileged, rather than malevolent, tone of the libertine meetings he describes, despite the fact that the rest of the passage is marked by a distinctly moralist tone. He also recognizes the need for individuality, wit, and originality in libertine interaction, though his own moral position is clearer in this portion as he describes the atheists (to whom he refers as libertines) and their desire to "render themselves singular by their heterodox Notions. Government was so toss'd and toloniz'd among them, as if the venerable Oeconomy was only fit to be made the Rabbles Football, and the Hierarchy worry'd with such unmannerly Contempt, between Jest and Earnest, as if they mistook the Church to be a Monster … as if every Man's Breast ought to be his holy Tabernacle, himself the Teacher, and his own partial Sentiments the only Gospel by which he was to preach" (45).

The connection between the socially subversive stance of the culturally privileged libertine and the dominant culturally determinative force of the Church is clear from these observations. The most obviously heretical approach to the social challenge essential to libertinism was to attack the dominant role of religion in much of Restoration and eighteenth-century society. While the grip of the Church on the English people had loosened greatly since the Renaissance, individuals who proclaimed themselves to be atheists and later societies like that of the Medmenham Monks attempted to wrest themselves, at least in terms of public image, entirely from the sphere of religious influence.[5] In any reference to the hedonistic extremity of groups like the monks of Medmenham, though, there is room for debate: Betty Kemp, for example, argues effectively in *Sir Francis Dashwood: An Eighteenth-Century Independent* that the tales of blasphemy and orgies have little factual basis, as most reports seem to be founded on accounts included in *Chrysal, or The Adventures of a Guinea*, the 1765 satirical novel by Charles Johnstone, an energetic enemy of known libertine John Wilkes and all things Wilkesean. Accounts of the Medmenham Monks are coloured in turn by a tradition of reports of their forerunners, including the Mohocks, the Hell-Fire Club, and the Schemers in the first part of the eighteenth century. Some of these groups clung tightly to the postures of Restoration libertinism through extravagant poses of atheism and debauchery, while others, particularly the Mohocks, were less libertines than gangs of rambling, disruptive young men: they lacked the originality and intellectual qualities of true libertines even of the Restoration mode. Such groups can really be linked only to the kind of shorthand libertinism constructed by outraged moralists to represent all things unorthodox.[6]

Roy Porter's "Libertinism and Promiscuity" outlines succinctly the traditions of free thought defying and parodying orthodox Christianity, and distinguishes between the "heroic" libertinism of extreme figures like Charteris and de Sade and a broader "popular" libertinism. Porter argues that popular libertinism took place in the social context of "a widespread ferment of opinion among those for whom the *ex cathedra* morality of the Church and traditional institutions now offered false frameworks for sexual values, or at least ones which squared ill with their own instincts" (6). He offers as evidence the public acceptance of the naturalness of sexuality, and Hume's representation of the Hellenistic idea of erotic attraction as the first and original principle of human society. The Church's assumption of the communal good superseding that of the individual could no longer be accepted by all of society, and particularly not by individuals who were already privileged members. The response of the Georgian libertine, though, is less the atheism of the earlier generation, and more a considered evaluation of specific doctrinal elements and their manifestations in the institutionalized religion of the Church.

In a time when institutionalized religion remained powerful despite the conflicts and challenges offered among the High and Low Church, public deism and atheism, continuing dissenting sects like Puritanism, and emerging ones such as Methodism, perhaps the most likely association to be made among the libertines and existing religious discourses (so far as such a thing is possible considering the individualist nature of the true libertine's selection of isolated elements to serve his or her own desires) is with Free-thinking. Free-thinking, in cultural ascendency primarily among the artistocratic and privileged over the first half of the eighteenth century, was traced back, by many of its adherents at least, to Locke's *Reasonableness of Christianity* (1695). Shaftesbury's influential *Characteristicks of Men, Manners, Opinions, Times* (1711) was often linked to Free-thinking by detractors, primarily for its suggestion of an ethical system lacking divine sanctions of any kind. A more explicit engagement of the discourse occurs in Anthony Collins's 1713 tract *A Discourse of Free-Thinking, occasion'd by the Rise and Growth of a Sect call'd Free-Thinkers*. Collins defines Free-thinking as "the Use of the Understanding, in endeavouring to find out the meaning of any Proposition whatsoever, in considering the nature of the Evidence for or against it, and in judging of it according to the seeming Force or Weakness of the Evidence" (5). In accordance with such values, Free-thinkers like Collins outraged the more conservative by arguing for natural over revealed religion, and criticizing the Bible as bibliographically corrupt and patently unreliable.[7]

This sense that if religion could no longer fulfill the needs of the libertine individual, the guidance of Nature could lead into at least individual fulfillment was not limited only to Restoration rakes and their followers, but was remarkably widespread. As Porter eloquently notes, the "naturalistic and hedonistic assumptions – that Nature had made men to follow pleasure, that sex was pleasurable, and that it was natural to follow one's sexual urges – underpinned much Enlightenment thought about sexuality. Thus Jeremy Bentham argued that the ascetic Pauline condemnation of fornication outside marriage was counter-utilitarian: 'when viewed in an unprejudiced point of view, and by the standard of utility, sexual gratification in those modes, against which popular antipathy is apt to rage with greatest fury, will be seen not to belong to the department of morality' " ("Mixed Feelings" 4–5). This historical understanding is central to the widening of the definition of libertinism past the realm of the sexual and into understandings of social utility and other larger questions, particularly as the Restoration embodiment of libertine sexuality reached its furthest possible extremity and the more moderate Georgian ideology began to emerge.

The widespread presence of prostitutes, bawdy prints, and titillating novels of the early eighteenth century all indicate that sexual indulgence and tolerance were not confined to a libertine fringe. Such markers were neither a result nor a cause of the continuation of the libertine subculture into the eighteenth century, but they indicated that challenges to ancient and prescriptive mores were more acceptable on a wider scale than they had been for some time. With such shifts in the broader cultural perspective, libertines became less indebted to the extremity of a subversive stance, and more open to the possibility of fulfilling individual desires without needing to upend entirely the culture around (and beneath) them. As sexuality became more publicly visible across a larger section of society, the cruelty and manipulation of Restoration libertinism became unnecessary, while the increasing dominance of the discourse of sensibility rendered such cruelty less attractive. Georgian libertines thus faced a differently constructed standard, where seduction was acceptable, but abuse was not.

We see both this shifting standard and its links to the broad tolerance of sexual and other indulgence in, for example, Hugh Kelly's essays in *The Babler*. In the issue for 30 April 1766, Kelly writes, "Unhappily, in this gay age, the depravity of manners has arisen to so enormous a degree, that it is in some measure necessary for a young fellow to give into the fashionable follies, and practise vices to which he has a real abhorrence, if he would establish the character of a man of taste, or shew himself tolerably well acquainted with the world." Kelly goes on to point out the predominant place in the libertine role of vanity and the desire to reinforce privilege and superiority: "A man finds his vanity tickled, as well as his inclination gratified, in the seduction of unwary innocence; and, abstracted from the transport resulting from possession itself, the generality of our sex think, with an infinity of satisfaction, upon their own accomplishments, and suppose they must be possessed of some extraordinary qualifications, when a woman shews her sensibility of them at no less a price than her everlasting disgrace." But Kelly also notes two of the more complex qualities of the libertine of his age: that the libertine is sufficiently good natured to appreciate traditional virtue in others, even if he chooses to reject it for himself, and that he has a vast capacity to form generous intentions, only to fall to the necessity of maintaining the libertine figure that he has constructed.

The first of these is established in the introduction to his essay of 3 December 1767: "In proportion to [a man's] repentance or atonement, we are apt to raise him in our esteem: and it is not the least part of his merit, that libertines themselves are lost in admiration of his behaviour, however slow, through a ridiculous fear of public contempt, they may be to imitate an action which they cannot, in spite of fashion or education, forbear to love." Later in the same essay, Kelly has Richard Bumper explain in his letter to Harry Rattle, Esq that he has endeavoured to avoid seducing Sally Poplar, his tenant's daughter, because of her innocence. Bumper later, however, obtains from the girl permission to "chat half an hour with her before she went to bed. This half hour was productive of another and another; til at last, the poor girl was worked up to such a pitch of tenderness, that she could refuse nothing; and then it was I found, in spite of all my humanity, that there was no possibility of getting off. It would have been very strange after pressing three hours for the last favour, which all the time I was in hopes would be refused, if I had withdrawn the moment it was granted." The couple has sex, is caught by the family, and in a fit of affection Bumper offers to marry Polly. Bumper's marriage is not the reformation it might initially seem, though. He makes even this choice in accordance with his libertine principles: "It is not for the satisfaction of others we are to live, but our own; therefore those actions which secure that satisfaction, since it must always be founded on a rectitude of principle, are the best tests both of the goodness of our hearts and the soundness of our understandings." Even in apparent acquiescence to social expectation, the libertine constructs his motivation so that he remains consistent in his principles: ever self-serving, even when he chooses also to serve others.

There was, of course, resistance amid the increasing tolerance of libertine sexuality and the beginnings of the Georgian understanding in which the libertine is not necessarily malevolent or even distastefully aggressive. Even Kelly chastises the libertine lightly in his essays (particularly those still attracted by cruelty as a signifier of power). Throughout the century, groups of outraged moralists formed broadly righteous organizations like the Societies for the Reformation of Manners and the Proclamation Society in order to battle what they saw as the undermining of the moral fibre of the nation. Though individual members of the groups may have planned only to lessen the presence of illicit sexuality in society, the groups themselves were fundamentally conservative, opposing not just freedom of sexuality, but also the general liberalization of society and religion that more open sexuality might represent. The Hutchinsonians, for example, attacked loose sexuality among the aristocracy at the same time that they rejected the thought of Locke and Newton, and the Vice Society's evangelicals were active in opposing rationalism, natural religion, and liberal politics in general. While opposition to sexual licence cannot be equated with an overly generalized opposition to liberalism and social progress, it is essential to note the extended web of connections between sexuality and other elements of social mutability, many of which were concretized in the Georgian libertinism that both encouraged and echoed the increasing acceptability of questioning hegemonic orders of all kinds.[8]

One important shift seems to have been agreed upon, however, in both the libertine and popular understandings of sexuality after 1700. The old-style Rochesterian image of the libertine with a whore on one arm and a young man on the other gave way by the Georgian period to new ideals of love, companionate marriage, and domesticity, resulting in a quite specifically heterosexual construction of the libertine. As Randolph Trumbach has demonstrated, sodomitical relationships, part of the splash of the old-style libertines who liked both women and boys, had become unacceptable in both popular and libertine society by 1700. Before 1690, "[s]odomy ... was the most extreme indulgence of the libertine rake" ("Sodomy Transformed" 107).[9] As we have noted, the central paradigmatic shift from Restoration to Georgian embodiments of the libertine discourse is one away from extremity, and public tolerance of bisexual libertinism seems to have collapsed under the same forces. Trumbach points out that the decline of bisexual libertinism was at least partly the result of the model, developing between 1698 and 1725, of the passive adult effeminate sodomite who was presumed to be interested exclusively in other males. Perhaps as a result of this shift, representations of the male Georgian libertine tend to be unmistakably masculine in appearance and proactive in demeanour.[10]

Constructions of sexuality, gender, and desire have been deconstructed and reassessed recently by a series of scholars, many of whom locate the emergence of the modern system of gender difference in the eighteenth century. Michel Foucault, Lawrence Stone, Nancy Armstrong, and Felicity Nussbaum, for example, have all analyzed the shifting discourses of gender and sexuality, and Jill Campbell's *Natural Masques* examines the function of gender and identity in Fielding's work. Such critical works rarely mention libertinism, but the studies of gender warrant consideration as we strive to understand the cultural significance of libertinism for both men and women. As Judith Butler's powerful assessment of the constructed nature of gender explains,

Gender can denote a *unity* of experience, of sex, gender, and desire only when sex can be understood in some sense to necessitate gender – where gender is a psychic and/or cultural designation of the self – and desire – where desire is heterosexual and therefore differentiates itself through an oppositional relation to that other gender it desires. The internal coherence or unity of either gender, man or woman, thereby requires a stable and oppositional heterosexuality. That institutional heterosexuality both requires and produces the univocity of each of the gendered terms that constitute the limit of gendered possibilities

within an oppositional, binary gender system. This conception of gender pre-
supposes not only a causal relation among sex, gender, and desire, but suggests
as well that desire reflects or expresses gender and that gender reflects or expresses desire. (22)

Butler outlines here the presupposed and naturalized codependence of
sex, gender, and desire generally unchallenged in the eighteenth century, and this set of assumptions is central to libertine constructs of sexuality and identity. The libertine depends on an established separation
of the sexes in order to construct relationships between them: even the
acknowledgment of the pleasure of sodomitical relationships outlined
by Trumbach exists primarily, if not exclusively, to emphasize an expan-
sionist desire, implying a broad scope of sexual prowess that facilitates a
more empowered heterosexuality. The libertine subverts social expectations of gendered behaviour not least through homosexual relationships
and flirtations and by encouraging the recognition of otherwise unacknowledged female desire, but there is little evidence for any substan-
tive questioning of the binary construction of gender that dominated
the culture of the day. It is perhaps another paradox of libertinism that
the libertine must subscribe fully to constructions of gender in order to
subvert those constructions, in ways that attempt to defy normative values constricting sexuality and to represent publicly a culturally distinct
individuality.

   Butler's explanation of gender bears a fascinating resemblance to the
construction of the libertine identity, particularly in cases where the individual is eventually subsumed by the libertine role, losing the very
identity that the external libertine stance was meant to embellish. Butler notes that gender is merely "the repeated stylization of the body, a
set of repeated acts within a highly rigid regulatory frame that congeal
over time to produce the appearance of substance, of a natural sort of
being" (33). Even the ostensibly compelling nature of the intentionality
of libertine subversiveness is unable to escape the cultural conditioning
that fosters prediscursive assumptions about the nature of masculinity
and femininity, and this reveals perhaps more clearly than any other approach the problematic nature of any attempt to manipulate the construction of identity, even within the comparatively open arena of the
privileged libertine. Even the most apparently subversive sexual act of
the libertine may ultimately be read to support the most prescriptive
sexual status quo: as Butler points out in the wider context of gender
and feminism,

acts and gestures, articulated and enacted desires create the illusion of an interior and organizing gender core, an illusion discursively maintained for the

purpose of the regulation of sexuality within the obligatory frame of reproductive heterosexuality. If the 'cause' of desire, gesture, and act can be localized within the 'self' of the actor, then the political regulations and disciplinary practices which produce that ostensibly coherent gender are effectively displaced from view. The displacement of a political and discursive origin of gender identity onto a psychological 'core' precludes an analysis of the political constitution of the gendered subject and its fabricated notions about the ineffable interiority of its sex or its true identity. (136)

The extravagant masculinity of many libertines of both the Restoration and eighteenth century thus is problematized: the passionate pursuit of sexual consent or conquest, of disruption of social norms, ultimately has contradictory effects – the individual may well transcend the prescriptive force of cultural values, but by positioning subversion fully within the individuated impetus, the localized 'self' of the actor, the forces that enable such prescription are concurrently entrenched and hidden, preventing recognition, perhaps even by the libertine, of the political, biological, and sociological assumptions underlying the limitations that enable transgression.

Despite our recognition of such paradoxes of conservative subversion, the eighteenth century seems to have embraced the apparently anti-conservative implications of libertinism, the increasingly widespread evaluation of limitations on sexuality, and the expanding space for feminized desire. Increased public acceptability of steps toward freedom of sexuality become steps toward the acquisition of power for the position of libertines as a group and for the individual libertine. Within this context, and as a foundation for examining the shifts in the sexuality of libertinism through the Restoration and the eighteenth century, I begin with Turner's assertion that "libertine sexuality … is inseparable from the cerebral triumph over the opposite sex, from mastery exercised though tactical reason" ("Paradoxes" 71). In Turner's traditional libertine context sex becomes a battle to reassure the libertine's sense of individual superiority not only over the defeated object, but also over all others who have not been so successful. Thus, the need for resistance by the object of desire was recognized in the most sophisticated forms of libertinism, and since the psychological power gained by seduction is short-lived, the libertine must continue to seek out new conquests in order to sustain himself.

This demonstrates the conformist nature of the sexuality of old-style libertinism. The libertine approach to seduction "undermines the libertine's claim to originality. The intense assertion of individual rebellion and individual libido turns out to be quite conformist, since it aims to prove an existing theory, an established (if scandalous) ideology of female submission and female arousal" ("Paradoxes" 72). The sexuality of Turner's libertine, then, would seem to be less physical than intellectual: the libertine strives for political and social status by contravening the norms which are agreed by the primarily aristocratic peer group to have been established to govern only the rabble. Turner's libertine thus both bends to social norms and contravenes them as he seeks psychological affirmation and individual dominance through briefly empowering but ultimately demoralizing sexual conquest.

Such triumphant cruelty, however, disappears from the sexuality of the Georgian libertine. To increase the enjoyment of both the psychological affirmation and individual power represented by libertine sexuality, the obvious steps to take are to enlarge the group that can confirm the elevating powers of privileged sexuality and to intensify the challenge of seduction by giving the opponent more freedom and more tools for opposition. In offering this freedom and the tools of self-determination, Georgian development of the female libertine past her limited roots in the Restoration discourse concurrently empowers and challenges the general qualities of libertinism. This occurs in the sexual realm of course, but it is particularly significant in the separate challenging of the different social norms and ecclesiastical controls imposed upon women. It is freedom handed to women by patriarchy, but it is a version of freedom nonetheless. Lady Mary Wortley Montagu, for example, documents the public acknowledgment of the developing equality of Georgian sexuality when she alleges that not only husbands but also wives were by 1724 freely committing adultery, so that "the Appellation of Rake is as genteel in a Woman as a Man of Quality" (2:32). The burgeoning public sexual awareness of women continued later into the century as well. Barker-Benfield argues that the eighteenth century's culture of sensibility provides "dramatic evidence of women's wishes for the individual pursuit of self-expression and heterosocial pleasure in a wider world, the unambiguous expression of which was epitomized by the figure of the rake. The expressive consciousness connoted by 'sensibility' extended even so far as women's own sexual wishes" (vxi–xvii). For all of Barker-Benfield's assertions that the roots of modern feminism are to be found in the culture of sensibility, though, one must also reconsider the same evidence of feminine sexuality and the subversion of existing socio-cultural structures to represent an inevitable continuation of the established discourse of libertinism rather than an inordinately speedy effect of the comparatively new sensibility.

In fact, the female libertine had existed since at least the Restoration, though she, like libertines in general, changed her self-construction as cultural forces like sensibility increased in dominance. Early female libertine writers such as Aphra Behn and Delariviere Manley need nod only briefly, if at all, toward the ostensibly morally educative capacities of their work, while later female libertines spent much of their lives and textual focus demonstrating their individualism and their privilege over the mechanisms designed to regulate the rabble, but returned to convention often enough to shore up the very same cultural values that enabled them to self-position above cultural limitation.[11] Turner's work shows clearly that libertines require conventional limits in order to represent themselves to be above them, and so must concurrently subvert and support the status quo, destabilizing the hegemonic order for the one while establishing it for the many; this paradox is almost inevitably missed in considerations of a feminine context. In an essay on women's amatory fiction, for example, Toni O'Shaughnessy Bowers argues that in the works of Behn, Manley, and others, "women actively desire, often initiate, and thoroughly enjoy heterosexual sex; but they consistently define and act out their desire according to the force-oriented ethic of the Augustan rake. Within such a framework, representations of female sexuality fail to exemplify a positively or uniquely female form of sexual desire" (57). This, of course, is a near perfect example of the libertine paradox: a female libertine's representations of sexuality are not about exemplifying positive examples of female desire, but about an individuated and autonomous expression of sexual agency and desire, dependent upon popular paradigms of sexuality only to establish the power of this individual figure to defy them.

Laurie Finke's major objection to the existence of a female libertine is similarly centred in the very generalities that the libertine by definition transcends. She argues that once a woman "gave herself sexually she ceased to be desirable, cast off in an endless search for variety and change ... For this reason, a woman could never achieve sexual conquest, because her only power lay in witholding sex" (27). This is true of the vast majority of women, but it is not true of the libertine woman: she rejects the assumption of feminine sexual powerlessness, and as a result is one of the few who achieves her status at least partly as a result of her ability to transcend mundane expectations of virtue and culturally prescriptive femininity. As is true of the male libertine, the defining quality of the female libertine is her *difference* from and privilege over other women.

The fundamentally individual and self-privileging nature of libertinism also reconciles the other common objection to the possibility of a female libertine: that, as Bowers argues, "amatory fiction's repeated – indeed excessive – reference to misogynist stereotypes signals its fundamental implication in androcentric codes that work to mitigate the threat of female subjectivity and sexuality" (58). This assertion is absolutely right, but it is only a problem if we expect female libertinism to equal feminism – and it doesn't. There is no movement in any form of libertinism to change the locus of power or the order of society, only to demonstrate the elevation of the individual libertine above that order. The female libertine needs no more than the male to attempt to elevate her peers or change social codes, only to manipulate them to fulfill her own desire.

Even in the face of such evidence of Georgian libertinism's potential as a discourse empowering for women, the issue of libertinism and women can still be a difficult one. But many of the apparent contradictions within female libertinism can be understood, if not remedied, by considering the shifting cultural contexts in which the female libertine continued her development and empowerment. Nancy Armstrong's work on desire and domestic fiction, for example, demonstrates the significance of the changes in publicly accepted constructions of women's roles when she explains the decreasing frequency of publication of conduct books for women. She argues that by the end of the eighteenth century, the conduct book ideal of femininity had passed into the domain of common sense where it provided the frame of reference for other kinds of writing, including the novel. Thus as the dictated normative function of women evolved over the eighteenth century, so also did the reactionary impetus of the libertines in challenging that which was normative. Instead of the sexual objectification of women in response to women's broader functional objectification during the Restoration, Georgian libertines offered a sexual empowerment and self-determination in opposition to the passivity and asexuality of the conduct book norm whose dominance as assumed knowledge became more and more entrenched.

If domesticity thus functions as the increasingly entrenched model of femininity so actively challenged by libertine understandings of sexuality, one must then determine whether the Georgian libertine concepts of femininity succeeded in their challenge. Popular understanding of the female libertine ranged from the image of the sexually aggressive woman informed by contemporary pornography to the role of the accepted challenger to society's double standard in support for libertine attempts to upend such strictures. The evidence suggests that the Restoration represents more of the former, while the latter began its development around 1700.

Jane Miller's "The Seductions of Women" addresses this issue clearly and powerfully, though, I think, problematically. She asserts that the tradition of the heroic individualist libertine focused on women only insofar as they were the generalized object of male desire. Miller views her representative woman, Clarissa Harlowe, as passive, voiceless, and left without choice or resistance by patriarchy and libertinism because of the historical and literary focus on the male tradition of seduction. Thus her conclusion that "so long as the narrative of male seduction [the only element of libertinism she discusses] ignores the woman as its reader or at best assumes her to be androgynous, the text will have closed in on itself, protecting its embalmed view of men's and women's libido, as *Clarissa* does, by identifying an independent sexuality in women – their refusal of the seducer – with the chaste and corpse-like" (60). I find Miller's conclusions problematic for a number of reasons, not least because of the assumption that the only independent sexuality for women is refusal. As well, in asserting that the libertine narrative excludes the female reader, Miller denies women the capacity for imaginative identification with anything other than a mirror image of themselves. The female reader is not abandoned by the libertine discourse, but liberated, even if in no way other than intellectually, to the potential for egalitarian thought and action.

In mid-eighteenth-century narrative, women have a voice, even if this voice was granted at least partly because the novel was considered a lesser genre. Deceived or not, Clarissa Harlowe chooses to risk running off with the undependable Lovelace and then to die gracefully after the elopement's horrible end. Her decision robs Lovelace of the affirmation of power that he so desperately needs to continue in the role of old-style egocentric libertine. It is not a happy ending, but it does represent choice.[12] John Valdimir Price's assessment of *Clarissa* recognizes this as well: "Clarissa does not take the easy way out in making her moral decisions. She rightly perceives that marriage to and sexual intercourse with a man whom she abominates would be morally more dubious than running the risks she does with Lovelace" (166). While Price's psychoanalytic interpretation and his assertion that "it is difficult for the reader not to feel that, all things considered, Clarissa is waiting to be raped" (165) strike me as hugely problematic both textually and theoretically, his sense of Clarissa's independence of thought is valid and useful to counterbalance equally extreme observations on the other side of the politico-sexual discourse.

More persuasive are suggestions like those of Lady Mary Wortley Montagu and texts of the period which show autonomous women being welcomed into the world rather than driven from it. Richard Braverman's discussion of the parasitical nature of the libertine augments such evidence as he demonstrates that the libertine does not have to support women's independence publicly to affect their situation positively: "If the bonds of gentry society are cemented by the circulation of women, the libertine-parasite interrupts marital exchange because the institution itself implies a legal limit to the power and potency of the heroic will" (78). The act of interrupting the male traffic in women may certainly be interpreted this way, but such a "parasitical" act also liberates women by negating the capacity of the offerer to participate in the exchange.[13] This is not to suggest that the Georgian libertine is somehow feminist, or that the female libertine was valued by her society for her agency and manipulation of difference, but the refusal to subscribe to traditional constructs of gender and sexuality in order to serve the individualistic pursuit of pleasure did enable a freedom for women of the right class.[14]

One of the ways in which both men and women traditionally manifested libertine identity and independence was through disguise, and for the Georgians a unique form of this device appeared in the masquerade. Harriette Wilson's words demonstrate the freedom thus accorded to women: "I love a masquerade, because a female can never enjoy the same liberty anywhere else ... It is delightful to me to be able to wander about in a crowd, making my observations, and conversing with whomsoever I please, without being liable to be stared at or remarked upon, and to speak to whom I please, and run away from them the moment I have discovered their stupidity" (Castle *Masquerade* 44). In her important work on the masquerade, Terry Castle lists the possible consequences of a woman's attending the event, including loss of reputation and falling victim to the very disguise that attracts her, resulting in rape or kidnapping by someone claiming to be a husband or friend. She rightly notes that "one must grant to that woman willing to compromise herself at the public masquerade a measure of courage and aplomb, as well as a will toward sensual self-determination that was, under the circumstances, both radical and compelling" (45). Much of the fear and moral dismay generated by masquerades was related to the belief that they encouraged the continued expansion of female sexual freedom and emancipation, a concern raised at least in part because the masquerade did allow women to gain control and power by escaping their socially-defined identities and their associated customs of conventionality.[15]

The nature of disguise in the popular thought and literature of the eighteenth century is as ambiguous as its effects on convention, as masks, disguise and mistaken identity all function as both allegorical demonstrations of deceit and evil, and the mysterious tools of Providence for good. Castle discusses the masquerade, but what she says is equally true of libertinism when she writes, "Like the traditional fantasy of the World Upside-Down, the masquerade was never merely an escapist reversal of the conditions of ordinary life. Its particular éclat always exceeded that of simple inversion, though inversion was of course the symbolic gesture on which the occasion was founded" (*Masquerade* 250). Weber concurs, albeit in reference to Restoration disguise rather than Georgian masquerade: "In the hands of a rake like Dorimant, disguise can become an anarchic act designed to subvert the conventional forms of society. Rakes' love of disguise is thus complex, indicative of their almost contradictory nature, their attractive high spirits and destructive will" ("Misrule" 25). While the desire for the subversion of hegemonic norms remains constant in libertinism of all periods, the destructive element described by Weber lessens by the end of the Restoration, according to the likes of Chesterfield, Fielding, and Saint-Evremond, and results in the still high-spirited Georgian libertine, combining hegemonic subversion and a rejection of abusive egocentrism.

The visor and the domino, then, as well as other forms of disguise, mistaken identity, and appropriation of identity, are tangible symbols of the almost unavoidable human (and particularly libertine) need for mystery and re-invention. The libertine uses disguise at times as a mere jest and at others as a device to deceive, so that he or she may emerge victorious and confirm a social status above the limitations of daily exchange. Disguise reveals another libertine paradox: denying their desire for disorder because they have so much to gain and enjoy from the existing order leaves libertines facing a contradiction which makes disguise even more appealing. Disguise or masquerade allows the libertine to behave outrageously and to contravene all tenets of good society while surrounded by an atmosphere of carnival in which none of the normative rules that so empower his or her privilege can be seriously or permanently eroded.

Disguise can be deeper than external appearances as well. Lisa Berglund's analysis of the "Language of Libertines" describes a libertine discourse which consists of a constant use of metaphor for sexuality (and, I would add, other elements of libertinism) which almost never mentions the tenor, once established, but only the vehicle. The libertine need never explicitly reveal his or her true focus on sexuality, subversion, or power when speaking to another versed in the discourse, creating yet another plane on which he or she can be elevated above the masses. The late seventeenth- and early eighteenth-century distaste among wits for fops who indulged in linguistic affectation and appearance demonstrates the usual disdain for the foolish imitators who cannot maintain full libertine originality, and parallels the distaste of society at large for the overly extreme libertine qualities that the fops aped. In effect, the true libertine moves back toward the centre in agreement with conventional opinion, in accordance with the Georgian embodiment of libertinism which softened the Restoration extremes of anarchic social rebellion. Once one is comfortably located within the libertine discourse, one can appropriate linguistic and external poses which can in turn locate a voice of moderation within the larger libertine mode without violating the central ethic of the philosophy. This is where, together with the inklings of liberation for women, individualism and power begin to develop the potential for variance within the mainstream, the potential for a libertine voice that speaks of good-natured pursuit of pleasure instead of Hobbesian brutality.

This individualism within the group identity is central to the libertine desire for originality and inimitability, but by the Georgian period there was little space left to expand in the direction of extreme debauchery or anarchism. It appears that many libertines began instead to develop their originality in directions that moved again toward the centre. Fulfilling all personal desires without resorting to cruelty became a new way to excel, and alongside figures like Saint-Evremond, Lord Hervey, Fielding, and Chesterfield, various fictions of the eighteenth century reveal a wide-ranging hierarchy of libertines in various stages of this recognition of the next natural development of libertinism.[16]

It is this naturalist focus of libertinism to which I will turn now, as the final point of evidence for the existence and significance of a Georgian libertine discourse, since naturalism is partially responsible for the presence of individualism and several of the sexual and religious challenges to social dogma that I have already discussed. John Traugott offers perhaps the bleakest understanding of libertine naturalism when he defines his rake in the most Hobbesian of terms: "He acts according to nature. And to act according to nature – if we refuse the reality of natural moral law – is to injure other people" ("Progress" 385). Underwood considers the concept in greater detail, though also from a position firmly entrenched in the Restoration milieu. Libertine naturalism depends in part on hedonistic and Epicurean elements determined by one's natural impulses and desires. Underwood interprets the philosophical origins of this idea such that the libertine denies the power of humanity to conceive reality through reason, and rejects the orthodox concept of universal order and of humanity's place therein. Such negative philosophical origins might lead one to believe that libertinism's sense of the natural evolves primarily from a Hobbesian view of the self-serving and violent nature of humanity, but Underwood also recognizes the other half of the tradition of the natural: the optimism of golden age primitivists who believe in inherently good human nature. "The one proposed freedom, indulgence, pleasure; the other self-interest, aggression and conquest. Together they produced an egocentrically oriented concept of nature in which indulgence was purchased through aggression, and pleasure through conquest, and in which by definition individual fulfillment and social order were in perpetual opposition" (28). In terms of Restoration drama, then, the audience sees "nature to advantage dress'd," since the publicly presented libertine is one who has had to strive to perfect the "natural" arts of appropriate behaviour in the world of the comedy of manners.

Certainly Underwood's interpretation of the balance of these two central elements of naturalism is appropriate to the Restoration comedy of wit. However, once the group identity fostered by the Church was lost to skepticism and intellectualism after the rise and fall of the Puritans, libertine thought developed rapidly from its origins in France and in earlier writers and thinkers like John Donne. The drama of the 1660s and 1670s reveals a hard-edged interpretation of such doubt and the subsequent need to reject social dogma, but as we have seen, by 1700 the rampant sexual and social abuse of others had lost its cachet, and as sentimentalism began its rise, so did the revised discourse of good-natured Georgian libertinism.

I argue, therefore, that the libertine did not die out after *The Way of the World*. The Georgian libertinism I propose is a continuation and development of the Restoration version, and it effectively parallels the movements in larger issues of both public and domestic society as outlined by Lawrence Stone, who contends that in the sixteenth and seventeenth centuries, "each individual thinks of himself as unique, and strives to impose his own will on others for his selfish ends. The result is a Hobbesian state of nature, the war of all against all, which can only be brought under control by the imposition of stern patriarchal power in both the family and the state."[17] By the very late seventeenth century and the eighteenth century, though, according to Stone's discussion of affective individualism, "all human beings are [understood to be] unique. It is right and proper for each to pursue his own happiness, provided that he also respects the right of others to pursue theirs. With this important proviso, egotism becomes synonymous with public good" (258). And this conflation of egotism and public good (which is generally itself synonymous with broad-scope morality) allows the development of my conception of Georgian libertine moralism, a perspective through which modern scholarship might resolve some of the apparent contradictions within the works and lives of figures such as John Wilkes, Sir Francis Dashwood, Samuel Richardson, James

Boswell, and others, including Fielding who, as a libertine moralist, was an intellectually and socially active and skeptical follower of the libertine tradition who could still maintain and even proselytize strong views on morality and society.

Fielding took advantage of the shifts within libertinism to develop the concept further in his essay-writing and fiction. Though Fielding was often charged with "an intention to subvert the settled notions of mankind in philosophy and religion" (Battestin *Moral Basis* 79), he points out in his preface to the *Miscellanies* that he is not "designing, in an Allegory of this Kind, to oppose any present System, or to erect a new one of [his] own" (*Miscellanies* I 4). He does not accept the status quo, and he does not set out to reinvent society. Instead, he contributes to the development of the tradition of libertinism – of which he clearly felt a part – into a viable moral, philosophical, and social alternative within the existing social organization of the Georgian period.

Certainly the tension between individual passions and broad social order played different roles in Fielding's life at different times. Battestin's biography of Fielding seems to be in agreement with those of Donald Thomas and Arthur Murphy when he asserts that Fielding made no attempt to conceal the libertinism of his youth. The documentation of Fielding's youth in Battestin's biography should effectively resolve the critical conflict between the image of Fielding as impious libertine painted by contemporary enemies (and others), and Fielding as devout moralist as painted by Wilbur L. Cross and by both Fielding and Battestin in their more defensive moments. Though Battestin fights to maintain his thesis of Fielding as latitudinarian moralist, he acknowledges occasionally what Pat Rogers announces confidently: "in general Fielding chose to abide by the standards of his age, and his pose of virtue strains our credence at times" (110).

As early as *The Old Debauchees*, Fielding expresses explicitly his sense of a libertine morality. Old Laroon, a likeable and victorious debauchee, announces that he has "no Sins to reflect on but those of an honest Fellow. If I have loved a Whore at five-and-twenty, and a Bottle at forty; Why I have done as much good as I could in my Generation; and that, I hope, will make amends" (III xiv). In *A Journey from this World to the Next*, a nearly identical passage appears as the speaker tells of his judgement by Minos: "I confess'd I had indulged myself very freely with Wine and Women in my Youth, but had never done an injury to any Man living, nor avoided an Opportunity of doing good; that I pretended to very little Virtue more than general Philanthropy, and private Friendship. – I was proceeding, when *Minos* bid me enter the Gate, and not indulge myself with trumpeting forth my Virtues"

(36). *Tom Jones* contains much the same speech yet again as Jones explains his moral system: "Lookee, Mr *Nightingale* … I am no canting Hypocrite, nor do I pretend to the Gift of Chastity, more than my Neighbours. I have been guilty with Women, I own it; but am not conscious that I have ever injured any – nor would I to procure Pleasure to myself, be knowingly the Cause of Misery to any human Being" (755). These elements of the freedom and social challenge of libertinism are with Fielding throughout his career, and to categorize them merely as elements of religion denies the sexual and potentially anti-social qualities of the ideas and the characters who convey them.

More than traditional scholarship has been inclined to accept, Fielding's concept of good nature includes these qualities and acknowledges the role that libertinism has to play in both reflecting and challenging public and private morality.[18] What Robert Etheridge Moore writes of Fielding's friend and influence William Hogarth is equally true of Fielding: "his satire is moral, certainly, but *moral* released from the limits of its usually restricted meaning. The blue-law, prayer-meeting quality is absent" (71). Fielding's manner of expressing such libertine and moralist tensions was in terms of "good nature," a concept with roots both popular and within the ongoing debate between sentimentalists and rationalists. Sentimentalists like Shaftesbury argued that pure, unself-interested motive, rather than outcome, determines the virtue of an act, while the Mandevillean rationalist interpretation was that instinctive benevolence is not virtue. We may love the person, but do not regard him or her as virtuous. Hume's *Treatise of Human Nature* (1738) challenged the dominance of such moral philosophers as John Locke and Samuel Clarke by arguing that reason is not a viable guide for moral judgments since there are no natural motives for many of the actions we term good or evil. All knowledge is relative since all of our understanding of cause and effect, right and wrong is based only on custom of thought and general consensus. Moral judgment for Hume is the domain of the sensitive rather than cognitive element of human nature. As he summarizes, "when you pronounce any action or character to be vicious, you mean nothing, but that from the constitution of your nature you have a feeling or sentiment of blame from the contemplation of it. Vice and virtue, therefore, may be compar'd to sounds, colours, heat and cold, which according to modern philosophy, are not qualities in objects, but perceptions in the mind."[19]

The phrasing in Fielding's own poetic definition of good nature reveals the ambiguity of the concept both philosophically and behaviourally as it refers to "the glorious Lust of doing Good" ("Of Good

Nature" l. 24). It is still a passion being indulged from its natural origins:

> The Heart that finds it Happiness to please,
> Can feel another's Pain, and taste his Ease.
> The Cheek that with another's Joy can glow,
> Turn pale, and sicken with another's Woe;
> Free from Contempt and Envy, he who deems
> Justly of Life's two opposite Extremes.   (ll. 25–30)

In the passage from "On the Knowledge of the Characters of Men" cited earlier, Fielding elaborates on this definition, offering the crucial explanation of motivation for true good nature, a quality which must be expressed "without any abstract Contemplation on the Beauty of Virtue, and without the Allurements or Terrors of Religion" (*Miscellanies* I 158). There is little need for publicly defined virtue or its roots in religion in true good nature. Instead, this model allows for both philosophical and behavioural challenges to the social constructs of good and evil, as long as no other person is intentionally harmed. Certainly it is allowable to violate socially constructed norms in order to serve another.

Other definitions of the period have even more explicitly libertine connotations, and Fielding cannot have been ignorant of the layers of meaning these would add to his definitions of good nature. Turner, for example, glosses the phrase "the best, good-natur'd things alive" (from Pope's epilogue to *Jane Shore*) as "Restoration slang for the sexually willing woman" ("Pope's Libertine" 127), suggesting a widespread understanding of the sexually libertine implication of the term. That the quotations from *Tom Jones, A Journey from this World to the Next,* and *The Old Debauchees* offering sexual and social allowances (and allowing doubt of the social structures that limit these things) all come from characters who are revealed by their actions to be good natured proves further the revisionist Georgian libertine quality of Fielding's most famous definition of human nature. Extended analysis of his plays and major works reveals the depth to which Fielding's redefinitions of the social constructs of libertinism, virtue, and morality actively mediate his fictive discourse throughout his career, from his earliest writings to *Amelia.*

2 Early Georgian Libertines: Fielding's Drama

Fielding's plays offer the earliest evidence of his understanding of libertinism and his development of the concept into something more appropriate for the Georgian period. Nearly every play offers representations of at least parts of the libertine ideology, and many offer specific discussions. Despite the critical commonplace that *Joseph Andrews* is Fielding's first full representation of good nature, the plays amply demonstrate Fielding's early sense of the relationship between good nature and libertinism which becomes so important in the later works. Since Fielding produced so many dramatic works of such varying quality and content, this discussion will focus on a representative sample of those plays that engage libertinism most specifically, rather than attempt to encompass his entire dramatic career in a limited space.

Love in Several Masques (1728), Fielding's first play, reveals that virtually all of the ideas on the tension between libertinism and morality that Fielding later developed concerned him from the beginning of his career. Many of the character types that come to dominate Fielding's fiction first appear in this work. The light comedies, here represented by *The Old Debauchees* (1732), *The Covent Garden Tragedy* (1732), and *Pasquin* (1736), were Fielding's most successful stage endeavors, and so are essential for study as representative of Fielding's understanding of his society and its sense of itself. *The Modern Husband* (1732) is Fielding's most serious attempt at social commentary within the five-act comedic form, with situations, characters, and social states resembling those to come in *Amelia*. *The Wedding Day* (1743), the last of Fielding's plays to be produced in his lifetime, offers a significant look back on the patterns established in his dramatic works. These six plays encompass most of Fielding's career, with first production dates ranging from 1728 to 1743, with an emphasis on the 1731–32 period, during which Fielding wrote or staged nine new plays. Further, though I deal with the three middle plays as a group of light comedies or farces, the plays selected also cover all five of Fielding's dramatic approaches as organized by stage historian Robert Hume (*Theatre* 257): traditional comedy (*Love in Several Masques* and *The Wedding Day*), serious satire (*The Modern Husband*), entertainment (*The Old Debauchees*), burlesque (*The Covent Garden Tragedy*), and topical satire (*Pasquin*). That these works cross the chronological and generic gamut suggests the continuing significance of libertinism to Fielding's work.

Fielding's invocation of libertine discourse in his plays functions as a challenge to socially imposed morals and as a support for the morally unorthodox. Biographers like Pat Rogers question Fielding's Christian orthodoxy, and represent him as punitive in cases of hypocrisy, but tolerant of errors of passion. This attitude is found in Fielding's plays as in his novels; both the outcome of the play and the implied authorial voice forgive the licentious and impetuous, but never the hypocritical. In his life as well, as Rogers explains, "Fielding was generous enough in that sphere of morality, however implacable he might be in his larger political and religious attachment. Provided that soldiers [accused of drinking, pilfering, and carousing] were brave and loyal he did not require their lives to be models of absolute purity" (147). Fielding constructs his plays in a similar way. His characterization and eventual punishment of the dishonest, deceitful and affected work together in admittedly thin plots, reconciling the social and intellectual independence of the libertine with a larger moral code that moves away from dependence on artificial social mores.

Even in production Fielding's plays contravened traditional social limitations. He ran plays, for example, on Wednesdays and Fridays during Lent until he was forcibly prevented from doing so. Certainly his perpetual need for income can be held partly responsible for this violation of religious decorum, but such an act demonstrates an irreverence and distaste for social limitations that prevent the individual from serving his or her own needs and desires. Furthermore, Fielding states clearly his disregard for public assumptions about the ostensibly didactic goals of some playwrights as he comments in his *Journey from This World to the Next* on the absurdity of the belief that any work on stage will really affect the morals or behaviour of an audience: "My Dramatic Works, replied the other [a playwright], which have done so much Good recommending Virtue and punishing Vice [should guarantee entry into Elysium]. – Very well, said the Judge, if you please to stand by, the first person who passes the Gate by your means, shall carry you in with him: but if you will take my Advice, I think, for Expedition sake, you had better return and live another Life upon Earth" (*Miscellanies* II 32–3). The playwright eventually gains entrance, but it is because he gave his benefits one night to save a friend's family, not for preventing the moral decay of his audiences. The narrator himself gains access under similar circumstances, acknowledging that he "had indulged [him]self very freely with Wine and Women in [his] Youth, but had never done an Injury to any Man living, nor avoided an Opportunity of doing good; that [he] pretended to very little Virtue more than general Philanthropy, and private Friendship" (*Miscellanies* II 36). Eliminating a moral imperative to drama (and to life in general) gives Fielding the liberty to create unconventional characters and to set plays anywhere from ballrooms to brothels without having to defend anything more than his own stance on issues. The necessity of even that defense, however, is usually negated by his libertine belief in privilege.

In his first play, Fielding establishes many of the ideas and assumptions that he will develop throughout his career, and elements of libertinism figure strongly. The couplet "Indecency's the bane to ridicule, / And only charms the libertine or fool" from the preface to *Love in Several Masques* both demonstrates Fielding's awareness of the discourse of libertinism in his society and reveals his rejection of the old understanding of the term. He has no respect for the purely indecent libertine, but the play that follows displays a growing recognition of a libertinism for his own time and his own philosophical inclinations. The three couples around whom the play revolves have evolved from the "gay couple" of earlier traditions: Merital is the libidinous rake (desired and pursued by the wife of the guardian of his intended, despite being apparently sexually reformed by the beginning of the play) who must manipulate the guardian Sir Positive Trap to win the spirited and independent heiress Helena; Vermilia is the indecisive lady whose maid gathers money and jewels from the jealous suitor Malvil in exchange for information (some true, some false) about the affections of her lady; and Lady Matchless is the wealthy and beautiful widow pursued by most of the other male characters, and won by the country squire Wisemore, whose use of disguise and disdain for the fops' flawed attempts at the inimitable originality of the true libertine characters reveal him to be part of the libertine tradition despite his tenaciously moralist public posture.

The change in the nature of the dramatic hero is not a shift between black and white, libertine and person of sense; it is a movement into a greyer locus of characterization. Between these six central characters, Fielding creates a community of Georgian libertines: young, witty, and socially and individually empowered figures who accept the central tenets of libertinism without surrendering to behavioural extremes to achieve their challenges to social, sexual, and gendered norms.

Merital's sexually libertine past is alluded to early in the play when Malvil refers to his friend as one "of you light, gay, fluttering fellows; who, like the weathercock, never fix long to a point till you are good for nothing" and as "a sort of sportsmen, who are always hunting in a park of coquets, where your sport is so plenty that you start fresh game before you have run down the old" (I i). Sir Positive Trap, Lord Formal, and Sir Apish Simple are the ridiculed extremist characters who suggest the need for challenge to the reigning moral order. Their very extremity points to the libertine centre of the play: before the first two hundred lines have passed, Sir Positive is established as the opposite of all that is valued in the play, and, interestingly, all that is libertine: "an old, precise knight, made up of avarice, folly, and ill-bred surliness of temper, and an odd, fantastic pride built on the antiquity of his family, into which he enrols most of the great men he ever heard of ... though he be monstrously morose to the rest of the world, he is as foolishly easy and credulous to his wife" (I i).

Fielding uses Sir Positive's "odd, fantastic pride" to mock conventional reverence for ancient families, and he makes the same point with Lord Formal, whose family is so old and so well placed that despite his outrageous vanity, he acts as arbiter of all that is acceptable: "Lord Formal is so perfect a master of good-breeding, that if he launched a little out of the common road, the world would esteem it a precedent, and not an error" (III vi). The young libertine characters recognize the ridiculousness of Formal, but others do not. Merital, for example, points up all of Formal's flaws in a brief scene at the end of the first act as he inverts the norms of old libertinism (to which certain foolish characters still attempt to subscribe) to demonstrate a central element of the Georgian libertine ethos: Formal compares women to a "fine house, I mean to entertain your friends with" and proffers the old misogynist chestnut that only ugly women are virtuous. He continues, "But beauty in the hands of a virtuous woman, like gold in those of a miser, prevents the circulation of trade." Merital, however, as the entirely modern Georgian libertine, has transcended such emotionless associations of femininity and possession, and suggests that the sexuality of men and women should not be so clearly differentiated: "A virtuous woman bestows her favours on the deserving, and makes them a real blessing to the man who enjoys her; whilst the vicious one, like a squandering prodigal, scatters them away; and, like a prodigal, is often most despised by those to whom she has been most kind" (I v). This speech certainly echoes standard moralist statements, but also, considering Merital's apparently quite recent past, suggests not a need for chastity of both sexes, but a need for the intelligent bestowing of favours. There is no indication that a virtuous woman will sleep with only one man in her lifetime. Women are neither victims of deceitful men nor overdefensive virgins, but individuals who can choose to "bestow" their favours on a man who will "enjoy" them. In the earliest example of the redefinition that develops throughout Fielding's works, virtue is no longer simply virginity, but something malleable and powerful in the hands of a woman granted the agency and intelligence to determine her own sexuality.

In fact, the most interesting element of *Love in Several Masques* in terms of libertinism is the development of the role of women in society, particularly courtship and sexuality. The play's lengthy dedication praises the learning and understanding of Lady Mary Wortley Montagu, "whose accurate judgment has long been the glory of her own sex, and the wonder of ours" and who is "a living confutation of those morose schoolmen, who would confine knowledge to the male part of the species" (7). This might seem a singular and thus insignificant comment except that Helena, the play's heroine, is described in similar terms by Merital, who opens his comments with a series of qualifications commonly used in reference to the magnetic male libertine: "Then my mistress is made up of natural spirit, wit, and fire; all these she has improved by an intimate conversation with plays, poems, romances, and such gay studies, by which she has acquired a perfect knowledge of the polite world without ever seeing it, and turned the confinement of her person into the enlargement of her mind" (I i). By discussing his mistress in terms of the discourse of libertinism, by describing her intelligence, naturalism, individuality, rebellion, and "natural spirit," Merital demonstrates her separation from the confines of her socially prescribed feminine role.

This passage is also one of many in *Love in Several Masques* that move toward collapsing the social differences between the masculine and the feminine. Wisemore mistakes two beaux for ladies in breeches and points out that the trend is already well entrenched in fashion. When his error is corrected, he notes, "But, perhaps, by them this amphibious dress may be a significant calculation; for I have known a beau with everything of a woman but the sex, and nothing of a man besides it" (I ii).[1] Centuries before modern theorists of gender and feminism articulated the position that "whatever biological intractability sex appears to have, gender is culturally constructed" (Butler 6), Fielding confirms that gender is determined as much by external social demands and appearances as by anatomy, and suggests again that the behaviour of the individual should not be determined by biological sex. It might be argued that since this comment is made by Wisemore, who is initially introduced as a stodgy and over-philosophical country squire, it suggests disapproval of collapsing genders rather than acknowledgment; however, Wisemore chooses to participate in the libertine practices of manipulation and disguise to gain the woman he desires just as do the more recognizably libertine characters. Furthermore, he despairs of the fops' attempts to appropriate the most frivolous qualities of socially constructed femininity while he admires the traditionally masculine qualities of education, independence, power, and control of the discourse of marriage and sexuality that Lady Matchless embodies. Only the weakening of humanity through cross-adoption of the most ridiculous qualities of either gender is attacked in Fielding's play.

This is most obvious not in the slightly effeminate fop Rattle (played by Colley Cibber), whose occasional wit maintains him as a minor character near the edge of libertine acceptability, but in the pompous and vain Lord Formal. Formal contributes to the conflation of gender roles by taking on the qualities of the silly Melanthaesque woman of Restoration drama when he tells Merital that "since the ladies have divided their time between cards and reading, a man, to be agreeable to them, must understand something of books as well as quadrille." Merital responds ironically, "I am afraid, if this humour continues, it will be as necessary in the education of a pretty gentleman to learn to read, as to learn to dance" (I v). Formal acknowledges that he himself does not actually read anything, but visits bookshops to record titles and authors, then mentions them in company and allows "good manners" to enroll him in the opinion of the first woman to offer hers. Such deferential behaviour and thoughtless and ultimately passive playing of the social game may be the domain of the female in traditional misogynist discourse, but it has long been left behind by the women who appear in *Love in Several Masques*.

Formal actually serves a dual function within the libertine discourse of the play: immediately after this discussion reveals him as the ironically masculine embodiment of all things presumed to be ridiculously feminine, he attempts to demonstrate his masculinity and his understanding of rakish libertinism, but displays instead the increasing irrelevance of the Restoration libertine as he mouths a series of platitudes about the possession of women and their potential in "circulation of trade." He is promptly corrected by "the gay Mr Merital," since such views are now unfashionable for the young and clever who seek the opposite sex as witty equal partners rather than mere objects of cruel conquest and purchase. The foolishness and unfashionable nature of such an understanding of relations between the sexes is confirmed later when the outmoded Sir Positive Trap announces that he hopes "to see the time, when a man may carry his daughter to market with the same lawful authority as any other of his cattle" (II vi). Merital's soliloquy closing the first act conflicts with these views as it voices the ideals of the genuine new libertine hero, that "good judgment only can discover and good nature relish" the beauties of "woman, that noble volume of our greatest happiness" (I vi). This is Fielding's first dramatic mention of that essential element of the new Georgian libertinism, "good nature." In this play alone the term is used in five scenes, and it recurs in almost every one of Fielding's plays, culminating in *The Fathers; or The Good Natured Man*, a work not performed until 1778, but one that was probably written early in his career.

Fielding does not make the error of allowing only the male characters to establish the value of libertine good nature and the increasingly powerful and self-determining role of female characters. Lady Matchless controls her fate fully and eventually chooses Wisemore because she loves him and because he values her for her qualities rather than her wealth and her status in the traditional social organization. Vermilia, too, controls her own fate, as she puts off her marriage to Malvil with no dominating male in sight to complete the triangle required for homosocial exchange in objectified female chattel. Young Helena is the most likely to be trapped by social constructs, but she responds to her uncle's desire to carry her off to market with, "Yes. But know, uncle of mine, that I am a woman, and may be as positive as you; and so your servant" (II vi). She bluntly negates the power of the existing social system over her own life and then exits in a physical expression of her individualism and disregard for socially constructed hierarchy. She further challenges Sir Positive's assumptions and the society he represents in act 5 when she reveals her knowledge of the sexual ways of the world (despite a near-cloistered upbringing). She responds to her uncle's comparison of fine fellows and snails with a reference to William Wycherley's *The Country Wife*, one of the most licentious of the libertine dramas of the Restoration: "Do you think so, sir? I have heard there is not a more dangerous place than a china-shop: take care my aunt does not bring one home in a jar, and then you may chance to see it pop forth its horns on the top of your cabinet." She then shows herself familiar with the social ways of the world as well when she threatens to reveal her aunt's regular infidelity: "Lookee, sir, I can make discoveries to you; and, since my aunt has falsely accused me with being the occasion of Sir Apish's behaviour to-day, I will tell you out of revenge what I would never have told you out of love" (V i).

Even Lady Trap contributes to Fielding's re-vision of libertinism. She participates to a certain extent in old-style libertine behaviour with her "morning rambles" which both Sir Positive and Helena know to be liaisons with young men, and she uses disguise to attempt to seduce the lover of her ward. After tricking Helena into copying out a letter setting up an assignation with Merital, Lady Trap has the letter delivered and waits at the appointed place in darkness. She pretends to be Helena when Merital arrives, and the couple embraces until Merital realizes he has been deceived. He discovers Lady Trap by feigning love for a "fine woman" rather than a "green girl" (III xiii), raising the volume of his murmurings in hopes of being interrupted before having to take his masquerade too far. The usual lovers' confusion arises when Helena witnesses part of the scene, but at no point in the play is Lady Trap tarnished or punished for her sexual licence. The play's libertine morality prevents any negative effects from sexual or social libertinism except that which is outmoded and unbalanced in the old-style Restoration incarnation. The only times the incident may be mentioned again are when Helena nearly reveals one of her aunt's acts of infidelity to her uncle (though it does not appear that this is the one she intends to expose), and when Merital's brief reference leads Lady Trap to quiet her husband's outrage over Helena's marriage to Merital.

Libertine subversion is further reflected in the use of masks and disguise, in no fewer than three other major scenes in the play. In the play's second incident, following Lady Trap's impersonation of Helena, Lady Matchless and Vermilia attend a duel "masqued." Just as Terry Castle shows that the masquerade allowed eighteenth-century women to abandon socially determined behavioural strictures, the masks here allow the female characters to exercise libertine control over the world around them. Like the use of disguise, the desire for an environment controlled by the individual rather than by external social constructs is a mark of the libertine, but the lack of manifestly cruel outcomes or trickery demonstrates the shift that has taken place within the paradigm. The women ensure that the duel will not take place by changing the direction on the note from "Merital" (whom Malvil mistakenly supposes to be his rival) to "Wisemore," thus removing the danger from the scene and determining a masquerade environment of flirtation and dissembling. When Lady Matchless asks, "Well, Vermilia, this sure is the maddest prank – what will the world say?" Vermilia's response demonstrates clearly the step the pair take in moving into the usually masculine realms of the duel and circumstantial control: "The world is a censorious, ill-natured critic, and I despise its cavillings. Besides, I am now grown careless of everything" (IV i). Lady Matchless encounters Wisemore and flirts aggressively with the man she will not yet fully admit she loves, concluding with a plan for a barefaced meeting at a later time. Vermilia's encounter with Malvil results only in Malvil arguing against the possibility of modesty in women and Vermilia's indignantly defending it until Malvil announces that he is no longer in love with his nameless ex-love, unaware that she stands before him. For the moment, he has failed the test that Vermilia's mask empowers her to administer.

The third masking incident is typical of eighteenth-century comedy as Merital poses as a parson, visiting Helena with Sir Apish. After Merital reveals himself and convinces Helena that her understanding of the scene with her aunt is mistaken, Helena dons the disguise and, in another obvious conflation of gender roles achieved through the tools of libertinism, the three "men" leave the house so that Merital and Helena can marry. This scene is derivative of Restoration comedies in the libertine stealing the sexually and socially desirable heiress through deceit and disguise. But the established tradition is transformed, since Helena does not marry merely to escape her oppressive guardian (which she might do with any of her suitors), but chooses as her husband the man she loves, after having established her agency and her libertine disregard for those cultural prescriptions of passive and passionless femininity and thoughtless acquiescence to social regulations that control those who lack her privilege and individuated power.

Finally, Wisemore enters Lady Matchless's home dressed as a sergeant to confront her other suitors. He violates the normative behavioural code by failing to remove his hat, a point ironically noted by the arbiter of all things social, Lord Formal, who entirely misses the other more significant violations of decorum going on before him. Wisemore declares that Lady Matchless's inheritance is being challenged and that she is, presently at least, uncertain of her financial standing. The libertine disguise reveals the disguises of motive – however thin – that the suitors Lord Formal, Rattle, and Sir Apish have sported from the beginning. Here again a libertine character (with the traditional or moral intent that will become even more significant in the novels and in plays like *The Modern Husband*) demonstrates that a device of power can serve only those privileged above the everyday concerns of society. Disguise can be used by the libertine, but it must be removed from those who should be ruled with the social rabble. Rules against deceit are necessary only for some, and the use of disguise by Lady Matchless, Vermilia, Merital, Helena, Wisemore, and even Lady Trap (who ends the play on the right side after all) shows that it is the witty, socially subversive and independent, rather than necessarily the socially well-placed, who are above the limitations of society.

Fielding's most successful group of plays followed *Love in Several Masques* both chronologically and thematically. Comedies and burlesques such as *The Author's Farce, The Tragedy of Tragedies, The Old Debauchees*, and *Pasquin* made Fielding the most popular playwright of the 1730s, and all of these plays contain characters, situations, and dialogues that invoke libertine philosophy in some way, though they vary in the explicitness of the depiction. I will examine the role of libertinism in *Pasquin, The Old Debauchees* and *The Covent Garden Tragedy*, the latter two of which Fielding himself paired on the stage as mainpiece and afterpiece. *Pasquin* was clearly the most successful and least scandalous of these three plays, running over sixty nights in all, including forty-three consecutively, and receiving generally positive reviews. Even the usually combative *Grub-street Journal* recorded that Alexander Pope had attended and enjoyed a performance, though this was quickly retracted. In the issue of 22 April 1736, though, 'Marforio' (probably Richard Russel) risked being contradicted and offered a patronizing explanation of the idea of irony when he published a long discussion of the moral flaws of the plays-within-the-play. He still found it necessary, however, to preface his comments with the admission that "the prodigious success of this [*Pasquin*] has fixed it secure beyond the attaques of any malicious Critic" (Paulson and Lockwood 84).

Unlike *Pasquin* and its critical acceptance, *The Old Debauchees* has been critically dismissed since its initial appearance. Nonetheless, the drama is successful as a piece of social commentary that is both entertaining and enlightening. It is also an excellent example of the movement that Fielding allows between public assumptions about morality and social representation, and the libertine understanding that underlies the social interactions he depicts throughout his work. *The Old Debauchees* is based on a 1731 scandal in which Catherine Cadière was seduced by her confessor, Father Girard, the director of the Jesuit seminary at Toulon, who reportedly used sorcery to aid in the seduction. Clearly, however, the scandal provided only the intellectual seed for Fielding's comedy. He uses his self-determined libertine privilege as a vantage point from which to demonstrate the validity of religious doubt and the folly of blind faith in social doctrine as he and his characters expose not the individual priest, but the manner of corruption and hypocrisy of the Roman Catholic Church and society as a whole.

But religion is only one area that Fielding attacks and undermines: the social and moral environment of his time also serves as a broad target. There were the private peccadillos of the court, for example, as

George II kept several mistresses who seem to have had almost the same social standing as the queen, and Sir Robert Walpole lived openly with Molly Skerrit while his wife played mistress to Lord Hervey. *The Old Debauchees* is thus recognizable as an early attempt by Fielding to comment on the behaviour of both the public and the leaders of the nation in a format and style to which the theatre-goer would pay attention. The voice, though, is not necessarily that of what Angela Smallwood calls a man "rightly famous for his Christian Moralist stance" (173); it is equally the voice of a libertine mocking those who thoughtlessly accept the constraints of social decorum, gender roles, and sexual repression. This understanding of the play, combined with Fielding's own unorthodox behaviour and frequent questioning of social doctrines at this time in his life, marks him to some degree as an advocate of the libertine tradition.[2] He constructs a play that, through the characters of an unrepenting libertine and a foolish man who submits to social domination, reveals his acceptance of morality and social goals for the masses and his denial of such things for his peers and fellow libertines. The play is unemphatic in its moralism, but as Georgian libertine drama it is typical of Fielding's work.

Whether Fielding was successful in his attempt to challenge and perhaps even redefine popular perceptions of both libertinism and moral concepts such as virtue is unclear from the contemporary critical reception of the play. Certainly some critics agreed with audiences in their approbation of the anti-papist tone of the play, while others saw only the libertine aspects of the production. An anonymous critic complained, "When such things are suffer'd on the stage, 'tis no wonder there are so many Whores and Pickpockets in the streets" (Paulson and Lockwood 60). In defense against such critical attacks on the moral implications of the play, 'Philalethes,' a correspondent to *The Daily Post* who was probably Fielding himself, uses a mocking tone to point out the ironic potential of allowing certain characters to espouse the alternative moral philosophies of the play: "The author is said to recommend *Whoring and Drunkenness*; how! Why a Rake speaks against Matrimony and a Sot against Sobriety: So Moliere in Don Juan recommends all Manner of Vices and every Poet (I am sure every good one) that hath exposed a vicious Character, hath by this rule contributed to debauch mankind" (Paulson and Lockwood 62). It appears that the social and moral implications of *The Old Debauchees* (and *The Covent Garden Tragedy*) were no more obvious to Fielding's contemporaries than they are to modern critics. Still, while it is certainly possible to read a moral message in the farce of *Debauchees*, a more explicitly libertine reading that denies an absolute morality and offers an alternative behavioural code, particularly in terms of the development and privileging of characters, is quite clear.

The Covent Garden Tragedy shared the stage with *The Old Debauchees* for one night, its scandalous setting and action contributing to the confusion about Fielding's stance on the shifting discourses of libertinism and morality. The play addresses issues similar to those of *Debauchees*, but adds other elements, notably a more explicit revelation of Fielding's own sense of libertine privilege. The procurers, prostitutes, bullies and culls represented here find even less in the doctrines of Church, family, and patriarchy that seems valid than do the characters of *The Old Debauchees*, and the play was attacked even more fiercely than its precursor. Audiences were angered by the depiction of a brothel and 'low' characters, and 'Dramaticus' expresses these sentiments in *The Grubstreet Journal* of 15 June 1732: "Such a scene of infamous lewdness, was never brought, I believe, before on any Stage whatsoever!" (Paulson and Lockwood 43). 'Publicus' joined the attacks in the same journal on 20 July by asserting that both plays were "so far improper for an *English Stage*, or to be exhibited to a *polite*, an *honest*, and a *christian* people, that, (unless Sodom and Gomorrah had been now undestroyed) they were only fit for the hangman's flames" (56). He goes on to assert that Fielding's "pen is not only void of *wit, manners*, and *modesty*, but likewise of the most common *rules* of *Poetry*, and even *Grammar*" (61). *The Covent Garden Tragedy*, then, was perceived in Fielding's time to be his most audaciously libertine play, subverting all that society deemed socially, morally, and sexually sacrosanct. Even Battestin, usually among the first to argue for Fielding's Christian moralism, agrees, suggesting that the play's characters and events were "meant to be savored by Fielding's fellow rakes in the audience" (*Life* 135). He further hypothesizes that Fielding "had no doubt sown his wild oats at Mother Needham's and had been entertained at the Rose through the obliging offices of the pimp Leathercoat" (145).

The play proves to be an evocative example of Georgian libertine comedy. Fielding does advocate a social code, but it is one in which figures like himself are raised above the need to bow to traditional standards. As he exercises the freedom to set a play in a brothel, Fielding exercises his choice to write a play devoid of a traditional moral, and it is only pedantic fools and members of the mercantile classes who worry about the omission. They cannot possibly understand the libertine privilege Fielding takes for granted. The Prologomena that he falsifies in the published version of the play offers a critic so dismayed at the lack of a moral statement that he feels compelled to find one, though the best that he can do is to mutter, "I cannot help wishing this may

teach all gentlemen to pay their chairmen" (107). From the play's prologue onwards an ironic statement against an artistic requirement of
moral didacticism is established. Here the usual moral lessons taught by
dramatic representations of "kings' and heroes' faults" are shown to be
useless to the masses who are ignorant of the privilege and distinction
of kings and heroes:

> Examples of the great can serve but few;
> For what are kings' and heroes' faults to you?
> But these examples are of general use.
> What rake is ignorant of King's Coffee-house?
> Here the old rake may view the crimes h'as known,
> And boys hence dread the vices of the town:
> Here nymphs seduced may mourn their pleasures past,
> And maids, who have their virtue, learn to hold it fast.

In fact, rather than offering a traditional dramatic moral or lesson,
Fielding presents throughout the play a series of Restoration-style libertine inversions of standard social mores. Mother Punchbowl offers a vision of heroism that echoes Rochester's "The Disabled Debauchee" as
she describes her glory days "[w]hen colonels, majors, captains, and
lieutenants, / Here spent the issue of their glorious toils; / These were
the men, my Bilkum, that subdued / The haughty foe, and paid for
beauty here" (I iv). Lovegirlo and Gallono engage in an equally Rochesterian debate over the superiority of women or wine, which is resolved
with Bilkum's "Either to other to prefer I'm loth, / But he does wisest
who takes most of both" (I vii). Lovegirlo's images of masturbation at
the end of act 1, as outrageous as Fielding's contemporaries seemed to
find them,[3] are also entirely within the old-style libertine tradition.
While it may be possible that these scenes are intended to be ironic,
since all of the speeches are given by debauched characters, I suggest
that the only irony here is that the male characters are out of fashion in
their attempts at libertinism; contemporary critics were right in their
suggestions that such a play simply cannot function exclusively as an
ironic satire of moral intent. Lovegirlo and Bilkum are products of the
Restoration tradition of libertinism of thoughtless excess, and Fielding
– always aware of the fashion – establishes the clownish qualities of
these characters not to evaluate them on moral terms (which is virtually
impossible, since there is no character in the play who can be held up as
a measure of moralist comparison), but to compare them implicitly to
the more fashionable libertines of Fielding's own age. That this group
includes Fielding himself is clear, and this is not surprising, since the

same sort of implied superiority of author over characters is one of the dominant characteristics of the intrusive narrative voice of the novels that followed Fielding's truncated dramatic career.

After the couples are paired off for their arrangements of keeping, Lovegirlo speaks the closing couplet of the play: "From such examples as of this and that, / We all are taught to know I know not what" (II xiii). The couplet reveals an ideology absolutely consistent with Fielding's libertine drama. One fails to recognize the moral of the story only if one feels that a moral is necessary; otherwise it is clear that the moral is that there need not be one. Public moralism is faulty, valued only by those who are not of sufficient standing to realize that one must act according to individual desires and autonomous knowledge, regardless of the rules of society.

Pasquin also addresses these issues of individuality and society, and it too is without a moral in the traditional sense. It is true that "The Election" contains social satire on the nature of the electoral process and on the prevalence of bribery in politics as well as the gullibility of various types of characters. It is probably also true that "The Life and Death of Common Sense" is a criticism of Walpole's corruption and a statement in favour of Bolingbrokean politics. However, it is equally true that a primary focus of the play as a whole is Fielding's attack on the frivolous forms of entertainment that had recently become popular in English theatres. Fielding's epilogue (which serves both "The Life and Death of Common Sense" and *Pasquin* as a whole) refers specifically to the other two plays under discussion here by stating that the epilogue will not be what audiences have come to expect from him and his libertine voice.[4] The author "begs a serious word or two to say" as he explains that "childish entertainments ... soft Italian notes ... and all the tumbling-scum of every nation" could destroy the deservedly privileged position of English drama. He evokes national pride as he asks,

> Can the whole world in science match our soil?
> Have they a LOCKE, a NEWTON, or a BOYLE?
> Or dare the greatest genius of their stage,
> With SHAKESPEARE or immortal BEN engage?

The central issue of the play is the one most explicitly suggested by the rehearsal format, the action of the second play-within, and the authorial comments in the prologue and epilogue: the need to return to English dramatic traditions and to attempt to rise above the foolish tastes of the town. The only places in which *Pasquin* addresses traditional issues of dramatic didacticism are points at which the lack of a moral is pointed out by overtly pedantic or mindlessly critical observers of the plays-within. The hostile Fustian asks Trapwit of the comedy, "Pray, sir, what's the moral of this act?" (II i), and Trapwit, either because there is no traditional moral or because he considers it obvious in his own obscure way, refuses to explain anything. The pedantic Sneerwell later notes his pleasure that at the end of Fustian's tragedy Common-sense speaks a lesson about the successes of Ignorance being haunted by the ghost of Common-sense, since he "was under terrible apprehensions for [Fustian's] moral" (V i). Again, the pedant expects a moral, and the parodied tragedian supplies one (though not of the usual focus), but neither possesses the libertine artistic independence that Fielding himself assumes, and so neither realizes that he has a choice. Not only do these fictional playwrights lack the talent to be successful, but they also lack the natural sense and superior understanding associated with Georgian libertinism, making their weakness impossible to miss.

While *The Old Debauchees* does technically end with the couplet-moral "when a Woman sets herself about it, / Nor Priest nor Devil can make her go without it," it is obviously not one that conflicts with the libertine ideology of the pointlessness of a staged moral statement. Like the others we have seen, this couplet advocates the freedom of the individual playwright to create work that suits his or her own taste rather than that of a socially constructed norm. The dominant moral scheme of *Debauchees* is that of libertine individualism, and though this play does not mock the stage as a place for moral statement (as do both *The Covent Garden Tragedy* and *Pasquin*), it does subvert the usual dramatic norm throughout. *The Old Debauchees* undermines the conventional dramatic moral and normative morality in general most strikingly in characterizations that show how that which is constructed as normative is frequently distinctly unnatural. Much of the play's satire relies on attacking not morality, but the contravention of human nature caused by the fear evoked by the power of socially determined moral and behavioural codes. Naturalistic libertinism is the dominant characteristic not only of Old Laroon's character, but of the play as a whole. Social challenge, sexuality, religious doubt, gender parity, and reinvention of identity are all essential here.

First, the rationalization of virtue and the abuse of religion-based fear derided in Fielding's definitions of good nature are satirized in the relationship between Father Martin and Old Jourdain. Martin states, and Jourdain accepts, that "[y]ou are to believe what the Church tells you and no more" (III vi). Though Jourdain's gullibility makes him appear ridiculous, Father Martin is the primary target of the satire against contravention of nature. There are two ways to view Martin's lust, sloth, lies, deceit, covetousness, and his abuse of the doctrines of forgiveness and tolerance. The first is that it is Martin's nature to abuse, lust, and lie, and that he disregards that nature by taking on the robes of a priest who ostensibly does good for no motive other than the benefit of others. In this view, Fielding attacks the falseness and hypocrisy around him as failures to accept natural order and motivation, using the priest as a common example, but not an exclusive one. Conversely, one could assume that Fielding indicates that all priests act to conceal their sinful natures by hypocritically hiding them beneath the cover of the Church. In this case it may be said that the nature of the priest is to be evil, but that he still betrays that nature by presenting an image of goodness to society at large. In either case, Martin fails to meet the libertine standard of naturalism and violates the doctrine of good nature.

Old Jourdain also contravenes the freer, more libertine nature shown in his youth in the vacillation and gullibility of his old age. Old Laroon tells us that Jourdain "was wicked as long as he could be so; and when he could sin no longer, why he began to repent that he had sinned at all. Oh! there is nothing so devout as an old Whoremaster" (I ii). The sins of Jourdain's youth range from common adultery to robbery and beating, denunciation of religion, and the administration of false justice. All but the last are sins not uncommon for a young rake, particularly of the high Restoration period in which Jourdain and Laroon would have passed their youth. Jourdain's internalization of the attitudes toward love and life that he attempts to deny by abandoning his own past is betrayed, for example, in his response to the false news of his unmarried daughter's pregnancy: there is initial surprise, and then he cries, "Oh! St *Francis*! St *Francis*! What a merciful Saint art thou!" (II iii).[5] The news is shocking, but not horrifying, since a pregnancy would not be at all an unknown or unforeseen situation for a libertine of old. The supposed pregnancy simply resolves the dilemma at hand, preventing Jourdain's daughter Isabel from being forced into a nunnery on Father Martin's orders to pray her father out of purgatory (and, conveniently, to be available for the sexual advances of Father Martin). Unlike Father Martin, Old Jourdain is not depicted as evil for denying his good nature and his own judgement, but as a gullible old fool who will not follow his true nature or even believe his own senses if the Church would contradict them: Isabel tells him that in her plot to reveal Father Martin, Jourdain shall witness all and believe his own eyes and ears, to which he responds, "Against the Church, Heaven forbid!" (III ix).

Characters who do follow their natures into spontaneous activity, love, and faith are represented in a far more positive light by Fielding, regardless of their virtue or morality in the conventional senses of the words. Young Laroon follows his "amiable temper of Mind" without any "abstract Contemplation of … Virtue," and disregards the "Terrors of Religion" (*Miscellanies* I 158) to reach the goodness inherent in a marriage for love. His fiancée Isabel uses her intelligence and self-empowerment and disregards Martin's hypocritical social views and threats in order to live in the world she loves. The lovers, who vow to marry each other or not at all because their love is naturally right, even if not aligned to religious expectation, certainly embody Fielding's ideal. It is Isabel's cousin Beatrice, though, who best demonstrates good nature. Beatrice's nature, in accordance with Fielding's statement, is to do good and avoid evil. She has great empathy and sensible judgement, the latter of which allows the events of *The Old Debauchees* to change her plans for the future – she decides to marry and not to enter a convent. The reason for her plans, however, is not changed: the heartfelt desire to do good. It is Beatrice, in her utter honesty and sterling intent, who shows that the way to Heaven is not blind faith, but good faith – a moral suggestion certainly, but one conveyed through unmistakably libertine means as she evaluates the institutionalization of religion and reaches her own conclusions, enabling an autonomous determination of her own future.

Beatrice represents the character type that is absent from *The Covent Garden Tragedy*. There is no one in Mother Punchbowl's world to represent an independent and thinking person who still chooses to follow some of society's directions. The single explicitly moralist speech in *The Covent Garden Tragedy* is that of Stormandra as she plans to hang herself because she has been spurned by Lovegirlo, the man who pays his women best:

> May good women be by my example taught,
> Still to be good, and never to be naught;
> Never from virtue's rules to go astray,
> Nor ever to believe what man can say.
> She who believes a man, I am afraid,
> May be a woman long, but not a maid.
> If such blest harvest my example bring,
> The female world shall with my praises ring,
> And say, that when I hanged myself, I did a noble thing.   (II vii)

Aside from the obvious irony attached to suicide as a noble act and the belief that anyone will even notice the suicide of a prostitute, this speech offers a blatant subversion of standard moral platitudes. That it is spoken by a prostitute and not just a woman seduced makes it ridiculous initially, and as she never finally does kill herself, she neither learns nor teaches any lesson. Further, she is rewarded at the play's conclusion for exactly the sins she professes to warn others against as in a "sudden turn of joy" she reaches an arrangement of keeping with Captain Bilkum (II xiii). *The Old Debauchees'* Isabel provides a compromise between the almost impossible goodness of Beatrice and the extreme Restoration-style sexual libertinism of Stormandra, but her character type is also absent from the *Tragedy*. It is this element of Fielding's naturalist characterization that reveals differences in the libertine ideologies of the two plays. A blunt sense of the authorial libertine privilege is represented by the very creation of *The Covent Garden Tragedy*. The play reflects old-style libertinism in its shocking explicitness and outrageousness, and contains fewer recognitions of the possibility of the compromise in the Georgian libertinism that is offered in *The Old Debauchees*.

Old Laroon has been the truest old-style libertine of *The Old Debauchees*, but he is also a good character if we use Georgian libertinism and good nature as guides. He functions as a character in transition from the Restoration libertinism of his youth to a more mature and thoughtful libertinism that he has adopted as it has developed around him. He is hot-headed when he denies the dominance of rationalism, but even in this he is motivated by the desire to "promote the ... Happiness of others." Though we know that Old Laroon is pleased by the wealth of his son's fiancée, he is more motivated by the desire for his son to enjoy his youth and to be as happy as Old Laroon was in his own.

Through both the traditionally favourable and detrimental aspects of the character of Old Laroon, Fielding is able to make a number of statements which use a specifically libertine discourse to demonstrate social and moral tensions. Old Laroon is a harmless and humorous teller of tales of a bygone era as he says, "Of all the Actions of my Youth, there are none I reflect on with so much Pleasure as having burnt half a Dozen Nunneries, and delivered several hundred Virgins out of Captivity ... Out of which Number, there are at present nine Countesses, three Duchesses, and a Queen, who owe their Liberty and their Promotion to this Arm" (I ii). In the end, though, despite the extremism of his libertine traits and speeches, Old Laroon has simply followed his nature, made himself and others happy, and avoided misfortune. He can honestly say that he has "no Sins to reflect on but those of an honest Fellow. If I have lov'd a Whore at five-and-twenty, and a Bottle at forty; Why, I have done as much good as I could, in my Generation; and that, I hope, will make amends" (III xiv). Old Laroon never deceives himself or others as to his true nature as a libertine, and so is both more honest and more attractive to the audience than Old Jourdain, who tries so hard to make his way to Heaven by denying his nature and his past that he almost ruins his daughter in the process. Old Laroon enunciates the libertine implications of this act: "And so, you would atone for all your former Rogueries by a greater, by perverting the Design of Nature! Was this Girl intended for praying!" (II ii).

A central focus of the intellectual element of libertine discourse is that of religious acceptance and religious challenge. The issue is almost entirely absent from *The Covent Garden Tragedy*, since that play is both set in and absorbed by a world where institutionalized religion not only has little influence, but is rarely even considered. On the other hand, *Pasquin* refers repeatedly to the failure of priests to fulfill their mandate and thus reflects Fielding's own reservations about thoughtless acceptance of the role of the Church in society. In an obvious repetition of the same point made in *The Old Debauchees*, he examines the supposition that the public must simply accept the word of a priest. The priest Firebrand tells us that Ignorance is such a "pious queen" that "she believes / Whate'er their priests affirm. And by the Sun / Faith is no faith, if it fall short of that" (IV i). Though Fustian defends his depiction of the grasping and false priest Firebrand by arguing that he intends only to show the difference between a heathen and a Christian priest, Fielding's satire is clear and sharp. Later in the scene Common-sense shows her irritation that Firebrand would tell her that despite her faith, she is "a most deadly enemy to the Sun, / And all his priests have greatest cause to wish / [She] had never been born." She accuses Firebrand of being a priest "who wears pride's face beneath religion's mask, / And make a pick-lock of his piety / To steal away the liberty of mankind." It is particularly significant that Fielding here combines the libertine desire for freedom of thought and behaviour (treated as an absolute good) with the use of disguise to gain one's own purposes and the need to challenge authoritative statements of any kind, particularly concerning religion. The various elements of libertine discourse are clearly connected in his mind, and thoughtless acceptance of appearances is the deepest foolishness of all.

Other readers such as Battestin also note the apparently anti-Church stance of *Pasquin*, but instead of accepting this as an interesting part of the libertinism that he documents in Fielding's youth, Battestin attempts to parallel Fielding's expression of distrust of the Church to the latitudinarianism of Bishop Hoadly: "to the more orthodox, High Church party in this age of theological controversy, the latitudinarian

Christianity even of Bishop Hoadly was scarcely less objectionable than the irreverent satire of *Pasquin*" (*Life* 199). Such special pleading is difficult to accept wholeheartedly. Other readings seem both more accessible and more acceptable, particularly that Fielding does not deny the validity of religion but uses satire and his Georgian libertine understanding to encourage a thoughtful approach to any doctrine.

Whether *The Old Debauchees* is a serious religious and socio-political commentary or a simple exercise in priest-baiting, the Church is essential to the most obviously moralistic aspect of Fielding's play as represented through the libertine understanding. He attacks the hypocrisy of the wealthy Catholic Church and of certain types of people who pretend to be what they are not in order to hurt others and gain for themselves. Father Martin is a priest on the outside and a sinner on the inside, but is ultimately a failure at both. Despite his attempts to convince Jourdain to the contrary, Martin is a far worse guide to Heaven than would be even Old Laroon, a libertine layman of true good nature. The apparently anti-Church theme of both *Debauchees* and *The Covent Garden Tragedy* is thus also libertine in its denigration of those who follow doctrine without adequate consideration of its social and individual implications. The characters in *The Old Debauchees* who are perceived as strong have examined their own values and developed an intelligent and informed world-view natural to themselves. They follow the doctrines of Church, family, and patriarchy only to the extent that seems valid to them.

Isabel, the heroine of *The Old Debauchees*, clearly has doubts about all three, and that she will not allow her father and the Church to ruin her is a significant manifestation of the gendered aspect of Fielding's representation of libertinism. Isabel demonstrates the relative empowerment of women through libertinism's challenges to social constructs: she is active not only in controlling her own life, but also in enjoying the world around her. When she announces, at her crucial first introduction in the play, "But this I am positive, till the World is weary of me, I shall never be weary of the World" (I i), she demonstrates the attractiveness of women who are free to have a role in the world and, further, are not frowned upon for enjoying it. Isabel is the clever heroine of Fielding's farce; her introduction cannot reasonably be seen as a negative or satirical presentation of active femininity. Her autonomous self-determination and its libertine undertones are present throughout the play, particularly as she tells Young Laroon, "the Commands of all the Priests in *France* shall not force me to marry another. That is, Sir, I will either marry you or die a Maid; and I have no violent Inclination to the latter, on the Word of a Virgin" (I vii). We see the error of a society that would have women be isolated and passive as Martin schemes to take advantage of these traditional elements to rape Isabel. He tells her, "While you are only passive, I'll answer for your Sins," and that in the isolation of a nunnery, "there are Indulgencies granted to people in that State, which would be sinful out of it" (III iv). His plan, of course, fails, and this is attributed in the last two lines of the play to the fact that "when a Woman sets herself about it, / Nor Priest, nor Devil can make her go without it" (III xiv).

Beatrice provides a second female presence powerful in independence of thought, despite her initial appearance of conventionality. She is not mocked for either her independence or her more traditionally acceptable initial plan to retire from a corrupt world and enter a convent (so unacceptable in the world of the play) in any sense that can be taken as more than bantering jest. Thus her character demonstrates a level of explicit moralism that attempts to make the prevalent libertinism more palatable, a nod to conventional morality missed by many of Fielding's critical contemporaries. Each woman decides her own fate for her own reasons. That Fielding creates female characters who are intelligent and active, and who do not allow themselves to be subjugated by their patriarchal surroundings suggests that he did indeed view women with a respect that was well ahead of his time, and yet was perfectly aligned with Georgian libertinism. Fielding could not offer an idea of a truly humane morality without mediating it with the forward-looking aspects of libertinism, unifying at a moral level the circles into which men and women were separated by his society. This involves much more than sexuality: he increases the number of qualities shared by the sexes, including individuated agency and worldliness in Isabel, faith and romance in Young Laroon, and intelligence and autonomy in Beatrice. The dominant construct of femininity as the binary angel/whore is violated, and sexual self-determination is just as valuable to the truly good-natured woman as perpetually guarded virginity; Fielding's sexually active women ("fallen" though they may be in popular contemporary discourse) are never cast out, and, in fact, generally close the play or novel rewarded with a happy marriage and financial stability.

Such conflation of artificial dichotomies is typical of Georgian libertinism and its shifting approaches to challenges of accepted ideas and practices of social, legal, and religious custom. Smallwood suggests that Fielding "opposes tyranny both national and domestic; and he exposes the bogus rhetoric which pronounces the merely traditional or customary to be natural and therefore right" (173). Fielding creates characters in his plays who negate the fundamentally immoral confinement and social abuse of women. This is again a dramatic embodiment of a view both moral and libertine: without the support of the philosophy and tradition of Georgian libertinism that demonstrate the significance of independence for women, the contradictions in his society's view of women remain unacknowledged. Fielding's recognition of this role of libertinism is of major consequence in *The Old Debauchees*, and an early manifestation of a pattern that will culminate in the libertine qualities of *Amelia*.

The libertinism of women in *The Covent Garden Tragedy*, as might be expected, is most conspicuous as a sexual quality that renders sexual relations somewhat more equitable, whereby both parties engage in an economic exchange based on some level of individual self-determination. The female characters are not confined by the value that society places on the standard conception of virtue; indeed, according to the play's discourse of sexuality, socially determined virtue is a vague and amorphous thing unnatural to humanity. In a move that echoes the tone of *The Modern Husband* (which ran immediately before the *Tragedy*), Fielding points out the ridiculousness of the public association between representations of morality and actual behaviour. The critic of the Prolegomena asks, "Leathersides desires her to procure two whores, &c., but then is she not continually talking of virtue? How can she be a bawd?" Mother Punchbowl's (historically accurate) vision of her own death in the pillory revisits the same apparent contradiction when she fears seeing "the sneer of every virtuous whore" (I iii).

The difference between that which is publicly determined to be virtuous and that which is truly virtuous is a longstanding interest of Fielding's, present in all of his novels, and demonstrated most explicitly in *Shamela*. The epilogue of the *Tragedy* expresses the need to recognize the uselessness of distinctions within a wide continuum of moral behaviour, since motivation – male or female – can never be determined, and desire is often co-opted by external forces. Kitty Raftor-Clive, one of Fielding's favorite leading ladies, played both Isabel in *The Old Debauchees* and Kissinda in the *Tragedy*,[6] and delivered the epilogue to *The Covent Garden Tragedy*:

> Pray tell me, sirs, in which you like me best?
> Neither averse to love's soft joys you find;
> 'Tis hard to say which is the best inclined.
> The priest makes all the difference in the case;
> Kissinda's always ready to embrace,
> And Isabel stays only to say grace.
> For several prices ready both to treat,
> This takes a guinea, that your whole estate ...

And virtuous women, though they dread the shame,
Let 'em but play secure, all love the game …
For prudes may cant of virtues and of vices,
But faith, we differ only in our prices.

Fielding's critics asserted that he was calling all women prostitutes and defaming the wives and sisters of all good men. Fielding's response fits exactly the naturalism and individualism of the libertine. In a letter as 'Philalethes' to the *Daily Post* 31 July 1732, Fielding denies that he terms all women whores, and that instead, "nothing more is asserted, than that it is natural for one Sex to be fond of the other" (Paulson and Lockwood 62).

In fact, Fielding's entire play offers naturalism and sexuality as challenges to existing social structures. The lack of moral outrage on stage marks the very act of writing the play as a libertine one. Fielding appropriates the traditional language of moralism and virtue to disrupt their popular significance, and to move toward a discourse celebrating the freedom and power of the individual. Kissinda's greatest desire is to be kept, but she fears love. She speaks in ways common to virginal heroines, but with small but significant divergences that mark the shifts Fielding sees as necessary to prevent hypocrisy in society. She reminds Lovegirlo, "Thou know'st too well a lady of the town, / If she give way to love, must be undone" (I ix). And Lovegirlo says what society's wilful blindness knows about human nature but denies: "Who but a fool would marry that can keep – / What is this virtue that mankind adore?" (I ix). Stormandra similarly uses the language of virtue to guard that which she values most:

Stormandra: Oh! Mother Punchbowl, teach me how to rail;
              Oh! teach me to abuse this monstrous man.
Punchbowl: What has he done?
Stormandra: Sure a design so base,
              Turk never yet conceived.
Punchbowl: Forbid it, virtue.
Stormandra: It wounds me to the soul – he would have bilked me.   (II ii)

Mother Punchbowl also mouths the platitudes of virtue in a libertine context of fulfilling individual desires, asking Stormandra to service Bilkum, and "with caution still preserve the bully's love." She rationalizes, "Forbid it, virtue, I should ever think / A woman squeezes any cull too much: / But bullies never should be used as culls" (II iii). Public virtue

functions as a series of platitudes to justify one's own actions or to coerce others into a design that serves the manipulator, but Fielding's own
libertinism frees him from bowing to such artificial constructions, opting instead for blunt honesty of action and motivation.

The politic of sexuality that Fielding offers in *The Old Debauchees*
does bow more to convention than does the version depicted in *The
Covent Garden Tragedy*. This may well explain why the former remained
on the public stage and the latter did not. The frequent sexual innuendo and general suggestiveness of the *Tragedy* are most significant for
their promotion of individuality, freedom of expression, and passion as
central values. That Fielding consistently denied that his work was any
more immoral than that of any other writer suggests that he is engaging
in a conscious reconstruction of moral discourse rather than simply be-
lieving that his obviously unconventional drama was morally corrupt.
He defended his play in *The Grub-street Journal* in 1732 by writing, "I
may aver [the critic] will find more [indecencies] in *Dryden, Congreve,
Wycherley, Vanbrugh, Cibber*, and all our best Writers of *Comedy*" (Paulson and Lockwood 64). Fielding does not specifically advocate the actual sexually libertine morality of Old Laroon in *The Old Debauchees*,
but he does use that morality to show that good nature and the following of doctrines natural to humanity are more relevant to the goodness
and true virtue of a character than the following of an artificial morality
established by an imperfect society.

Pasquin also demonstrates the effect on women of the confining ideals of that imperfect society. Much of the play offers the same critical
assessments of the female characters as of the male. Mrs Mayoress is as
gullible as her husband and his associates in accepting the addresses of
Lord Place and Colonel Promise, and she is mocked for her pride in
having been "woman to a lady of quality," in much the same way that
her husband is mocked for his pride at his social position as a mayor in
such an unfashionable place as the country. The ambition and manipu-
lativeness of Mrs Mayoress are also satirized to allow the domestic realm
and the political realm to parallel one another, and to expose the folly
of human nature and those who would so involve themselves in the
politics of the day. Miss Mayoress is naive but innocent as she accepts
Lord Place's suggestion that it is the fashion to go into keeping rather
than to marry, and the entire discussion demonstrates Fielding's sense
of social superiority and privilege as he reveals the emptiness of middle-
class attempts to keep up with the behavioural and intellectual flair of
the libertines. Miss Mayoress and Miss Stitch also serve as the vehicles
through which Fielding satirizes the lack of public understanding of is-

sues, the dependence on potentially scurrilous columnists for information, and the fatuity of the low and uneducated discussing topics of any importance.

In examining the place of women in *Pasquin*, however, it is useful to consider the players as well as their characters. Charlotte Charke took on the role of Lord Place from the eleventh performance until the end of the run. This is another example, like those discussed earlier, of Fielding's interest in the conflation of gender roles. Sexual innuendo now arises out of otherwise innocuous statements, as when Lord Place asks Mr Mayor to "give me leave to squeeze you by the hand, in assurance of my sincerity" (I i) and declares, "Gentlemen, be assured, I will take care of you all; you shall be provided for as soon as possible" (II i). The fop and the woman, whose similarities Fielding has depicted in *Love in Several Masques*, have actually become one. And that Fielding created the opportunity for Charke to enact on the public stage the transvestism that she also enacted in much of her own life confirms the playwright's willingness to represent alternative constructions of sexuality and gendered agency even in a context that encourages spectatorial slippage between fictional and historical culture. As Kristina Straub argues, "When the actress puts on masculine sexuality, even as she functions as its object of desire, she opens possibilities for challenging the stability and authority of that sexuality" (134).[7]

Throughout Fielding's plays, in fact, the refusal to accept traditional moral, social, sexual, or formal limitations reveals his sense of his own libertine privilege, though this is most apparent in terms of traditional morality in *The Covent Garden Tragedy*, and of form in *Pasquin*. In *Pasquin*, for example, Mrs Mayoress explains to her daughter that going into keeping is not necessarily immoral because "that can't be, if your betters do it; people are punished for doing naughty things; but people of quality are never punished; therefore they never do any naughty things" (II i). It is valuable to note the doubled role given this passage. Some of the audience would have accepted such a thing as truthful (for better or worse), and others might have read an irony into the passage considering its source, thus allowing it to function as a satiric comment on the social knowledge of the middle class from the position of a playwright who considered himself far above that class and thus sufficiently privileged to say so. Either way, the statement that nothing done by people of quality can be naughty manifests the libertine acceptance of rules only for the low and the belief in a superior position of understanding. Similarly, the general attractiveness of the character of Lord Place and Fielding's apparent respect for the woman playing him also reveal a sympathy with the figure who manipulates those beneath him

– without cruelty – to gain that which he desires. Lord Place was assumed by audiences to be "addicted … to gaming and whoring" (Paulson and Lockwood 84) as well, but is never punished for his arrogance
and manipulation, and he plans his departure for London on the assumption that he will be greeted happily on his return in the next election year. Certainly he looks down on the "Canaille," but he is not
satirized himself as much as he is a tool for the satire upon the laughable middle classes.

   This sense of Fielding's self-positioning within the circle of those
protected and elevated by libertine privilege is only reinforced by *The
Covent Garden Tragedy* and his responses to public criticism. The first
fictional critic of the Prolegomena to the *Tragedy* reveals Fielding's belief that many critics simply cannot understand the difference in standards to be applied to the privileged libertine and the lower citizens.
The second critic, with notes "ORIGINALLY INTENDED FOR THE
GRUB STREET JOURNAL" (104), exemplifies the low critic who bows
thoughtlessly to all social and even grammatical rules. He pedantically
complains of the "meanness of the diction, which is some degrees lower
than I have seen in any modern Tragedy," of phrases like the oxymo-
ronic "virtuous whore" (108), and of the word "rep,"[8] of which he notes
"I find, indeed, such a word in some of the Latin authors: but, as it is
not in the dictionary, I suppose it to be obsolete. Perhaps, it is a proper
name; if so, it should have been in Italics. I am a little inclined to this
opinion as we find several very odd names in this piece" (110). The prologue suggests that perhaps moral examples need to be staged for the
low, since the low cannot possibly follow the examples of kings and heroes, and the opening scene continues this disdainful tone toward the
artistic judgement of the mercantile classes. Fielding mocks the critics
in the *Grub-street Journal* by making Leathersides a contributor, and
notes that a tailor catcalls and cries out "Sad stuff!" and an apprentice
hisses and cries "'twas low" (I i).

   Fielding admitted his sense of the social privilege that elevated him
above the demands of society when he was drawn into critical debate
over the immorality and technical incorrectness of his works. As 'Philalethes' in *The Daily Post* of 31 July 1732, Fielding refutes claims that he
has "abus'd the Ladies" with his statement that "the Poet is so much a
Gentleman as to think [this] the worst Thing could be said of him." He
responds to attacks against his work as violations of "*the most common
Rules of Poetry, but even Grammar*" by calling this "a most barbarous Assertion; how true it is I shall leave to the Opinion of the World: As for
the strict Rules which some Criticks have laid down, I cannot think an
Author obliged to confine himself to them; for the Rules of Grammar,

the Education which the Author of the Debauchees is known to have had [at Eton], makes it unlikely he should err in those" (Paulson and Lockwood 63). This ringing statement of social superiority, excusing Fielding from the rules of drama and precluding the possibility of error all in the context of his most unabashedly sexually libertine play, makes clear his self-positioning within the discourse of libertinism. Writing and mounting this play which denies or inverts to libertine ideology all traditional socio-sexual standards concretizes both this self-perception and Fielding's lack of concern over the behavioural strictures encountered by the majority of society.

These behavioural strictures are considered with more seriousness, however, when Fielding moves away from light comedy and toward serious social satire, as is the case in the five-act play *The Modern Husband*. In this play Fielding engages more fully the idea of Georgian libertine morality that is hinted at in his entertainments and farces. The similarities between *The Modern Husband* and *Amelia* are clear,[9] but less obvious is the fundamental connection between the philosophical and social implications of *The Modern Husband* and all of Fielding's later writing. The serious issues raised here appear repeatedly throughout Fielding's novels; that even minor interests, such as surprise and outrage at the idea of "the virtue of a man!" (III viii), and that one of the central typological precursors of Squire Western appears here, demonstrates the continuity in Fielding's work.

Fielding appears to have spent more time in writing and perfecting *The Modern Husband* than he did in his other plays. There is now general consensus that *The Modern Husband* was written and circulated in 1730,[10] though it was not performed until 1732. The play is serious, with little outright comedy that fits smoothly into the action, and with an explicit attack on certain types of illicit activity. Initially the work appears to be in direct opposition to the devil-may-care comedies for which Fielding is famous, but, in fact, its ideologies are consistent with the pattern of his lighter comedies. The difference is not one of understanding but of circumstance; here the central figures are married. It is clear from the contrast between the standards applied to the married Moderns and Bellamants and the unmarried Gaywits and Bellamants (Emilia and the Captain) in their distinct subplots, that Fielding has not surrendered his libertine socio-sexual understanding, but instead presents his Georgian libertinism in combination with his understanding of the necessities of married life.[11] This pattern obviously recurs in both *Tom Jones* and *Amelia*, albeit in different ways. Like Tom Jones, the privileged Gaywit and Captain Bellamant can engage in socially and sexually libertine behaviour without shame or punishment, but they must surrender the sexual element of that privilege once they marry, as the closing quatrain of the play makes clear:

> However slight the consequence may prove
> Which waits unmarried libertines in love,
> Be from all vice divorced before you wed,
> And bury falsehood in the bridal bed.   (V xv)

An understanding of revised Georgian libertinism helps to explain many of the problematic elements usually associated with *The Modern Husband*. The continuity of libertinism resolves any apparent ideological conflict between this play and the next one Fielding produced, the unabashedly and arrogantly libertine *Covent Garden Tragedy*. It also clarifies the traditional critical assessment of *The Modern Husband* as unsuccessful, despite the fact that it ran fourteen nights, and that even the *Grub-street Journal* acknowledged its popularity. There is a great temptation to regard as a failure a play in such apparent contradiction of all that Fielding's successful comic plays are assumed to be. With the Georgian libertine context that I suggest here, however, the play fits more comfortably within Fielding's pattern of artistic and philosophical development, and so an acknowledgment of the success of the piece no longer contradicts any general thesis concerning Fielding's drama.

The difficulty in reconciling the apparently conflicting moral and libertine impetuses in *The Modern Husband* also affected contemporary understandings of the play. Even within the printed version, the presence of two at least partially contradictory epilogues makes divergent readings possible. Colley Cibber's epilogue, spoken by the actress who plays Mrs Modern, is almost purely moralist, emphasizing the play's commentary on the hypocrisy of privileging reputation over deed, and concluding with "Thus each extreme is for instruction meant / And ever was the stage's true intent, / To give reward to virtue, vice its punishment." Fielding's own epilogue, though, offers Mrs Modern her chance to argue that she has merely been caught living up to the values of the town. She supposes that prudes will condemn her "[n]ot because naughty – but because – found out." She offers a nightmare vision of all husbands of the town hanging out their wives to "draw beaus in throngs." And, since the town is so bad in any case, she will not leave her "sister-sinners, / To dwell 'mongst innocents, or young beginners ... So, hang the stupid Bard! – I'll stay in town." Delivered with panache this speech loses any traditionally moralist undertones in a sea of pro-license, pro-libertine enthusiasm for independence from public opinion and limitations, particularly at the always significant close of the performance. In its acknowledgment of the dearth of consequences for any act of the unmarried libertine and its concurrent admonition in favour of marital fidelity, the play's closing quatrain on vice and marriage crosses between the two diametrically opposite interpretations of the play and between the two epilogues; however, contemporary critics (and many more recent) still missed the collapsing of extremes into the compromise which I have termed Georgian libertine moralism. Some contemporaries accused Fielding of not exposing vice, but creating it. In *The Grub-street Journal* of 30 March 1732, 'Dramaticus' asks "what business Capt. BELLAMANT and EMILIA, Mr GAYWIT and Lady CHARLOTTE have with the main design of the play" (Paulson and Lockwood 33). He deplores the lack of any lesson that can be learned from such entirely frivolous or entirely evil characters as Lady Charlotte and Lord Richly, and then asks "what instruction or pleasure can be gathered from this heap of absurdity?" (36). In an article probably written by Fielding's friend Thomas Cooke, *The Comedian* responded to the accusations of 'Dramaticus.' The article suggests that Fielding's own class is superior to that of his critic and that the playwright would be in a position to know the behaviour of young ladies of fashion. Cooke goes on to argue that Fielding's "Intent was to expose particular Vices and Follys, and to make these ridiculous and those odious, to give his audience Pleasure and himself Profit" (Paulson and Lockwood 39). The readings of Cooke and 'Dramaticus' are both plausible, but more useful is a combination of the two, bringing traditional libertinism and moralism into a viable system of Georgian libertinism that provides an alternative to unnatural social confines – libertine permissiveness and privilege outside of marriage where no one is injured, and, within marriage, at least sexual fidelity, though not necessarily adoption of other social rules.

The epilogue, and the play itself, show Fielding's awareness of the conventions he manipulates, formal, moral, and libertine alike. After Lord Richly and Mrs Modern are interrupted in their plotting by the arrival of Mr Modern, Richly swears, "Pox on him, a husband, like the fool in a play, is of no use but to cause confusion" (III iii). Of course, this has been exactly Mr Modern's function here, and Fielding's identification of such a place where he does follow convention makes more explicit and powerful those places where he subverts it, establishing Georgian libertinism as a viable approach to social organization. Fielding offers in his prologue a standard aim to "divert, instruct, and mend mankind," but he has already explained that his work will not be standard, since it focuses upon a "pair of monsters most entirely new!" The traditional dramatic goals of delighting and instructing to a moral purpose will be met, but the methodology and devices will be those of the libertine as Fielding reveals the "true nature" of his society in various forms. He uses his revisionist libertinism to create a developing and relevant social moralism, different from the confines that the youthful libertine playwright saw as unnatural and uncomfortable.

Various elements of the libertine serve the slightly altered moral ends of Fielding's serious social satire. The good man Bellamant commits adultery and is then forgiven in an act that suggests a libertine understanding of the way of the world on the parts of both Mr and Mrs Bellamant. Both Gaywit and Captain Bellamant, the play's heroic young men, have at least sexually libertine pasts, and Gaywit has clearly participated in the old-style libertine discourse of masculine possession of women before the opening of the play. But Gaywit values good nature: it is listed as one of the primary qualities that attract him to Emilia, and his own good nature leads him to use the knowledge gained from his past to help those caught up in the scandal of the play, while refusing to "take advantage of the misfortunes of any; but surely not of the woman I love" (V vii). Of course, in preventing any more scandal than is necessary, he also enables himself to keep his inheritance as he marries Emilia, the woman he desires. He thus maintains the individualistic, powerful, and privileged nature of the romantic libertine hero.

Other libertine characters in the play also bring to mind the harmless, active, and devilishly attractive libertines of Fielding's other plays and his novels. The levee scene, for example, seems at first to have been inserted into an action to which it does not contribute simply to procure a comedic scene amidst the more serious elements of the play. However, it does demonstrate the innocuousness of certain manifestations of libertinism. Colonel Courtly, Lord Lazy, and Mr Woodall are licentious, clever, and witty, joking that "a parliament-man should always bring his wife with him, that, if he does not serve the public, she may," and mocking the failed attempts at true, considered libertinism by "toupet coxcombs" (I ix). The characters are funny, and effective in their wittiness and their privileged disinterest in the causes of the low, and they show that Fielding has not abandoned his sense of superiority or his place in the libertine tradition even in his most explicitly didactic play. The only sour note sounded in the scene is that of Lord Richly, who suggests to Mr Modern that he believes in the virtue of Mrs Modern "as firmly ... as thou dost thyself," and implies that Bellamant is a "prudent" and "dangerous man" who may well be pursuing Mrs Modern's virtue. Richly then reminds the audience that the levee has been a waste of time for Captain Merit and Mr Modern, since "great men, justly, act by wiser rules; / A levee is the paradise of fools." The enjoyment of privilege is entirely appropriate for the Georgian libertine, but his enjoyment of the misery of the lower characters is not.

Lord Richly represents the line of Restoration-style libertinism that continued to coexist with the rising Georgian libertinism in historical figures like Colonel Charteris and John Wilkes, and fictional ones like Richardson's Lovelace and *Amelia*'s Noble Lord. Indeed, as we have seen, Georgian libertinism to some extent defines itself through differentiation from such old-style libertinism carried over from a period long past. Richly's libertinism denies any influence of good nature or sensibility. He rejects common sense as well as the good nature through which Gaywit meets his desires, in favour of his own interpretation of good nature – that others must surrender to his desires or be punished, since he is the most powerful figure in the play. In direct opposition to Gaywit's appreciation of good nature, Richly tells Mrs Modern that she must "do a good-natured thing" for him and "act like other prudent women in a lower station; when you can please no more with your own person, e'en do it with other people's." And his reasoning is a cutting version of the old-style libertine naturalism: in relations between the sexes, Richly explains, "In using you so we follow the dictates of our natures" (II vii). All of Fielding's other dramatic libertines either understand that passions must be tempered with good nature, or, if they cannot understand this, are represented as harmlessly silly or fruitlessly foppish characters.

Lord Richly's sense of his libertine privilege, which also violates the outlines of good nature, might initially be mistaken for that which Fielding approves and manifests himself in other works, but Richly's sense of privilege is a Hobbesian one quite different from Fielding's. As Gaywit summarizes, Richly "is arrived at a happy way of regarding all the rest of mankind as his tenants, and thinks, because he possesses more than they, he is entitled to whatever they possess" (II vi). He manipulates women with large sums of money left for small gambling debts, and he controls men with promises of preferment and interest. Richly's money is his power, and he tells Mrs Modern bluntly that "money shall always be the humble servant of my pleasures; and it is the interest of men of fortune to keep up the price of beauty, that they may have it more among themselves" (IV ii). Fielding's sense of privilege certainly includes ignoring the opinions of the low about his own work and about the subjects and positions which that work encompasses. He even acknowledges his own sense of privilege briefly – in a play that nearly rants about abuse of privilege – when he has Captain Bellamant refuse to beg Lord Richly's blessing with "I would not kneel any longer to you though you were the Great Mogul" (V xiv). Though this scene predates the creation of the Great Mogul's company at the Little Haymarket Theatre, I think it is quite clear that Fielding is self-referential here, and that he thus manages to privilege himself above all of the fictional characters he creates and the psychologies they represent. Self-elevation is not in itself a bad thing to Fielding, but self-elevation at the cost of unilaterally debauching and humiliating others does not fit into his construction of the modern libertine. Lord Richly is the most obviously old-style libertine character of the play, but he ultimately fails at true libertinism even in the Restoration paradigm: he fails to examine his own motives intellectually or philosophically, preferring instead to depend on the general excuse of the thoughtlessly "natural."

Lord Richly's abuse of and disdain for women is also in clear opposition to the Georgian vision of libertinism. None of the major female characters in this play fulfills the position of the straightforward feminine libertine as we have seen it in Fielding's other plays. Lady Charlotte is entirely self-absorbed, Emilia is passive, and Mrs Modern, though highly sexually available, is almost entirely controlled by her avaricious husband. She seems to have loved and had an affair with Gaywit, but we are not offered enough information about this couple to make any real judgments about her behaviour. An argument can be made for certain libertine qualities in Mrs Bellamant, but even that does not begin to align her with the female libertines of Fielding's drama. In any case, Lord Richly is entirely devoid of appreciation of the independence and potential of women, and considers them only chattel to be manipulated, conquered, and discarded. This attitude is explicitly stated in a scene with Gaywit, where the young hero demonstrates his progress, but still imperfection, in the role of good-natured libertine as he expresses his desire to "possess" the woman he loves. Richly then expands upon the linguistic usage in a distasteful economic metaphor that brings to mind piracy in trade and piracy of name and social position in the event of the usurpation of a man's presumed possession of a woman. While Gaywit's comments express primarily desire, Richly's demonstrate the psychological and economic colonization of the disempowered by those still guided by the old need to prove control and dominance: "You know, Harry, you have my consent to possess all the women in town, except those few that I am particular with: provided you fall not foul of mine, you may board and plunder what vessels you please ... Then the principal thing to be considered is her cargo. To marry a woman merely for her person is buying an empty vessel: and a woman is a vessel which a man will grow cursed weary of in a long voyage" (V vii). Richly is certainly a villain, even by the libertine standards according to which he assumes he is to be judged, and he provides a Hobbesian contrast to the more acceptable young Gaywit, who is in both literal and libertine terms of the next generation. It is the good nature that Richly lacks and Gaywit possesses that separates the two and allows Fielding to establish the role of the libertine, old and new, in this essentially revisionist-moralist drama.

Richly's abuse of women, though, is not the only behaviour involving gender relations attacked in *The Modern Husband.* The general understanding of women as property as manifested in the process of a criminal conversation charge is also attacked, partly because it violates the libertine view of women as presented in Fielding's plays. Until the Matrimonial Causes Act of 1857 was passed, criminal conversation was a charge under which the lovers of adulterous wives could be sued for damages resulting from the appropriation of the feminine property of another man, and for the public shame of the cuckold. Trials were public, and eventually this procedure became almost necessary as a prerequisite to having a private divorce bill approved in Parliament.

The implied position of a woman as chattel in this charge, however, violates the Georgian libertine understanding of the necessary independence of women, even within marriage. While Fielding clearly opposes the adultery of Mrs Modern, his satire is harshest when directed at Mr Modern's attempt to procure money by procuring his wife. The satire on the Moderns also opposes the idea of marriage as a financial institution or social stepping stone: it is not sexual misbehaviour that Fielding takes exception to, but the fact that Mr Modern uses his wife solely as an objectified tool of greed. According to Fielding's libertine paradigm, Mr Modern's request violates all standards of good nature, and his argument in support of his request violates all standards of humanity. He tells her, "Your person is mine: I bought lawfully in the church; and unless I am to profit by the disposal, I shall keep it all for my own use" (IV i). Such a thoughtlessly patriarchal assumption about an institution as inviolable in Fielding's mind as marriage must be held up as an evil even worse than the aggressive libertinism of Lord Richly. Smallwood refers to Fielding's attacks on such patriarchial domination and abuse as a part of his "significant degree of sympathy with contemporary rationalist-feminist thinking" (62). While I am reluctant to apply later labels like "feminist" to Fielding's thought, choosing instead to align such things as his views on women to his often unorthodox and libertine ideologies, I think Smallwood is correct in pointing out the acceptance and even advocacy of the independence of women in Fielding, particularly in this instance.

The Modern Husband, then, presents attractive young heroes who are, as Tom Jones is later called, good-natured libertines, and contrasts them with cruel, self-absorbed old-style libertines and the anti-libertine abuse of a wife by a husband. Once again Fielding distrusts the existing social organization and its apparently continuing moral decline. The imperative is one of assessment and challenge of hegemonic orders and of a libertine freedom of intellect and behaviour until one independently chooses to marry, at which point sexual activity is, in Fielding's moral sphere, finally to be limited to a single partner.

I conclude this lengthy discussion of Fielding's dramatic career with the one play that in itself encompasses more than fourteen years of theatrical and novelistic representation of eighteenth-century culture. *The Wedding Day*, a five-act traditional comedy, was written in 1729 but not staged until 1743, when Fielding revised it for David Garrick's performance; it was Fielding's last new play to be mounted in his lifetime.[12] Again the undeniable attractiveness of the rake, and the essential rejection of established cultural norms in favour of individuated agency and the pursuit of pleasure are paramount. Like *Love in Several Masques* and *The Modern Husband*, the play also confirms that Fielding did not limit his investigations of subversive cultural perspectives to the intentionally licentious afterpieces that occupied theatrical margins with *The Old Debauchees* and *The Covent Garden Tragedy*.

The Wedding Day is in many ways a conventional love plot, complete with Frygian *senex iratus* and *dolosus servus*, or heavy father and tricky slave. Millamour is the rake, driven by witty libertine sentiments: "Reputation, like the small-pox, gives you but one pain in your life. When you have had the one, and lost the other, you may venture with safety anywhere you please" (I ii). He neglects but secretly loves Clarinda, who has responded to the apparent end of their affair by marrying Mr Stedfast, a Jonsonian humours character "whose resolution is immovable as the predestinarian's fate" (I iv). Stedfast in turn is father to Charlotte, who is pursued by the good Mr Heartfort (friend to Millamour), but promised to Young Mutable by her imperious father because Stedfast "hath laid it down as a maxim, that all men are wild at one period of life or another; so he resolved never to marry his daughter but to one who hath already passed that period" (I iv). To Stedfast, Heartfort is suspiciously and dangerously good, thus disrupting again any expectation of an unproblematic representation of the qualities of virtue in Fielding's work. Through Millamour's disguises as Lord Truelove and Doctor Gruel, the consummation of the Stedfast-Clarinda marriage is put off, and Charlotte's wedding to Mutable is delayed long enough for Heartfort to convince her to marry him. Just as Millamour and Clarinda are about to conquer their desire in favour of a sad but chaste relationship, one of Millamour's bawds provides the *deus ex machina* that resolves all. After a brief conference with Millamour, Mrs Plotwell confronts Stedfast with the news that she is the lover he abandoned years before, and that his new wife Clarinda is really their daughter. Stedfast agrees to the marriages of both of his daughters, "for it is impossible for a man to keep his resolutions while he hath one woman in [his house]" (V xii).

This conclusion obviously echoes that of *Joseph Andrews*, but it is significant for more than that. The happy ending of the play is not the result of a reformation by the libertine character, nor of any form of repentance. Instead, the final scene is made possible only by Millamour's libertinism. His schemes prevent the incestuous relationship from being consummated, and, most significantly, his continued association with the bawd Mrs Plotwell is responsible for the fatal information. His full reformation would have resulted in incest and a forced marriage. It is the power, sexual freedom, and rejection of established rules of appropriate public relationships embodied in Millamour's libertinism that enable his heroic status as good-natured servant of true desire.

The role of Mrs Plotwell as an independent and unrejected woman associated with unsanctioned realms of sexuality brings to mind the often affectionately rendered women of *The Covent Garden Tragedy*. Both Plotwell and Mrs Useful shocked audiences in much the same way as did the earlier play, but even in revision in 1743, Fielding did not remove them. Once again he refused to be limited by the voice of public opinion; the libertine playwright is still determined by his own privilege above the artistic and cultural rabble. Fielding's first biographer Arthur Murphy makes clear that this is not merely a modern critical assumption. He argues that Fielding's refusal to revise his work for public taste was in part the result of "that sovereign contempt he always entertained for the understandings of the generality of mankind ... he doubted the discernment of his auditors, and so thought himself secured by their stupidity, if not by his own humour and vivacity" (in Battestin *Life* 362).

This libertine negation of entrenched social values and those who hold them is not represented merely in the presence of procuresses on stage. The forms of patriarchy manifested in tyrannical masculinity are denied again in Stedfast, just as they have been in Sir Positive Trap and Old Jourdain, as is the objectification of women as mere chattel for trade in homosocial relationships among men seeking status. Feminine agency is again well beyond contemporary standards, as Charlotte resolves "never to marry, 'till I have found a man without one single fault in my eye, or a single virtue in any one's else. – For my part, I take beauty in a man to be a sign of effeminacy; sobriety, want of spirit; gravity, want of wit; and constancy, want of constitution" (III ix). She uses her father's decree against Heartfort as an excuse to reject him, but also rejects her father's choice, briefly pursues Millamour, and then decides on Heartfort after all when Millamour's marriage to Clarinda is made possible. She refuses to be manipulated even by the great schemes of Millamour, though, if they do not also serve her own desires: when Millamour's plan is about to rob her of her ability to choose whether or not to marry Mutable, she recognizes and reveals the trick to the senior Mutable, who has been waffling between Charlotte and the wealthy (and fictional) Miss Truelove as the right bride for his son. She disrupts this plan to transfer her from one man to another without her consent, and then leaves the room with the same determinedly dismissive gesture as Helena offers Sir Positive Trap in *Love in Several Masques* when he wishes for the power to take her to market. Charlotte announces, "your son, sir, happens to be a person for whom, ever since I had the honour of his acquaintance, I have entertained the most surprising, invincible, and infinite contempt in the world … This gentleman ["Truelove"], sir, is no lord, and hath no estate … And he hath contrived, sir, to marry your ingenious son to some common slut of the town. So I leave you to make up the match, and am, gentlemen, your most humble servant" (IV vii). She parodies the very patriarchal discourse that she rejects with the increasingly emphatic repetition of "sir"; we next see her enabling Clarinda to continue her ruse of sickness to delay the consummation of her marriage.

Even Clarinda takes control of her romantic and domestic future. After her affair with Millamour sours, she takes advantage of the wealthy Stedfast to ensure her continued status and wealth; she refuses either to wait for the return of the unfaithful Millamour or to slip passively into the social hinterland of the fallen woman with Lucina and Millamour's other implied lovers. Such agency draws Millamour to her again in a way that traditionally passive femininity cannot. Fielding's rejection of adulterous liaisons (established in *The Modern Husband*) prevents Clarinda from actually having intercourse with Millamour after her marriage, but her desire is powerfully expressed both to other characters and to Millamour himself, as is clear in his rebuke after their temptation scene has faded to black: "Cruel Clarinda – Thus to stop short when we are at the brink of happiness: to show my eager soul a prospect of elysium, and then refuse it the possession" (IV iii). Clarinda refuses to commit adultery even with the man she was supposed to have married, and it is this managed expression of passionate desire that makes her as worthy of the *deus ex machina* as Joseph Andrews was in the novel published only a year before *The Wedding Day* was produced.

The male characters of the play are rather less chaste than Joseph Andrews, but it is not only in the sexuality of Millamour and the independence of the female characters that the libertine significance of *The Wedding Day* is made clear. Traditional religion finds itself under suspicion again, for example, but more subtly than in the earlier burlesque entertainments. As the procuress Mrs Useful ironically chastises Millamour for continuing on in his "profligate way" until he loses Clarinda, she mouths what might otherwise have been a fairly standard moral: "It is very true, what religious men tell us, we never know the value of a blessing till we lose it" (I ii). Though various characters marry and plan nuptials, the first of two contexts in which religion is raised in the play is that of a bawd's explanation of sexual loss. The second is no kinder to institutionalized religion, though it does remind us again of the evolutionary nature of libertinism as a culturally responsive discourse, mediating itself with broader movements of culture from the Restoration to the mid-eighteenth century. The exchange begins with Millamour's Restoration-style witticism that he "always thought love as foreign to a speculative man as religion to an atheist."

Heartfort: Perhaps it may: for I believe the atheist is as often insincere in his contempt of religion as the other in his contempt of woman. There are instances of men who have professed themselves despisers of both, that have at length been found kneeling at their shrines.

Millamour: Those two things I never intend to trouble my head about the theory of – I shall content myself with the practice –

Heartfort: With the practice of one, I dare swear.

Millamour: In my youth I believe I shall; and for being old, I desire it not. I would have the fires of life and love go out together. What is life worth without pleasure?   (II ii)

Millamour's speeches imply a position that does not claim atheism itself, but does reject religion as a force relevant to the young who refuse to reject all pleasure. His libertine construction of religion has much in common with the position of *The Old Debauchees'* Old Laroon: institutionalized religion denies pleasure, so those who seek pleasure deny religion. Even the "grave sober man of sense" Heartfort's contradictory argument does not value religion other than to note that few men reject it when "at length" they can no longer indulge in pleasure. As Millamour has quipped earlier, "sins, like places at court, we seldom resign, till we can keep them no longer" (I iii).

Millamour's wit is just one of the qualities that make his libertinism so attractive: his facility with disguise to serve the desires of his friends, and his ability to manipulate the perceptions of others to fulfill his own desires (perhaps, as we shall see, even including constructing the whole story of Stedfast's paternity) also contribute to his charm. Still, Fielding renders his character less specifically good-natured than some of his other dramatic libertines. This suggests that both early and late in his dramatic career, he investigates and evaluates the fluidity of libertinism rather than simply proselytizing a specific static definition of such a slippery cultural discourse.

Perhaps the most interesting aspect in this representation of the ambiguous or transitional libertine figure is the question of Millamour's reformation. As Robert Hume describes it, Millamour "repents spectacularly" after being taken to task by Heartfort, but Hume also notes that Millamour's "unrepentance two pages later, and re-repentance four pages after that ... are, at best implausible." Hume argues that *The Wedding Day* is not intended to "burlesque reform comedy, but neither was [Fielding] writing it effectively ... the tag-moral is totally unconvincing" (*Theatre* 48–9). I think that Hume is correct about the tag-moral (and this, as we have seen, should not be surprising, as it has been equally true of a whole series of tag-morals in Fielding's work). Less clear is the significance of the apparently deterministic qualification of a prescriptive dramatic genre. In the reformation scene Heartfort informs Millamour that the only reparation he can now make Clarinda is to see her no more:

Heartfort: How! what privilege dost thou perceive in thyself to invade and destroy the happiness of another? Besides, though shame may first reach the husband, it doth not always end there: the wife is always liable, and often is involved in the ruin of the gallant. The person who deserves chiefly to be exposed to shame is the only person who escapes without it.

Millamour: Hey-day! thou art not turning hypocrite, I hope. Thou dost not pretend to lead a life equal to this doctrine?

Heartfort: My practice, perhaps, is not equal to my theory; but I pretend to sin with as little mischief as I can to others: and this I can lay my hand on my heart and affirm, that I never seduced a young woman to her own ruin, nor a married one to the misery of her husband. Nay, and I know thee to be so good-natured a fellow, that what thou dost of this kind arises from thy not considering the consequence of thy actions; and if any woman can lay her ruin on thee, thou canst lay it on custom ... Custom may lead a man into may errors, but it justifies none; nor are any of its laws more absurd and unjust than those relating to the commerce between the sexes: for what can be more ridiculous than to make it infamous for women to grant what it is honourable for us to solicit, nay, to ensnare and almost compel them into; to make a whore a scandalous, a whoremaster a reputable appelation! Whereas, in reality, there is no more mischievous character than a public debaucher of women.

Millamour: No more, dear George; now you begin to pierce to the quick.
(V iii)

What leads to Millamour's "spectacular reformation" is not any religious revelation or recognition of immorality, but two very different epiphanies: Heartfort's explanation of the doctrine of libertine good nature almost exactly as it is phrased in *The Old Debauchees*, *A Journey from this World to the Next*, and *Tom Jones*, and his expression of the unfairness of the sexual double standard. These arguments do not point to a conventional fifth-act conversion into the latitudinarian moral man, but to a mediation of the cruel edge that has coloured Millamour's character to this point. This is why his "unrepentance" and "re-repentance" follow this crucial scene. Millamour considers attempting again an adulterous relationship with Clarinda after his conversation with Mrs Useful in the next scene, but it is not for the same reasons. Useful is unable to convince him to serve his own appetites, and changes tack so that Millamour is placed in the Tom Jones-like position of being accused of ill nature for declining a sexual opportunity. Useful argues that Clarinda pretends to be ill only so that Millamour's persona Dr Gruel can see her: "What can you think else? Can any thing hurt a woman equal with being refused?" (V iv). In this sudden turn, Millamour's newfound good nature pushes him back to the arms of his married love, whispering, "since we cannot be what we wish, let us be what we can" (V vii). Clarinda, however, cites her honour and rejects him again, after which Millamour orders Useful away, threatening to expose publicly the qualities for which she has been so useful privately.

Even after this, though, he cannot truly be described as reformed. He continues in his ruse as the doctor until his disguise is exposed, and then leaves the room talking privately with Plotwell. When he returns, Plotwell has been left in the supposed sick room with Clarinda, and then all three reunite for the announcement of Clarinda's surprising parentage: Stedfast and Plotwell (known as Cleomela then). One of two things has happened here. Either Millamour has had the answer to his situation for some time in his knowledge of Plotwell's history and only decides to use it when he is sure he is willing to marry Clarinda, or he has fabricated the entire story on the spur of the moment after learning of the ancient relationship between Stedfast and Cleomela.

Either way, Fielding has created another hero attractive for his privilege, power, wit, skill, and confirmed sexual prowess who remains the centre of libertine control over the situation, whether the conclusion is brought about by a libertine deception or by his continued and unrepentant public association with a bawd. And either way, Millamour confirms Fielding's youthful interest in libertinism in the late 1720s and his continued willingness to offer that interest for public consumption in the 1740s, long after the obscenity of *The Old Debauchees* and *The Covent Garden Tragedy*, the politico-philosophical ribaldry of *Pasquin* and the problematizing anti/moralism of *The Modern Husband* had been superseded by the popularity of *Joseph Andrews*. Millamour's manipulative success and his libertine-to-libertine conversion confirm that for the libertine, as *The Modern Husband*'s Bravemore tells us, "grandeur and the gallows lie on the same road." And we will see that Fielding examines the directions of that road even more closely in the travels of Joseph Andrews and Tom Jones.

3 Georgian Libertinism and the Reclamation of Virtue: *Shamela* and *Joseph Andrews*

Shamela and *Joseph Andrews* form a transition between Fielding's dramatic career and his career as a novelist, and both works are informed by the developing Georgian libertinism. *Shamela* (1741) is a brief but brutally effective satirical revision of Samuel Richardson's *Pamela* (1740). It exposes what Fielding regarded as the moral complacency of the novel, particularly Pamela's conscious virtue, which is held up as a commodity that treacherous servant girls might exchange for marriage and high life. *Joseph Andrews* (1742) moves past the clever parody that informs *Shamela* and into the novel proper; it is a panorama of eighteenth-century life that reveals more effective examples of individual morality and libertinism than are tendered in either *Shamela* or *Pamela*.

Like *The Modern Husband*, the deliberately titillating main action of *Shamela* is tinted with a representation of a more established morality. This, of course, is exactly what Fielding perceived Richardson to have done, except that Richardson successfully marketed his version as a moralist tract without regard for its obviously self-contradictory nature: the title page of the equally titillating *Pamela* states that it is "[p]ublished in order to cultivate the principles of virtue and religion in the minds of the youth of both sexes." Fielding appropriates the events of *Pamela*, actively subverts the novel's voice, and rejects its construction of morality. He replaces Richardson's "virtue" with a new implied morality in which honesty and individualism are more important to goodness than thoughtlessly prized traits of technical virginity and consciously enacted modesty and humility.

Shamela and Parson Williams are contemptible not for their sexual relationship (especially before Shamela's marriage), but for their hypocrisy and dishonesty in denying their relationship, and for the ridiculous ways in which Williams guides Shamela to rationalize her sexuality as a part of healthy religious worship. Fielding's derision of these characters' manipulations and rationalizations clearly manifests his libertine frustration with such pseudo-moralism. The two characters challenge socially imposed limitations on individual sexuality, yet allow themselves to be so burdened by social mores that they must attempt to reconcile their actions to social constructs of religious morality. Thus do they fail at both good nature (which would preclude the mercenary goal of the deceit) and libertinism (which would celebrate their independence of social stricture). Here is the first clear fictional embodiment of the failed libertine, begun in dramatic characters like the priest-ridden Old Jourdain of *The Old Debauchees*: a character attains all or most of the qualities that enable libertine autonomy of thought, action, religion, and sexuality, but eventually lacks the social privilege, personal empowerment, or will necessary to emerge as a self-determining individual. That these men and women fall repeatedly back into their socially constructed roles suggests that Fielding recognized the difficulty of achieving the powerful and individuated position of fully integrated good-natured Georgian libertine.

By writing a book as explicitly bawdy as *Shamela*, and mocking a work as widely admired as *Pamela*, Fielding again exhibited the libertine independence of thought and position which allowed him to defy so ably entrenched public morality with plays like *The Covent Garden Tragedy*. He positions himself as intellectually and morally superior to the gullible masses who, like Mr B., are susceptible to the mercantile virtue of Richardson and Pamela. As Claude Rawson suggests, "Fielding's limited but hearty freedoms with 'low' matter and language doubtless sprang from natural gusto combined with a pointed superiority to the straight-laced middle class form" (*Order* 287). Such critical observations about Fielding and his narrators are not uncommon, but none of the critics who make them observe the obvious connection to the discourse of libertinism in which elements such as naturalism, the energy and individualism implied in "gusto," and the "pointed superiority" of position form a coherent and consistent platform from which Fielding and other libertine writers declaim.

As a part of the ongoing reclamation and redefinition of the ideology of libertinism for the Georgian period, Fielding first denies the validity of the popularly constructed understanding of virtue, which, particularly for women in eighteenth-century England, had become almost fully equated with sexual virginity. The absence of definition thus created by *Shamela* is remedied most fully in *Joseph Andrews* (and augmented by the subsequent novels), but Fielding also addresses the constitution of virtue in sources like the *Champion*. His essay of 24 January 1739/40 offers an extended definition of virtue that, in accordance with his more permissive and individualist understanding, aligns virtue with the new moralist Georgian libertinism developing in parallel to the traditional conceptions of virtue and libertinism. Standard definitions of both virtue and libertinism are rooted in their Restoration discourses, but they eventually collapse into the false and extreme positions that Fielding rebuts with his new virtue and the Georgian libertine moralism to which it contributes:

Virtue is not that coy, nor that cruel mistress she is represented. Nor is she of that morose and rigid nature, which some mistake her to be … Nor hath the virtuous man less advantage in the ways of pleasure. Virtue forbids not the satisfying our appetites, virtue forbids us only to glut and destroy them. The temperate man tastes and relishes pleasure in a degree infinitely superior to that of the voluptuous. The body of the voluptuous man soon becomes impaired, his palate soon loses its taste, his nerves become soon unbraced and unfit to perform their office: whereas, the temperate body is still preserved in health, its nerves retain their full tone and vigour, and convey to the mind the most exquisite sensations. The sot soon ceases to enjoy his wine, the glutton his dainties, and the libertine his women. The temperate man enjoys all in the highest degree, and indeed with the greatest variety: for human nature will not suffice for an excess in every passion, and wherever one runs away with a man, we may generally observe him sacrificing all the rest to the enjoyment of that alone. The virtuous and temperate man only hath inclination, hath strength; and (if I may be indulged in the expression), hath opportunity to enjoy all his passions.

Poverty is so far from being enjoined us by virtue, that parsimony, which she expressly prescribes, is a certain way to wealth. Indeeds [*sic*] she suffers us not by any base or mean arts, by imposing or preying on others, to rush, as it were, into immense fortunes … It is needless to run through any other instance, we shall find in all, that virtue indulges us in the use, and preserves us from the abuse of our passions.

In Fielding's definition virtue is an active process of consideration of each set of specific circumstances, rather than a set of prescriptive social limitations of thought and action. His virtue allows the individual to participate in the world intellectually, economically, socially, and sexually as long as no other individual is intentionally injured in the process: one cannot gain power "by all means whatever," but one should be able to indulge natural appetites without censure. This is the virtue that informs Fielding's vision of the libertinism of his day: virtue takes on "its proper function as the external sign and the inward spirit of England's social and political elite" (Ruml "Gentleman" 196).

Shamela similarly challenges blind acceptance of religious dogma without consideration of a given situation or the needs of the individual. But even more, Fielding demonstrates through the character of Parson Williams the naiveté inherent in any generalized assumption that religious association infallibly manifests good nature or true virtue. He uses Williams to attack not the clergy as a whole, but the specific behaviour of specific members of the clergy, who would injure others spiritually, socially, and economically to satisfy their own appetites. Fielding later implies in the events of *Joseph Andrews* what he states explicitly in another *Champion* essay: if "a few unworthy members creep in [to the clergy], it is certainly doing a serviceable office to the body to detect and expose them; nay, it is what the sound and uncorrupt part should not only be pleased with, but themselves endeavour to execute, especially if they are suspicious of, of offended at contempt or ridicule" (29 March 1740). Fielding serves equal blame and ridicule, however, to those who would indulge blind faith over good faith, much as he did in the more vitriolic attacks on Catholic priests in *The Old Debauchees*. As Parson Oliver states in the penultimate frame letter of *Shamela*, "what Scandal doth it throw on the Order to have one bad member, unless they endeavour to screen and protect him?" (304). Institutionalized Christianity deserves censure when it too loses the qualities of good nature that are supposed to serve congregations. If, by failing to censure, the Church ceases to bring comfort and happiness and prevent misery and misfortune, it is as deserving of scandal as the hypocritical parson or the thoughtlessly victimized parishioner. Fielding's libertine requires not atheistic rejection of religion, but conscientious moral evaluation at each of these levels, even as he recognizes that just by hinting that a member of the holy orders had behaved ill, one might be "arraigned for spreading such invectives, with a malicious design of bringing the whole body of the clergy into contempt" (*Champion* 29 March 1740).

Williams might be termed a libertine by those who misunderstand libertinism to represent only sexual licentiousness, but it is clear that his damaging and aggressive self-serving character does not belong among Fielding's other actively libertine characters such as Old Laroon, Julian the Apostate, and Tom Jones. He is instead one of the failed Restoration-style libertines against whom Fielding's heroes are held, from Squire Western and the youthful Mr Wilson, to Mr Modern and *Amelia*'s

Noble Peer, for he uses his knowledge and position to coerce sexual acquiescence from young women. While Shamela is at the time of the fictional exchanges of letters a jaded and conniving woman of the world, she was once, we must suspect, a younger and more innocent servant girl who entered into an illicit, but natural and pleasurable sexual relationship with Williams, which resulted in the birth of a bastard child. Other than carelessness and the unreasonable social barrier against women (virtuous or not) who are not virgins, such a scenario – assuming that it was entered into willingly by both parties – is not particularly damaging.

The relationship reveals its anti-libertine elements, however, when one considers that Shamela, while clever at deceiving her dull master, is herself passive and trusting when it comes to the spiritual guidance of her parson. Instead of offering well-considered, if non-traditional, exegesis of Biblical texts or even the hegemonic Church stance, Williams intentionally misreads texts in order to get what he can from Shamela and his other parishioners. Since Fielding apparently believes in an afterlife (he repeats that Heaven is where one should anticipate rewards for earthly virtue), Williams does Shamela a great spiritual wrong as he persuades her to plan for "Pleasures, which tho' not strictly innocent, are however to be purged away by frequent and sincere Repentance" (287), a plan that smacks of purchasing pardons against future sins. He preaches "Be not righteous overmuch" in a way that twists the generally understood anti-sanctimonial meaning of the text into an encouragement of unconsidered sin. Shamela records that she has also learned from Williams's sermon that "those People who talk of Vartue and morality, are the wickedest of all Persons. That 'tis not what we do, but what we believe that must save us" (288). While these suggestions obviously echo the teachings of Whitefield and the Methodists (consistently a subject of derision in Fielding's works), they are also, in Fielding's mind, dangerous to the soul. Using such enticements to manipulate others violates the doctrine of good nature and its admonitions against damage to others (as well as the necessary rejection of "the Allurements or Terrors of Religion" [*Miscellanies* I 158]).

Finally, Williams acts against Fielding's libertinism when he counsels the willing Shamela to commit adultery. Consensual and non-manipulative sexual contact between two unmarried adults is quite acceptable in Fielding's Georgian libertine code, but, as we have seen in *The Modern Husband*, adultery is not tolerated, as it no longer involves only the two sexual partners. Williams explains to Shamela that "the Flesh and the Spirit were two distinct Matters, which had not the least relation to each other … Therefore, says he, my Dear, you have two Husbands, one the Object of your Love, and to satisfy your Desire; the other the Object of your Necessity, and to furnish you with those other Conveniencies ... as then the Spirit is preferable to the Flesh, so am I preferable to your other Husband, to whom I am antecedent in Time likewise. I say these things, my Dear, (said he) to satisfie your Conscience" (301). Shamela's complicitous conscience may be satisfied, but Fielding is not, and neither is the standard of Georgian libertinism.

It is unusual to view Shamela as something of a victim; she is traditionally read as the "monster of selfish ambition" (Smallwood 51), the scheming victimizer of the ludicrously gullible Mr Booby. This standard reading is also appropriate, and I will discuss it shortly, but I think it is necessary to look at both sides of Shamela's character. She is considerably less knowing, for example, than is generally assumed. She does manipulate and pursue Booby (with help from Williams and her mother, who encourages her to "make a good Market" of her person), but she is uneducated and unsophisticated, and so is herself easily manipulated by Parson Williams. Further, for all of her affected innocence of flirtatious discourse and the revelations of sexual knowledge which invariably follow, Shamela consistently misses puns and jests of which she is the object: her position outside of the hegemonic masculinist grouping of wit, power, and worldly knowledge remains unchanged. In one scene, Shamela pretends not to know what Booby means when he tells her "you can give me Pleasure if you will" and then immediately confirms her knowledge of Booby's sexual arousal as she reports being pulled into his lap: "O Mamma, I could tell you something if I would." In the same paragraph, however, Mrs Jewkes "took a Glass and drank the dear *Monysyllable*" (291), a standard bawdy toast which Shamela admits to her mother she does not understand. More significant is the echo of this incident near the end of the letters and after Shamela's marriage to Booby. Both Williams and Booby make toasts to "*et caetera*," another pun on the female genitalia. Shamela again is ignorant of the joke of which she is the object, and the joke only gets extended when she asks "if it was not a Health to Mr *Booby's* Borough, and Mr *Williams* with a hearty Laugh answered, Yes, Yes, it is his Borough we mean" (301-2). At the same time that Shamela triumphantly uses her "vartue" and sexuality to connive her way into marriage with Booby, she surrenders much of her autonomy and becomes the objectified sexual possession of her husband: his "burrow."

She continues her affair with Williams, of course, but since Fielding's goal is to reveal the mercenary qualities of *Pamela*, since we are intended to sympathize at least somewhat with the obviously victimized Booby, and since adulterous sexuality is beyond the protection of libertine self-determination, she is caught and punished for her adultery, and loses all that she has gained through her cleverness and empowered agency.

Shamela is something of a victim of both the anti-libertine drives and thoughtless manipulation of power by Parson Williams and the long-standing tradition of a masculinist social organization (with both a husband and a lover who do not subscribe to any form of belief in an expanded gender equality). This is not to say, however, that she does not herself attempt to use, in the grasping and self-serving way of the Restoration, the tools of libertinism to dissemble her way into the master bedroom. Though Fielding's belief in and support of the class system, which enabled him to write with his tone of confidence and superiority, aligns him ideologically with Mr Booby and against the upward mobility of Shamela, he also clearly finds both Richardson's Mr B. and his own Mr Booby foolish and credulous. The result is a work that satirizes both central characters, Booby for being gullible and driven by uncontrolled and unconsidered appetite (despite his social power) into the untenable position of either an unequal marriage or rape, and Shamela because she uses the tools of libertinism not to enable love or even desire, but out of avarice and lust for an adulterous lover.

Shamela enacts the role of old-style libertine effectively, demonstrating exactly the type of interpretation of independence and social subversion that Fielding rejects in his more positively represented Georgian libertinism. Most significantly, she manipulates social constructions of virtue and generalized moral beliefs by playing the very role she violates by knowingly playing it. She appropriates the behaviour and simulates the beliefs of the virginal and beautiful but subservient and powerless servant girl Booby assumes her to be even as he accuses her of manipulation. She tells Mrs Jewkes, "I would not be Mistress to the greatest King, no nor Lord in the Universe. I value my Vartue more than I do any thing my Master can give me" (289). She announces this, however, only after realizing that her initial goal of "a regular taking into Keeping, a settled Settlement, for me, and all my Heirs, all my whole Lifetime" (283) has become too easy to attain from her lustful master, and she decides to "make a great [fortune] by my Vartue" (293). As she flirts verbally, pulls down her stays to expose her breasts, and enacts numberless ruses to arouse Booby and then deny him, Shamela exemplifies exactly James Turner's assertion that for libertines of the old style, "Libertine sexuality cannot be understood simply as a surrender to spontaneous physicality; it is inseparable from the cerebral triumph over the opposite sex, from mastery exercised through tactical reason" ("Paradoxes" 71). After her marriage, Shamela writes to her mother that

"Times are finely altered, I have entirely got the better of him, and am resolved never to give him his Humour. *O how foolish it is in a Woman, who hath once got the Reins into her own Hand, ever to quit them again*" (301). She has won power through her tactical superiority over her ostensible master, and holds the reins over his uncontrolled animal appetite. To Shamela, the social form of virtue becomes "vartue," and is only "*a charming Word.*" Though she blesses the "*Soul who first invented it*" (290), she reinvents it as she reinvents herself, both marketable commodities in the distorted values of popular England.

This reinvention of virtue as a tool to entrap the very class that would banish a woman for lacking the traditional version is echoed in the multiple reinventions of Shamela in her various autodiegetic endeavours. She both gains and demonstrates individual power and a sense of superiority as she reports her clever deceits and manipulations to her mother by letter.[1] She controls not only the representation of her own character (as not traditionally virtuous, but witty, ingenious, and, of course, stunningly beautiful), but also that of Mr Booby. While Booby holds the publicly recognized power in the fictional reality of the relationship, Shamela has the power in her reporting to make him more ridiculous than he may be, thus tempting the reader to believe he deserves his fate, married (however briefly) to a treacherous and adulterous wife.

Rawson addresses this issue briefly, but instead of recognizing the libertine empowerment of Shamela via her independent thought and fictional control in dictating her own story, he grants those qualities directly to Fielding. It is true that, as I have noted above, the ultimate power of narrative and all of the privilege that comes with it are Fielding's, but Shamela's role in her own fictional and metafictional world must also be considered. Rawson, for example, suggests that the placement and frequency of markers like "says she" and "says I" emphasize the satiric issues of self-absorption by the speaker and, significantly, "become part of Fielding's managerial self-display" (*Order* 270). Again, this is accurate, but Rawson does not examine the impact of those same elements on the fictional narrator of Shamela's tale: Shamela enacts the same "managerial self-display," and that is where she most effectively gains not only a libertine authority and power of self-representation, but also the feminine independence valued in the Georgian libertine model. Shamela's autodiegetic exercise grants her the power of author and authority that Fielding's later narrators teach his readers to value. The majority of the actions and schemes she records align her with selfish and often cruel Restoration libertinism, but the act of recording itself shows the shifting nature of the search for individualism and autonomy in the early eighteenth century. Shamela's self-narrative is only the first in a series of feminine autodiegetic exercises to appear in Fielding's fiction. This device enables his female characters to demonstrate their powers of self-determination, originality, and creation in accordance with Fielding's own libertine belief in the necessity of increased equality between the sexes.

Ironically it is not Shamela's own exercise of narrative authority that causes Parson Oliver's outrage, but that of a third hand hired by Booby to tell their story, presumably in the form of *Pamela*. Parson Williams assures Shamela that the final version will contain nothing of the truth: "So far on the contrary, if you had not been acquainted with the Name, you would not have known it to be your own History" (303–4). Shamela's final comment is that "all these Matters are strange to me, yet I can't help laughing to think I shall see my self in a printed Book" (304). She does not see herself, however, nor even her own reported version of herself, but Booby's perception of her, mediated by the dramatic sense of the hired hack writer. She has lost control over her story, and in losing that control she is left open to the accusation of deceiving the public, including credulous but influential clergymen like Parson Tickletext, who apparently not only expects blind faith, but exercises it too: when her deception moves from the private sphere to the public domain, her one unintended (and thus uncontrolled) deception results in public humiliation and punishment. It is for her adultery with Williams that she is ultimately turned away by her husband, but it is the deceit for which the public has fallen that makes Tickletext, Oliver, and the implied reader cheer her downfall. Shamela becomes vulnerable to the effects of social limitations on feminine sexuality and autonomy only after she loses her power of autonomous self-representation.

The libertine challenges that Fielding throws down in *Shamela* reveal his frustration with the reductive and thoughtlessly accepted vision of human behaviour dominating social organization and individual action in his society. As Ian A. Bell suggests, "Fielding sees a society driven by money and outward show, hopelessly gullible and lacking in substance. By engaging in dialogue with that culture's most celebrated literary document, Samuel Richardson's *Pamela*, Fielding is able to begin to build a platform from which he may announce his own oppositional concerns and attitudes" (76). *Shamela* only begins, though, to tear down traditional standards; the positive engagement, offering an alternate model incorporating many of the central tenets of challenge and independence in Georgian libertinism was still to come in *Joseph Andrews* and the novels that followed.

In *Joseph Andrews* Fielding continues his assessment of the moral and intellectual (mis)understandings of *Pamela* and of the society that so readily accepted Richardson's perspective. This engagement with Richardson's work is only a part of Fielding's first major novel, however. Fielding also develops further a number of themes found in his plays: the chaos caused by "the virtue of a man!" earlier established in *The Modern Husband*; marriage between a footman and his lady, as in *The Virgin Unmasked* (1735) and *Miss Lucy in Town* (1742); the flaws of the existing legal system and the consequences of false imprisonment, in *The Coffee-House Politician* (1730); and the spiritual and practical weaknesses of some of the clergy, previously examined in *The Old Debauchees*, *Pasquin*, and others. Still, as was true of audiences for the plays, readers of *Joseph Andrews* were left confused at times as to whether the central impetus of the work was moral or something more subversive. As one contemporary reader, Elizabeth Carter, wrote to another, Catherine Talbot, on 1 January 1742/3, "It must surely be a marvellous wrongheadedness and perplexity of understanding that can make any one consider this complete satire as a very immoral thing, and of the most dangerous tendency, and yet I have met with some people who treat it in the most outrageous manner" (Paulson and Lockwood 123). But this sort of contradiction in responses is to be expected in a work that, among many other things, explicitly manifests Fielding's sense of a libertine moralism.

It is true that neither Joseph Andrews nor Abraham Adams indulges in a sexuality which should be termed libertine. It is also true, however, that the challenges Fielding's characters offer to the existing hegemonic structures at various times, along with the novel's underlying implication that true libertinism is the capacity to choose the activities in which one indulges, together demonstrate one of the generalized philosophies of the novel: a combining of the subversive elements of the libertine's challenging of an ineffective status quo and the new morality of true virtue asserted by Fielding in places like the *Champion* essay. The novel's combination of new morality and libertine subversion into a viable socio-cultural alternative is reiterated in small in discussions such as that in book II chapter xvii where Adams announces that experience without reading is dangerous, and the generous innkeeper counters with the fruitlessness of reading without experience. Neither is exclusively correct, of course, but the argument exposes the necessity of considering multiple positions to find truth. As he does in the process of generic definition in the preface, Fielding filters and recombines ideas that are usually oppositional. In the most significant reconsidera-

tion occurring in *Joseph Andrews*, Fielding appropriates the definition of
virtue as virginity, and combines it with his libertine desire to challenge
and subvert those limitations on individual behaviour imposed by society. The new definition that emerges, like his *Champion* discussion,
permits social, sexual, and even religious freedom to consider all possibilities and emerge with a sense of an appropriate personal path. Like
Joseph's chastity, which turns out to be devoted not to an abstract social
respect for virginity, but to his passion for a specific woman, Fielding's
virtue is not an inviolable code of prescriptive acts or assumptions of
value, but a morality that resides in context, circumstance, and the individual.[2]

If Shamela gains a certain amount of libertine power of self-determination and representation of others from recording her own actions in
violation of reductive political and social *exempla*, Fielding's narrator in
Joseph Andrews demonstrates this power and privilege tenfold. Narrative
libertinism is a device perhaps first made possible in English fiction by
Fielding and his intrusive narrators. Epistolary fiction and narratives
claiming historical veracity lack space for the sort of play that enables
the narrator to take on a stance or persona informed by the privilege of
libertinism. The libertine narrator manipulates the reader's understanding of the fictionalized world in the same way that the libertine more
generally strives to subvert popular understanding of prediscursive standards of religion, morality, society, and sexuality. A libertine narrator
relishes his control over information and representation, alternately
masking as the naif and the omniscient to establish further both his
control over all elements of his own fictionalized community and the
implied ability to ignore or manipulate the presumed values of the culture that such a fictionalized community purports to represent. The
power to problematize cultural values is inherent in representing a society to itself, and that subversive capacity is not lost on the libertine narrator of *Joseph Andrews*. His desire for originality is revealed in the
preface with the explanation that he is creating a "Species of writing,
which I have affirmed to be hitherto unattempted in our Language"
(10). He similarly demonstrates his sense of libertine superiority over
the literary masses as he lists in the prefatory chapter to book I titles of
the popular romances from which his work is distinct and to which it is
superior (I i 18). At one point, Fielding's narrator even tacitly equates
himself to God as Mr Wilson intones, "I am thankful to the great Author of all Things for the Blessings I here enjoy" (III iii 224). At other
times, the narrator makes clear that any sense of superiority and privilege the reader may have in his or her encounters with the fallible characters of the novel is granted only by the more privileged omniscient

narrator, who chooses to reveal information only as he deems it necessary to the reader's limited understanding. This becomes particularly clear upon the introduction of Fanny as a belated explanation of Joseph's arduous and thus far potentially ridiculous defense of his chastity:

It is an Observation sometimes made, that to indicate our Idea of a simple Fellow, we say, *He is easily to be seen through*: Nor do I believe it a more improper Denotation of a simple Book. Instead of applying this to any particular Performance, we chuse rather to remark the contrary in this History, where the Scene opens itself by small degrees, and he is a sagacious Reader who can see two Chapters before him.

For this reason, we have not hitherto mentioned a Matter which now seems necessary to be explained ... Be it known then, that in the same Parish where this Seat stood there lived a young Girl ...   (I xi 48)

The narrator manipulates the reader's knowledge once again when he interrupts Fanny's kidnapping by the servants of the Roasting Squire to offer "*A Discourse between the Poet and the Player; of no other Use in this History, but to divert the Reader*" (III x 259). It is unclear whether he means by "divert" to amuse or to misdirect, and it is not until chapter xii that the narrator finally gets around to acknowledging that "NEITHER the facetious Dialogue which pass'd between the Poet and Player, nor the grave and truly solemn Discourse of Mr *Adams*, will, we conceive, make the Reader sufficient Amends for the Anxiety which he must have felt on the account of poor *Fanny*, whom we left in so deplorable a Condition. We shall therefore now proceed to the relation of what happened to that beautiful and innocent Virgin" (III xii 269).

The narrator's potentially libertine function within the novel is not limited to demonstrating managerial power and superior knowledge, however. His is also the voice through which Fielding challenges literary mores and traditional forms in the same way that his characters challenge social and cultural strictures. His reconsideration of the nature of the conventional masculine epic hero is one literary challenge that is significant to an understanding of the developing Georgian libertine figures of his work. In Adams's battle with Fanny's first attacker, Fielding mocks the tradition of the hero as thoughtless fighter, ignorant and low:

Nature, (who, as wise Men have observed, equips all Creatures with what is most expedient for them;) taken a provident Care, (as she always doth with those she intends for Encounters) to make this part of the head [where brains should be] three times as thick as those of ordinary Men, who are designed to exercise Talents which are vulgarly called rational, and for whom, as Brains are necessary, she is obliged to leave some room for them in the Cavity of the Skull: whereas, those Ingredients being entirely useless to Persons of the heroic Calling, she hath an Opportunity of thickening the Bone, so as to make it less subject to any Impression or liable to be cracked or broken; and indeed, in some who are predestined to the Command of Armies and Empires, she is supposed sometimes to make that Part perfectly solid.   (II ix 137–8)

This hero is only slightly more than animal, violent and aggressive without the conscious thought necessary to the new hero, and though Fielding's narrator is ironic here, the implied need to reform the popular archetype of the hero is clear. And so a new model is constructed, out of the combination of Fielding's sense of virtue and the new Georgian libertinism in figures still willing to do battle when circumstances and consideration reveal it to be necessary.

Considering the most common direction for critical discourse on *Joseph Andrews*, the appropriate place to begin our search for Fielding's revisionist model hero might be with Parson Adams, Fielding's "Man of good Sense, good Parts, and good Nature ... as entirely ignorant of the Ways of this World, as an Infant just entered into it could possibly be" (I iii 23). Adams is obviously successful as a model and perhaps even a hero on a number of levels, but he ultimately lacks the qualities to represent fully Fielding's standard, which integrates both spirit and intellect, good nature and active evaluation. Adams has too much a Pamelian excess of naiveté to be effective as even a purely traditionally moralist hero, and certainly not as a libertine hero of the new Georgian virtue. He entirely lacks the necessary balance to his great faith; he needs to learn the lesson that Fielding quotes with approbation from Rochester in the opening paragraph of "On the Knowledge of the Characters of Men": "*Man differs more from Man, than Man from Beast*" (*Miscellanies* I 153). Adams certainly represents all that is required of Fielding's good nature, but his is a good nature unmediated by the essential libertine understanding of the truth of real society. In fact, Adams's is a good nature that appears *unmediatable*, regardless of the lessons which should be learned if only from the incidents recorded in the journey of *Joseph Andrews*.

Adams's ignorance becomes explicit when he misses blatant revelations of the fallibility of human nature such as that of the Promising Squire, in whom Adams still wholeheartedly believes, even after a series of fabulous promises are broken and explained away only by weak and repetitive excuses. He exclaims, "Bless us! how Good-nature is used in this World" (II xvi 175). He is entirely wrong in his assessment of the situation, of course, as both the reader and Adams's fellow travellers recognize immediately. Ironically, however, there is truth in what he says since his own good nature is so abused, but as he does not recognize the correct context of his truth, he learns nothing about human nature or society from this incident, nor from his encounters with the hypocritical brave man and the avaricious Parson Trulliber, who knows "what Charity is, better than to give to Vagabonds" (II ix 137; II xiv 164–8). Our suspicion that Adams gains nothing from his experiences is confirmed when, even after being attacked by the Roasting Squire's dogs on their master's orders, Adams agrees to dine with him, though the results are fully predictable.

Fielding explains in the *Champion* of 27 March 1740 that good nature "makes us gentle without fear, humble without hopes, and charitable without ostentation, and extends the power, knowledge, strength and riches of individuals to the good of the whole." Certainly Adams strives toward this goal, but he cannot achieve even this sense of true good nature since he lacks the power, knowledge, and riches that signify the worldly elements equally necessary for a genuinely effective good nature. Adams is vain, but without any sense of a libertine conscious vanity of a tangible superiority: he deeply regrets the fact that he travels without his "Master-piece," a sermon on vanity that he wishes to read to Wilson not to educate him, but because he is "confident you would admire it" (III iii 214). The point is reinforced as the reader discovers that Adams "thought a Schoolmaster the greatest Character in the World, and himself the greatest of all Schoolmasters" (III v 232). For all that Brian McCrea might argue that "Adams has never struck readers as self-contradictory" ("Rewriting" 183), the parson does consistently violate his own dicta. He does not intentionally subvert or even thoughtfully consider the hegemonic assumptions that he has accepted deeply, personally, and blindly as truth, and this must, as it does, eventually leave him without adequate independence or self-determination to function effectively in Georgian England. He is led back to his room after concluding the night-ventures scene in Fanny's bed, confused and still self-righteous, failing to think actively about the paths he has chosen,[3] and muttering about witchcraft rather than accepting the obvious truth of the evening's events. Like those of Old Jourdain in *The Old Debauchees*, Adams's beliefs have been explicitly contravened by actuality, but still he will not evaluate them. Like Parsons Tickletext and Oliver, Adams operates according to the same thoughtless blind faith in his own sagacity that he expects from his parishioners; he reveals himself to be a fundamentally conservative character without potential for growth or development as a self-empowered individual.

Finally, Adams cannot function within *Joseph Andrews* as the good-natured libertine hero embodying Fielding's sense of authentic virtue as he is repeatedly unable to understand the emotion of another human being. A central element of Fielding's definitions of good nature, and thus of the ideal of good-natured libertinism toward which his best heroes move, is that, as I have noted, good nature "disposes us to feel the Misfortunes, and enjoy the Happiness of others; and consequently pushes us on to promote the latter, and prevent the former; and that without any abstract Contemplation on the Beauty of Virtue, and without the Allurements or Terrors of Religion" (*Miscellanies* I 158). Adams certainly enjoys the happiness of others as he snaps his fingers and dances about various rooms throughout the novel, but he absolutely lacks the ability to feel the misfortunes of others. Over and over again we see Adams offering no recognition of heartfelt and justifiable misery, only consolations on the worthlessness of earthly passion and even love, so that the allurements and terrors of religion finally replace empathy. When Joseph's beloved Fanny has been kidnapped by the servant of the Roasting Squire, who plans her rape, Adams's first response to Fanny's danger and Joseph's misery is:

You cannot imagine, my good Child, that I entirely blame these first Agonies of your Grief; for, when Misfortunes attack us by Surprize, it must require infinitely more Learning than you are master of to resist them: but it is the Business of a Man and a Christian to summon Reason as quickly as he can to his Aid; and she will presently teach him Patience and Submission ... It is true you have lost the prettiest, kindest, loveliest, sweetest young Woman ... You have not only lost her, but have reason to fear the utmost Violence which Lust and Power can inflict upon her ... but on the other side, you are to consider you are a Christian, that no Accident happens to us without the Divine Permission ... nor have we any Right to complain.   (III xi 265)

Adams's character is too dominated by standardized religious and social dogma even to think of beginning his consolation with empathy, and here again we see his weakness as hero and guide to virtue, or even complete good nature. Joseph's response to this ineffective consolation is much more appropriate both in its truth and its balance of natural and essential human passions and abstract understandings of traditional morality. He quotes Shakespeare's *Macbeth*:

Yes, I will bear my Sorrows like a Man,
But I must also feel them as a Man.
I cannot but remember such things were,
And were most dear to me - (III xii 267)

This balance between virtue as Fielding interprets it and the vast demands of human passion is the heroic quality that makes the new libertinism viable in Georgian society. Joseph is a much closer approximation of Fielding's ideal than the dogmatic and closed-minded Adams can ever be. The parson's responses to the misfortunes of others are not only misplaced but also hypocritical: he urges passive acceptance of circumstance as Joseph and Fanny encounter barriers to their marriage (IV viii 308), yet as Fielding points out, his own anguished reaction to the false news of his son's drowning is hardly consistent with the doctrine he so willingly offers to others.[4] This insensitivity caused by excessive absorption in abstraction and culturally standardized thinking recurs as Adams ecstatically congratulates the lovers on their good fortune in discovering the possibility of their filial relationship, completely blind to the agony that this news brings: "he continued all the way up to exhort them, who were now breaking their Hearts, to offer up Thanksgivings, and be joyful for so miraculous an escape" (IV xiii 329).

To point out these weaknesses in Adams's ability to fulfill Fielding's standard of the true virtue of Georgian libertinism is not, I hope, to blacken the general character of Adams. As I noted earlier, his character is successful as a hero on other levels and in terms of a number of the other cultural threads running through the novel. He never consciously acts with anything but good intention. He defends the weak with his ham-fists and his crabstick, and he tries to ensure that even the poor can marry for love, since "it would be Barbarous indeed to deny them the common privileges, and innocent Enjoyments which Nature indulges to the animal Creation" (IV viii 283). He defends the efficacy of good members of the clergy (though his own behaviour damages clerical credibility at times), and preaches ardently what he believes to be the single spiritual and moral truth.[5] He even violates hegemonic prescription occasionally, as he refuses to deny Joseph and Fanny the right to marry, even in the face of Lady Booby's wrath, and as he chastises Squire Booby and Pamela for inappropriate behaviour in church. Though McCrea suggests that Adams's belief that "he was a Servant of the Highest" (IV xiv 342) is one that "combines humility and deference to rank ('servant of') with an egalitarian assertion of quality ('the Highest')" and that thus "Fielding uses Adams to mediate between submission and defiance" ("Rewriting" 144–5), there is evidence that Adams in fact fails at that mediation. He is a good man, but one too bound by religious dogma and closed-mindedness to emerge as an effective model of the virtuous, empowered, and self-determining hero that Fielding has established in his plays, and which will become fully enshrined in the character of the good-natured libertine hero, Tom Jones.

In the extended recounting of the story of his youth, Mr Wilson shows himself to be anything but bound by religious dogma. But in spite of his ultimately sentimental reformation from his ostensibly Restoration-style libertinism by the love of a good woman and rural retirement, Wilson too lacks the broad virtue of Fielding's new heroic and the active and thoughtful balance of Georgian libertinism. In the dreary telling that Fielding uses to parody the self-absorbed spiritual autobiography, Wilson inherits a substantial sum at a young age, only to lose his wealth, his health, and his innocence in his attempts at attaining the "Character … of a fine Gentleman" (III iii 202). His failure at libertinism is implied in this introductory phrase even before any of the action: he attempts not to *become* a fine gentleman, but merely to gain a reputation. The libertine values originality, the power of creation, and the control of self-representation, but Wilson's very goal states that he will leave his "character" in the hands of others as he attempts only to imitate the truly independent thinking and considered social subversion of authentic libertinism. He becomes merely a fop, led by others and thoughtlessly accepting their doctrine, just as he had earlier accepted traditional social constructs and constraints in the country. Thus he pursues not the equal and enjoyable sexual relationships with women of Georgian libertinism, nor even the unmediated and controlling sexuality of the Restoration version, but "the Reputation" of "an Intrigue" (III iii 203). He lives a life "hardly above Vegetation" (III iii 205) as he follows the same patterns of activity every day, appearing at auctions, coffee houses, play houses, and drawing rooms, without any meaningful human contact or social interaction. He "mak[es] very free with the Character of a young Lady of Quality," and thus violates the central ideal of good-natured Georgian libertinism that no harm shall be done to others in the course of one's own pursuit of pleasure. When young Wilson refuses the opportunity to duel with the soldier who gives him the lie for his comments on the lady, he must retire to the Temple, where he becomes one step even further removed from real libertinism: "the Beaus of the *Temple* are only the Shadows of the others. They are the Affectation of Affectation" (III iii 205–6). It is in the company of these twice-removed artificial representations of libertinism that Wilson begins his decline into debauchery. This is significant to Fielding's libertine interest since, as Turner explains, a "central problem of libertinism, once it had rejected traditional religious beliefs, was to maintain an authentic self in a world increasingly constituted by 'representations' " ("Paradoxes" 73-4).

In this world of reflections, Wilson seduces a young woman, grows tired of her, and then is left by her after she has been corrupted by the influence of the other kept women to whom he introduces her (and after she has infected him with his third bout of venereal disease). He commits adultery with the wife of a citizen and is prosecuted for criminal conversation. While we have seen from *The Modern Husband* that the objectification and possession of women implied in a suit of criminal conversation marks the complainant as a violator of the Georgian libertine sexual ethos, so does the act of adultery, since, as becomes increasingly explicit in Fielding's novels, possessing multiple sexual partners is the only libertine privilege that Fielding expects his lovers to give up upon marriage. Once one has chosen to pursue the spiritual and social convention of marriage, its function must be upheld for the good nature of the genuine libertine to survive.

Finally, Wilson joins the Rule of Right club, "Fellows who might rather be said to consume Time than to live. Their best Conversation was nothing but Noise" (III iii 211). He accepts this new doctrine quickly and with as little serious evaluation as ever. This incident offers Fielding the opportunity to demonstrate explicitly the need for the new type of virtue. Typically, Fielding does not deny the validity of elements of the philosophy of the club, but rejects the extreme applications of a potentially useful ideology. As Battestin's extensive notes relate, the brief summary of the Rule of Right contains both the sentimental Shaftesburian insistence on the cultivation of an innate moral sense and a contradictory Hobbesian and Mandevillean sense of moral relativity derived from an assumption of an innate animal aggression in humanity. Members of Wilson's club use relativity to explain away clear violations of the "intrinsick Beauty and Excellence" of virtue, and thus rationalize self-serving acts like adultery and refusal to pay legitimate debts. Conversely, the true Georgian libertine depends not on abstract and undefined virtue, nor on Hobbesian rationalist pursuits, but on naturalism and good nature, considering the desires of the individual and the joys and miseries of others. As Dale Underwood explains in the standard definition of Restoration libertinism, "the libertine considered human laws and institutions as mere customs varying with the variations of societies and characteristically at odds with Nature as, of course, with 'right reason' " (14). 'Right reason' thus is not even a traditionally libertine concept, and must certainly fail the test of authentic Georgian libertinism for both its extreme, rather than thoughtful, application of doctrine (however ostensibly subversive that doctrine is assumed to be) and its lack of the mediating element of good nature that is so essential to Fielding's redefined understanding.

As often as critics choose to term Wilson a libertine, then, these are acts of faulty taxonomy dependent on a cursory understanding of libertinism as merely a debauched lifestyle. Both traditional libertinism and Fielding's revisionist understanding are much more complex and require a much more careful application than such classification implies. Even after his redemptive marriage to Harriet, Wilson is not entirely effective as a model of Fielding's libertine hero. Having tasted the result of a disastrous attempt at imitating his second-hand models of libertinism, thoughtful examination, and social subversion, Wilson retires to the country, where he also retires from any serious attempt at challenging hegemonic strictures beyond sheer splendid isolationism. He imitates the golden age more effectively than he imitated the libertine, but he cowers beneath the power of the brutish young Squire, who tramples Wilson's crops and kills his animals without Wilson's challenge or even apparent anger. He simply accepts the status quo in the realm of public power and that of private interaction. He denies the "Inferiority of Understanding which the Levity of Rakes, the Dulness of Men of Business, or the Austerity of the Learned would persuade us of in Women," but he immediately refers to his wife with the possessive "my Woman" even as he compliments her understanding. Even more than the patriarchal Adams, Wilson supports the separation of spheres of men and women as he smilingly explains to the parson that he would not wish his wife knowledge of Greek or any "Understanding above the Care of her Family" (III iv 226–7).

In fact, Fielding uses *Joseph Andrews* in part to articulate his thesis that the sexes in fact must have the same opportunities and freedoms in order for society to avoid ridiculous over-simplifications of complex issues such as that offered in *Pamela*'s equation of virtue with technical virginity. As Smallwood writes, Fielding regards "the gendering of moral conduct as a pressing social evil" (3). And though Smallwood later asserts that "*Joseph Andrews* is in fact by far the most masculine of Fielding's novels in its emphasis, being the least positive of all in its presentation of female characters" (124), her assessment is appropriate only insofar as one evaluates the female characters on traditionally moralist criteria. Certainly the critical commonplace is that the series of attempts on Joseph's chastity implies a judgmental evaluation not of feminine sexuality but of the opposition between good nature and hypocrisy. As Leo Braudy, for example, explains, book I "offers us a small social panorama of sexually aggressive women, beginning with Lady Booby, the sexual hypocrite, moving down the social scale and up the moral one to Slipslop, the maid-in-waiting who is at times almost honest about her lust, and concluding, still lower socially and higher morally, with Betty the chambermaid, in whom physical desire is associated with generosity of mind as well as of body" (134). This good-na-ture-versus-hypocrisy sense of Fielding's characters may well be appropriate in terms of his redefined virtue and libertine moralism, but there is more to the representations of women in this novel than such a direct analysis of generalized qualities of human nature cleverly inverted by gender in tandem with Joseph's non-traditional chastity. Fielding surely hints at his intent to establish play between expectation and fictional reality when he names his ostensible heroine Fanny. A man of Fielding's linguistic wit and skill at innuendo is not one who would use such a name without anticipating the titters of his readers.[6] The slyly named Fanny functions as the archetypally virtuous (and virginal) heroine, exercising a moment of passionate and self-determined agency when she abandons the cow she is milking to seek her injured love, but eventually surrendering to the masculinist hegemonic order as she objectifies herself as a prize to be won and then hands herself over to the possession of her future husband: "O *Joseph*, you have won me; I will be yours for ever" (II xiii 160).

Other female characters, though, are much more interesting in their individualized and libertine quests for social and sexual autonomy in the patriarchal society exemplified in the novel by dominating husbands. This latter group includes the conservative Parson Adams, who attempts to control the actions of his strong-willed and pragmatic wife by quoting "many Texts of Scripture," the ultimate guide of all of his actions, "to prove, *that the Husband is the Head of the Wife, and she is to submit and obey*" (IV xi 323, Fielding's italics). The chambermaid Betty is generally held up as the best example in *Joseph Andrews* of Fielding's good nature and its ability to overbalance traditional sexual morality. Betty has "Good-nature, Generosity and Compassion, but unfortunately her Constitution was composed of those warm Ingredients, which, though the Purity of Courts or Nunneries might have happily controuled them, were by no means able to endure the ticklish Situation of a Chambermaid at an Inn" (I xviii 86). She is dominated not by conservative moralist discourse, but by nature, and she explains to Mrs Tow-wouse, "if I have been wicked, I am to answer for it myself in the other World, but I have done nothing that's unnatural" (I xvii 85). Betty's only centre of power in her position as a poor servant woman is her sexuality: she chooses to share her favours with men to whom she is attracted, but is deaf to the "sufferings" of other lovers. It is ironic, then, that the not unnatural sexual encounter she has with Mr Towwouse after being aroused by Joseph's beauty is perhaps the one incident in which she is not necessarily in a position to consent or withhold. She is guilty of adultery, and so, despite her generosity, even in Fielding's scheme, she must be turned away. The narrator does not dispute the severity of her punishment as we might otherwise expect. However, his description of the event does hint at removing from her the full responsibility for the transgression. Tow-wouse begins to seduce her, already aroused as she is, but the description of her consent to intercourse recognizes the hierarchical implications of the seduction: "The vanquished Fair-One quietly submitted, I say, to her Master's Will" (I xviii 88). Fielding's morality signifies more than simple acceptance of prescriptive behavioural guidelines. The rules must be evaluated and challenged according to the individual's own perception and worldly experience, and this essential process often results in contradictory impetuses. Even as we recognize that Betty's unconventionality marks her as triumphant in her own way, we realize too that for all of her generosity and good nature, she ultimately fails at negotiating the complex demands of virtue, morality and desire.

If neither Fanny nor the often cited Betty successfully manifests the libertine qualities of social and sexual self-determination, control, independence, and considered evaluation of social constructions of virtue, the reader must look to the female character Fielding calls "the Heroine of our Tale" (I viii 38): Lady Booby. Lady Booby is the only woman in the novel to hold both the social status and cultural privilege necessary to the libertine position. Though she does not gain the love of the man she seeks, and thus is generally treated as nothing more than a limited character functioning only to impede the progress of the lovers, Lady Booby in fact embodies more than any other female character in *Joseph Andrews* Fielding's interest in the revised Georgian libertinism. All of the acts that lead many readers to characterize Lady Booby as a simple, lust-driven villainess are motivated by her desire for Joseph, but she does not hope to seduce and abandon him, but rather to marry him and live out her idealized vision of married life after she has survived her clearly incompatible husband. Fielding informs his readers of Joseph's physical attractiveness, and his intelligence and confidence are implied by his rise to the leadership of the other footmen in London. It is not at all improbable to suggest that these qualities, encouraged by the mornings he and Lady Booby have spent walking arm in arm at Hyde Park, might lead Lady Booby to feel real affection for her foot-

man. Joseph's perfect decorum and demeanour on these and other occasions was behaviour "which she imputed to the violent Respect he
preserved for her, and which served only to heighten a something she
began to conceive, and which the next Chapter will open a little farther" (I iv 28). Without knowing the outcome of the story, many readers will expect a declaration of love, not the unmediated and lewd
attempt at seduction that many critics take as given, particularly since
Lady Booby's first words to Joseph are to ask "*if he had never been in
Love.*" She flirts openly, offers her submission ("Would you not then be
my Master?"), and acknowledges that a footman's designs on his mistress "may not be wicked, but the World calls them so" (I v 29–30).
Lady Booby's intention here may be seduction, but to assume this is to
miss the cues Fielding offers us that she honestly believes she loves Joseph and pursues him in her natural desire for his response. I suspect
that it is because she loses out in the end that unsuspecting readers label
her as a conventional one-dimensional villainess, when she is actually
little removed from Fanny in the quality of her passion, and perhaps
even love, for Joseph.

More than any other character in the novel, Lady Booby actively
evaluates her emotional and physical responses to her circumstances.
After being rebuffed by Joseph, she engages Slipslop in the first of a series of discussions in which she considers the contradictory forces of
passion and reason. She finally overcomes her pride and decides on one
more attempt at expressing herself. She first slips into jealousy "with
great Discomposure of Countenance, and more Redness in her
Cheeks" at Joseph's confession of having kissed women in the house,
and then is again rebuffed, this time with Joseph's speech on his (thus
far unexplained) inviolable value for his virtue. Her rage is that of a
woman humiliated and rejected by a lover, as is made clear when she
protests too much in accusing Joseph of having had "the Assurance to
imagine, I was fond of you myself" and when, alone, she berates herself
for having "exposed [herself] to the Refusal of [her] Footman" (I viii
39–43).

Lady Booby then disappears from the narrative after having dominated book I. She reappears in book IV, where we are reminded of her
love for Joseph: "the Arrow had pierced deeper than she imagined; nor
was the Wound so easily to be cured. The Removal of the Object soon
cooled her Rage, but it had a different Effect on her Love" (IV i 278).
Fielding spends two pages here reporting her struggle with her passion,
ending with Lady Booby's blaming Slipslop for the false information
that led to Joseph's dismissal. For four pages in chapter vi, Lady Booby
guardedly discusses with Slipslop the ridiculous cultural limitations on

women and classes that would prevent a marriage for love if it would subvert existing hierarchies of conventional behaviour. She mentions socially prized but worthless men whom she could acceptably marry, and continues, "And yet these we must condemn ourselves to, in order to avoid the Censure of the World; to shun the Contempt of others, we must ally ourselves to those we despise; we must prefer Birth, Title and Fortune to real merit. It is a Tyranny of Custom."

Lady Booby struggles yet again with her desire to marry Joseph in chapter xiii, and here her awareness of the libertine significance of her anticipated subversion of the traditional role of women is made clear. She agrees with Slipslop's query, "and why should not a Woman follow her Mind as well as a Man?", and then acknowledges that her affection is based not only on the long list of Joseph's "Beauty and Virtues" that she cites, but also on a sexual desire that women in her culture are not permitted to admit openly. Having considered the question at length, she dreams of attaining that which she desires, regardless of the opinion of her peers. She wishes to "retire from them [the eyes of her acquaintance]; retire with the one in whom I propose more Happiness than the World without him can give me! Retire – to feed continually on Beauties, which my inflamed Imagination sickens with eagerly gazing on" (IV xiii 327). While her appetite is not necessarily admirable, she, like Betty, is honest in her confession of desire, and her dream of a marriage for love combined with desire is consistent with Fielding's conception of the Georgian libertine naturalism of love and sexuality.

Lady Booby does resort to an abuse of power more typical of the old style of libertinism in her attempt to have Joseph and Fanny imprisoned for the theft of a twig in order to prevent their marriage. We must acknowledge, however, that given Fielding's values as represented in *Joseph Andrews* and elsewhere, were the context different and were Lady Booby the rightful bride (in a structure we have seen in the plays and will see again later when Sophia is nearly forced to marry Blifil in *Tom Jones*), such machinations and trickery would be entirely excusable in the name of love. Our final vision of Lady Booby is as she leaves the room "in Agony" after the discovery of Joseph's parentage removes the final barrier to his marriage to Fanny (IV xvi 339), and destroys her last hopes as well. Throughout the novel, though, she has been "a Woman of a bold Spirit" (IV xiv 332), ready to investigate screams in the night, to query the cultural mores of her day, to subvert traditional limitations on the power of feminine self-determination, to admit and pursue her sexuality in the name of love, and to employ all means in her power (sometimes to Restoration-style excess) to fulfill her well-considered desires. While perhaps not entirely representing Fielding's ideal, Lady

Booby's character certainly deserves a re-evaluation, particularly considering Fielding's broad definitions of virtue and his obvious sympathy with the social challenges that Lady Booby's libertinism represents.

Joseph, of course, does not love Lady Booby, but the two characters share a series of traits that clearly delineate Joseph as the novel's hero and as a virtuous Georgian libertine. Since one of the central preoccupations of libertinism is that of the power to choose one's own path after actively considering various options and their consequences for the autonomous self and others, the fact that Joseph chooses to maintain his virginity does not preclude him from contributing to Fielding's process of defining and representing a libertine moralism. Certainly, for example, using a trait traditionally associated only with women as the initial identifying characteristic of his hero contributes to Fielding's questioning of gendered divisions of discourse and behaviour, as Jill Campbell's work demonstrates so effectively. And in another inversion of traditionally gendered discourse, Joseph's speech to Lady Booby and his letter to Pamela both wonder why any trait so valued in a woman can be any less so in a man. Though many critics have not been able to move past Joseph's chastity into the other interesting aspects of his character,[7] and others have strained to establish in Joseph a more powerful secret sexuality than is readily visible,[8] Joseph's choice to remain celibate until marriage demonstrates only that he rejects the amorous approaches of other women not out of love for some abstract understanding of Pamelian virtue, but simply out of respect for the woman he loves. He asserts his will in the face of a situation in which his response is assumed, and he disrupts conventional assumptions about his gender and his apparent class. Fielding's suppressed merriment at Joseph's priggish speeches in answer to sexual invitations confirms that there would be no real shame in a healthy young man's indulgence with a consenting partner; after all, Fielding's virtue is not "of that morose and rigid nature, which some mistake her to be … [and] forbids not the satisfying our appetites." Virtue forbids us only to "glut and destroy them" (*Champion* 24 January 1739/40), and it is, for example, that gluttony and destruction rather than basic indulgence, which seem to have been Wilson's error.[9] Real shame or not, however, Joseph chooses to privilege the Georgian libertine's moderately equitable view of women over the sexual pursuit of any woman other than his Fanny.

Moving past this usual focus, then, to consider other elements of Joseph's character in the context of Fielding's libertine moralism, we begin in Joseph's childhood. The description of his self-directed reading suggests an early independence of mind, as he searches for a broader understanding than could be achieved through the thoughtless activities of childhood. Later, when Lady Booby takes him to London, he chooses not to game, drink, or swear, but he almost immediately establishes himself as a connoisseur of music: he offers at the opera his own considered judgments, and his fellow footmen accept his opinion and his leadership. He takes a principal role in the footmen's riots at the playhouses, challenging the assumption that servants can easily be intimidated into silence (both personal and political) because of the powerlessness of their positions. He even behaves with less devotion than formerly at church on the rare occasions he attends his Lady there as he perhaps begins to evaluate actively the religious interpretations he has accepted passively for most of his life, as in fact he does later in various encounters with Adams's extreme dogmatism. In short, he has found the "Spirit" and "Life" which he had previously lacked as an individual. He is still good-natured, open, and honest, but no longer naive and unable to determine his own opinions and beliefs. Even before his process of maturation is fully begun, then, Joseph exhibits indications of meeting at least some of the criteria for Fielding's new virtuous libertine hero.

The source of Joseph's major developments of character, though, is his love for Fanny Goodwill. For this love, as we have seen, Joseph contravenes expectations of the sexuality of his gender and his apparent class. And for this love, he confronts the deeply held and hegemonic religious beliefs and cultural assumptions of his mentor Adams. He answers Adams's overpious consolations on the loss of Fanny and the fear that they might never be wed with acknowledgements that he knows his duty, but that practical circumstance prevents such abstractions from dominating natural responses of grief. In quoting from *Macbeth* (III xii 267), Joseph uses the world of the theatre, itself traditionally considered subversive and immoral, to represent the best balance of the demands of religion and passion: bearing sorrows, but also acknowledging them. He later points out the unintentional hypocrisy of even the good Parson Adams, and thus the fallaciousness of overexalting the value of purely abstract religious consolation as Adams shrieks in agony at the apparent death of his son mere moments after citing Abraham and Isaac as a model for religious duty. Adams responds that Joseph is "ignorant of the Tenderness of fatherly Affection," but Joseph defends his passionate love for Fanny as he cries in frustration, "Well, Sir … and if I love a Mistress as well as you your Child, surely her loss would grieve me equally." This immediately tumbles the two into another dispute about the validity of matrimonial love, wherein Adams recommends loving even one's wife "with Moderation and Discretion." Joseph disputes this doctrine as well before Mrs Adams ends the discussion by reminding her husband, "you do not preach as you practise" and informing him that a "Wife hath a Right to insist on her Husband's loving her as much as ever he can" (IV ix 310-1). In order to serve his desire and love, Joseph challenges conventional piety and religious abstractions; he accepts the natural quality of his passion and refuses to deny its validity; and finally, he defies the attempts of his more powerful relations to prevent his marriage, thus defending the individual's right to self-determination in love and life.

Mr Booby tries to force Joseph to "decline any Thoughts of engaging farther with a Girl, who is, as you are a Relation of mine, so beneath you." He suggests that the marriage "would break the Hearts of your Parents, who now rejoice in the Expectation of seeing you make a Figure in the World." Again Joseph denies such external authority: "'I know not,' replied *Joseph*, 'that my Parents have any power over my Inclinations; nor am I obliged to sacrifice my Happiness to their Whim or Ambition.'" This is the voice of a man demonstrating the thoughtful independence and agency of the privileged libertine in the face of those who would dominate him. He denies Booby's assertion of "the wide Difference" between them based only on the criterion of wealth, stating, "My Fortune enables me to please myself likewise ... for all my Pleasure is centred in *Fanny*, and whilst I have Health, I shall be able to support her with my Labour in that Station to which she was born, and with which she is content" (IV vii 301–2).

In the novel's conclusion the final barrier to the full identification of Joseph Andrews as good-natured Georgian libertine is lifted by the revelation that he is a gentleman born. Joseph has taken a series of apparently inappropriate stances, which, included in Fielding's considerations of the libertine, might confuse the established classes with the rabble from whom the libertines distinguish themselves. After all is revealed, however, these stances are absolutely appropriate for a man who turns out to be a well-born good-natured libertine, promoting a right to choice based on the privilege of the individual. Fielding thus cleverly manages to preserve the privilege essential to libertinism at the same time that he places that quality in a character who, externally at least, does not initially seem fitted to it.

Joseph ultimately refuses to sell the story of his "Appearance in *High-Life*" (IV xvi 344) because he does not need to be re-formed, autodiegetically or otherwise. He represents easily the qualities of Fielding's Georgian libertine in his revisionist virtue, good nature, naturalism, independence of thought, occasional subversion of conventional stricture, and even the power he exerts over his own sexuality. He chooses his partner, offers her the same independence of spirit that he manifests, and refuses to be distracted from his passionate desire for her. Though the hero is not so actively and explicitly libertine as Tom Jones will be, and the most self-empowered and honest female libertine is not rewarded with the man she loves, *Joseph Andrews* effectively demonstrates Fielding's continuing participation in the discourses of libertinism and virtue, and, still in its early stages, his exploration of the viability of a combination of the two in the good-natured Georgian libertine.

4 Threads in the Carpet: *Jonathan Wild*

In spite of the absence of a specifically Georgian libertine character like Joseph Andrews or Tom Jones, libertinism illuminates the action of *Jonathan Wild* (1743), and colours the implications of its characters and events. In fact, considering this problematic novel within the framework of Fielding's libertinism contributes powerfully to the longstanding critical debate over the ambiguous nature and actions of controversial figures like Jonathan Wild and Mrs Heartfree. Instead of setting up essentially good characters who manifest qualities of libertinism according to his understanding of the discourse, Fielding creates an underworld counterculture which, in its semblance to the world of Gay's *The Beggar's Opera*, would seem to be a natural home to both the more exuberant and the uglier aspects of libertine life. Rather than allow his criminals to relish any privilege, power, or freedom, however, Fielding represents Wild and his entourage as failures in a wide array of cultural contexts. There is precious little scholarly agreement on what exactly *Jonathan Wild* is *about*, and I do not suggest here that it is a novel *about* libertinism in any of its forms. This chapter will argue, though, for the recognition of libertinism as one of the contributing influences on the novel, and for its place in the wider literary and cultural implications of this immensely complex and contradictory text.

Wild and his peers attempt to grasp the idea and the privilege that libertinism entails, but have neither the capacity to understand its need for thoughtful action in rebellion, nor the originality, independence, and grace essential to the successful Georgian libertine. What emerges from an examination of the echoes of libertinism in *Jonathan Wild*, then, is a demonstration of the flaws of those who cannot engage that philosophy effectively. Unlike the direct and positive representations of Georgian libertines that occur elsewhere within Fielding's works and culminate in *Tom Jones*, the elements of *Jonathan Wild* informed by libertinism offer a view akin to that of a photographic negative, suggesting libertine qualities by showing their corruption and absence in Wild and his peers. Like the failed and Restoration-style libertines we have seen elsewhere, Wild emerges as a weak and thoughtlessly egocentric creature of fashion and appearance. His characterization particularly explicates that, for Fielding, some moral depth is essential to all humanity, and to libertinism, which has long since moved away from simple extremes of behaviour and "the fetishization of greatness … [in which] energy tended to be valued over ethics, and satire and panegyric were forced closer together" (Turner "Sublime" 103).

As he has done before, Fielding positions himself as a libertine and consistently takes advantage of his artistic privilege. In *Jonathan Wild* he uses that privilege not only to set the novel in a criminal underworld (with much the same attitude of *The Covent Garden Tragedy*), but also to parody literary genres such as criminal biography, travel narrative, romance, and familiar letters, at the same time that he re-evaluates and subverts the dominant social and political norms of his day. Fielding uses the ironic inversion within his central criminal biography to reveal the flaws of his society, and the hollowness of those who would use their own liberties (or the various definitions of liberty manufactured in the novel) not to challenge the existing social structure, but merely to gain from it.

As is true of all of Fielding's works, any number of paradigms and ideological perspectives can be applied with varying degrees of success to elucidate the patterns in Fielding's social and political thought in *Jonathan Wild*. The irony that permeates the novel, combined with its political aims and the differences between its structure and content and those of Fielding's other works, has made *Wild* perhaps the most vehemently debated of Fielding's works. Over the course of the novel, Fielding manages to render ironic to some degree almost every character, situation, and cultural presupposition he represents. Wild's character in particular is composed of constantly shifting comic inflections; he cannot be taken at face value, but he must be taken into consideration in any attempt to assess the novel. Even the novel's apparently direct satire on greatness has been shown by Claude Rawson to be undermined by the hero's anarchic clownishness (which often seems to provide its own comic justification).[1] A straightforward reading of the novel or any of its components is thus impossible, but analysis of those components that contribute to the understanding of culture and humanity that fosters Fielding's ironic representation is not.

The difficulty in determining exactly when *Jonathan Wild* was composed contributes to the critical contradictions about the significance of Fielding's irony and his truth. The work was probably drafted between 1737 and February 1741/2, with revisions, probably including much of the Heartfree plot, completed in 1742 after the fall of Walpole and the completion of *Joseph Andrews*.[2] Fielding also revised the novel extensively for publication in an edition separate from the *Miscellanies* in 1754. This extended period of composition and revision thus stretches from initial drafts up to ten years before the formal beginning of Fielding's magistracy, to final revisions near the close of his judicial career. Scholars usually discuss Fielding's novels in the context of other contemporaneous work, and validate the methodology by the existence of a specific period of composition. This approach is obviously problematic in the case of *Jonathan Wild*; however, since Fielding's conception of a Georgian libertine moralism carries throughout his fictional works (and is consistent with the role of an independent justice who strove for social change in occasionally unorthodox ways), the conflicts and contradictions that arise from forcing *Jonathan Wild* into a limited political and social site do not occur in the same way when approaching the work using the libertine paradigm. For all of the alterations in the specific political ramifications of *Jonathan Wild* between the 1743 and 1754 editions, allusions to libertinism remain significantly consistent.

The titular character of the novel is the obvious place to start as we examine the representation of libertinism and the failure of anyone in Wild's circle to function effectively within the revised version of libertinism that interested Fielding throughout the long composition process of the novel. It is interesting to note that one of the first aspects of the life of the historical Wild that Fielding alters is that of his time. Wild was born in 1683, shortly before the death of Charles II (which was followed by the more constrained rules of James II and William of Orange in 1685 and 1688/89 respectively), and hanged in 1725. Fielding's Wild is born almost twenty years earlier, in 1665, at the start of the plague (as the narrator tells us) and in the midst of the development of the Restoration libertinism of Rochester and the court wits. Instead of coming to maturity after the turn of the century and in the era of sentimentalism, Fielding's Wild matures in the middle of the 1680s, with old-style libertinism still at its height in the public eye and on stage. Wild thus becomes not the young would-be libertine failing at both the libidinous and cruel old style and the good-natured new one, but simply a figure attracted by Rochesterian extremity of appetite and subversion, but who is not rich, powerful, or clever enough to attain the privileged agency of the great men and great libertines of the Restoration.

As the libertine ideal of independence and individualism shifts position across the Restoration from a marginal view to one, if not hegemonic, certainly the subject of widely muttered agreement, Wild is caught in this transition between a society focused on the good of the many and one much more concerned with the place of the individual. As the narrator takes pains to point out with ironic regret, Wild is not purely self-absorbed and grasping – he is not undilutedly "great." As with Fielding's libertine heroes, Wild's character is a mixture of goodness and greatness, but the mix in this case is wildly disproportionate. Wild's twisted understanding and manifestation of libertinism depends on his incomprehension of naturalism, anti-rationalism, and the central moral and social doctrine of Fielding's good nature.

The novel's first page establishes that Fielding's own sense of good nature has not shifted from the vision he has always represented in his works. The narrator explains that of heroes, "far the greater number are of the mixt kind, neither totally good nor bad; their greatest virtues being obscured and allayed by their vices, and those again softened and coloured over by their virtues" (I i 39). The implied presence of Fielding's good nature and libertinism is thus confirmed before the reader enters Jonathan Wild's world upside down. Wild bases his actions on his faulty definition of good nature: "he carried good-nature to that wonderful and uncommon height that he never did a single injury to man or woman by which he himself did not expect to reap some advantage" (I xi 67). Wild's character is not absorbed in questions of good nature or libertinism any more than it is absorbed in any other single cultural discourse, but the central philosophical and social misperceptions that mark his character do echo many of the broader issues of libertinism, and confirm its continued presence.

Claude Reichler's work on the three phases of French libertinism seems particularly pertinent to a discussion of that presence of libertinism in the cultural assumptions underlying *Jonathan Wild*'s satire. Turner summarizes Reichler's view that in the second phase of libertinism (in late seventeenth-century France),

[t]he libertine's supple, detached conformity to social and stylistic expectations, the ease with which he slipped from place to place in a 'verbal geography,' effectively redefined *all* beliefs as local customs and all truths as received opinions, without actually running the danger of defying official ideologies ... The self may cleave to its mask, losing the capacity to distinguish the authentic but

veiled interior from the ironically compliant exterior. Inverting the error of the first stage, this second generation gave so much weight to social representations that their autonomy was threatened, the inner self collapsing into 'its own vacuity.' ("Priapism" 4)

According to Reichler, this phase then develops into the 'double im-passe': the self-fulfilling trap always threatening to appear within the otherwise comfortable existence of libertinism. Reichler's trap becomes unavoidable when both extreme behaviour with illusions of mastery and full autonomy with excesses of simulated compliance to existing social systems (in efforts to manipulate from within the social system) lead to the eventual collapse of the philosophy of libertinism into one great set of characters in the social theatre.

Wild's very life, of course, is a costumed role in the public theatre, from his youth with Count LaRuse when he "made a considerable fig-ure, and passed for a gentleman of great fortune in the funds" (I vi 57) to his maturity, in which he expends great effort avoiding public and personal recognition of what he really is. To his associates (one hesitates to say friends) such as Bagshot and Heartfree, Wild can offer "a counte-nance full of concern, which he could at any time, with wonderful art, put on" (II ii 86–7). Fielding makes explicit from the beginning the breadth of this continuing effort at disguise: the preface to the *Miscella-nies* reminds us that "without considering *Newgate* as no other than Human Nature with its Mask off, which some very shameless Writers have done, a Thought which no Price would purchase me to entertain, I think we may be excused for suspecting, that the splendid Palaces of the Great are often no other than *Newgate* with the Mask on" (*Miscella-nies* I 10). The difference between Wild and those who inhabit the splendid palaces of the great, however, is that Wild is eventually lost in his own attempts to disguise himself as both socially acquiescent friend and powerful, fearless libertine: he is caught out and hanged at the end of the novel by the combined efforts of both of the groups he has tried to deceive. Even before this happens, though, we discover that he has lost all sense of any real individual identity amid the layers of public de-ception. Wild lies alone in his boat cast adrift by the French captain, denying that he fears death, "[a]t which words he looked extremely fierce, but, recollecting that no one was present to see him, he relaxed a little the terror of his countenance" (II xi 116). Wild can no longer react honestly even within his own mind, and has thus surrendered his po-tential for the libertine individualism, self-determination, and control that provides part of the impetus for his self-construction. He cannot remove his masks even to himself, and without any private identity, he is unable even to determine his own desires, much less act to achieve them.

Wild also – with the assistance of the narrator – attempts to manipulate and control language. Manipulation of the semantic instability of words like honour and liberty occurs on at least three levels – Fielding, the narrator, and Wild – and simultaneously demonstrates Wild's failure in the language of libertines, and Fielding's success in wielding it. This is particularly fitting since Fielding rails in the *Champion* of 17 January 1739/40 at the common squandering of words and the use of certain phrases that have "by long custom arrived at meaning nothing, though often used." At the first level of linguistic manipulation, Fielding uses *Jonathan Wild* as part of a redefinition of the concept of liberty.[3] The concept is subjected to semantic contortion of various types throughout the novel, as it is used, for example, to suggest simultaneously both freedom of sexuality and a sense of disgust in the description of Laetitia Snap's unsupported breasts (I ix 63), as a term used in opposition to virtue in Heartfree's response to Wild's suggestion of a murderous escape (III v 137), and as a system of extortion (as well as a geographical area) in the references to the liberties of Newgate. But Fielding leaves behind such games when he presents his preferred definition of liberty in the speech of the grave man in Newgate, a speech which Fielding recommends to his readers in the brief "Advertisement from the Publisher to the Reader" appended to the 1754 edition. The grave man's speech proposes that the essential form of liberty is that of separation from those who would abuse freedoms by those for whom liberty is a useful tool of good nature rather than avaricious priggishness: "Every *prig* is a slave. His own *priggish* desires, which enslave him, themselves betray him to the tyranny of others. To preserve, therefore, the liberty of Newgate is to change the manners of Newgate. Let us, therefore, who are confined here for debt only, separate ourselves entirely from the *prigs* ... not to give up the interest of the whole for every little pleasure or profit which shall accrue to ourselves. Liberty is consistent with no degree of honesty inferior to this" (IV iii 174–5). This passage almost certainly functions as the political allegory suggested by Thomas Cleary and others, but it also suggests the same construct of liberty that informs Georgian libertinism: challenging the social order that frustrates security and true liberty while at the same time preventing descent into the violently egocentric realm of Wild and the Restoration libertines, which still privileges extremism as a central device of self-definition.

Fielding's semantic experimentation is subtle, however, compared to the efforts of Wild and the narrator. The two cannot easily be separated in a discussion of voice and language since Wild's communication is accurately recorded only once in the course of the novel: in the orthographically disastrous letter to Laetitia. The narrator explains immediately after that "if it should be observed that the style of this letter doth not exactly correspond with that of our hero's speeches, which we have here recorded, we answer, it is sufficient if in these the historian adheres faithfully to the matter, though he embellishes the diction with some flourishes of his own eloquence" (III vi 140). Because of this admission, the reader must question the motivation and representation of every act of verbal manipulation attributed to Wild. Thus his impressive rhetoric and apparent libertine self-determination and originality are revealed to be only additional failures. His great speech recontextualizing honour for Bagshot, full of lamentation that "a word of such sovereign use and virtue should have so uncertain and various an application that scarce two people mean the same thing by it" (I xiii 74), would be a brilliant statement of the libertine capacity to redefine society except that the narrator acknowledges two books later that Wild is not capable of making it.

Wild's alternative discourse does occasionally distinguish him from the mass of other characters, as when his priggish language confuses the debtors at Newgate and they select him as their new leader. Over and over, though, the lowness of the language he uses to separate himself, combined with the socially untenable site of his distinction, renders him ridiculous and without the control he so desperately seeks. The laughable grammar and spelling of his letter to Laetitia, the one instance in which he does speak in his own voice, do not serve simply to make Wild the subject of humour in his inability to express himself even adequately, far from doing so with the superiority he desires. Combined with the narrator's earlier reference to Wild's inability to spell his own name consistently (I ii 42), the letter also serves as yet another example of Wild's failed attempts to take advantage of libertine privilege. Fielding himself exercised part of the libertine privilege of self-creation when he changed the spelling of his own name from Feilding to Fielding (Battestin *Life* 7); but instead of demonstrating a like capacity for self-determination or challenge to familial or linguistic limitations, Wild's discordant spelling of his own name and his other orthographical errors demonstrate only another example of ignorance and failure in Wild's effort to pursue a self-creating, sexually attractive, socially and intellectually autonomous persona.

Even the members of Wild's gang see through his attempts at verbal manipulation; Wild's long rhetorical speeches need repeatedly to be backed up with the threat of violence to convince even those who have agreed to follow him. The eloquent redefinition of honour ends with Bagshot acquiescing not to Wild's ideas, but to his sword, and Wild gains ninety percent of the money taken from Heartfree "partly by argument, but more by oaths and threatenings" (II iii 91). The narrator too fails to give Wild any power or privilege through linguistic machination as his narration gives way to alternating ironic slippage and reclamation. The repeated attempts, for example, to establish Wild above the "vulgar" populace, only accentuate Wild's own vulgarity and lowness, and, in speaking for his anti-hero, the narrator takes from Wild any power he might have gained from self-representation. The more the narrator uses the overblown language of "greatness" to convince the reader, the more the reader is struck by the inordinate amount of effort required to confer any privilege, power, or originality onto Jonathan Wild.

Rendered voiceless in his own story, Wild from the beginning falls short of all of his own expectations, including those that so echo the libertinism of Fielding's other heroes. Each successive failure suggests in growing detail the novelist's own sense of the liberty and libertinism of his age as one philosophical quality underlying the action of the novel. It is particularly significant that Wild fails sexually not only in his inability to allow women the limited power and self-determination offered by the Georgian libertines; he fails even at the power-driven seduction and rape that typify the worst element of Restoration libertinism. After his first attempts to force himself on Laetitia are fought off with little apparent difficulty, Wild appears not as the great conqueror he aspires to be, nor as a nobly defeated warrior, but as a boy in a public school whose naked backside has been whipped by his tutor (I ix 64). Wild's attraction to women is described not in terms of a man guided by the love of a good woman, as might be said of Joseph Andrews, Tom Jones, and William Booth, but entirely in terms of power and dominance. He strives for independence from and control over the sexuality of his partner: "The hero, though he loved the chaste Laetitia with excessive tenderness, was not of that low snivelling breed of mortals who, as it is generally expressed, *tie themselves to a woman's apron-strings*; in a word, who are tainted with that mean, base, low vice, or virtue as it is called, of constancy" (II iii 91–2). But he fails even in his infidelity: though he intends to impose upon Molly Straddle, not only is he imposed upon as he must pay for her services, he is then robbed by her.

Shortly after this incident the narrator admits Wild's inability either to accept the love valued by Fielding's revisionist libertinism, or to maintain any real power as an individual. He describes Wild as afflicted by "that weakness of suffering himself to be enslaved by women, so naturally incident to men of heroic disposition; to say the truth, it might more properly be called a slave to his own appetite; for, could he have satisfied that, he had not cared three farthings what had become of the little tyrant for whom he professed so violent a regard" (III iv 132–3). The truth comes out in the second part of the sentence, of course. Wild fails at the masculine sexuality of the powerful man and the libertine both because he lacks the good nature that characterizes the balanced or even virtuous appetite of the Georgian libertine, neither neglected nor glutted, and because he cannot control his own actions in the face of his lustful desires. In convening their marriage, Wild sacrifices Laetitia's and his own happiness to fulfill a passing craving for a woman who is independent and confident enough to control her own sexuality and to be available only when and to whom it pleases her. Bagshot, Fireblood, and others are entertained by Laetitia, LaRuse fathers a child by Theodosia Snap,[4] the Heartfrees have a fruitful marriage, and even Wild's mother dreams during her pregnancy of being enjoyed by Mercury and Priapus. Wild's only successful sexual encounters are purchased: intentionally with gifts and unintentionally with the theft of £900 by Molly Straddle, and through a marriage forced on Laetitia by Snap and Wild Senior for their own economic gain.

Wild's acts of purchasing women reveal his un-libertine lack of sexual attractiveness as well as his objectifying view of women. He repeatedly refers to Laetitia as the object of his appetite, while Mrs Heartfree is called a "charming dish" (with the subsequent pronoun being "it") (II viii 110) which Wild schemes to conduct "from the proprietor" Heartfree (II ix 110). Even after agreeing with Laetitia to conduct separate lives within their marriage (an agreement perhaps acceptable to Restoration libertines, but another failure within Fielding's vision), Wild considers his wife a part of his property. He applies the sexual double standard anathema to Georgian libertinism when, after pursuing Mrs Heartfree, he berates Fireblood for his sexual conduct with Laetitia, as "a stab in the tenderest part, a wound never to be healed," and asks, "doth not everything of the wife belong to the husband?" For all that Wild's rant focuses on the dishonour he faces (and for which he has given his wife consent), his response is exactly that of the anti-libertines Sir Positive Trap and Lord Richly of *Love in Several Masques* and Mr Modern of *The Modern Husband.* In fact, Fielding seems to bring the latter example to mind intentionally as Wild announces his plans for a divorce and a criminal conversation suit: "I will apply to Doctors' Commons for my redress against her; I will shake off as much of my dishonour as I can by parting with her; and as for you, expect to hear of me in Westminster Hall; the *modern* method of repairing these breaches and of resenting this affront" (IV x 197–8, italics mine). Since criminal conversation suits have already been established in Fielding's plays as manifesting patriarchal perspectives of women as chattel, this scene reveals Wild's utter lack of understanding of the movement toward feminine agency.

Wild has been ineffective at the language of libertines, the domination of others through publicly accepted privilege, and both the sexual dominance of the Restoration libertine and the acknowledgement of the need for independence of women in the world of the Georgian libertine; next, he is subjected to the test of the attainment of control and power. However, true to the established pattern of establishing Wild as the clownish failure at so many cultural criteria, including those involved in a successful embodiment of Georgian libertinism, Fielding ensures that Wild never really attains true power either. He is not motivated by the standard human desire for gain; he is driven instead by the need to prove his ability to perform great deeds and some – almost any – level of superiority. Wild's failure emerges from the extremity of his need. More than once, he struggles to gain power by positioning himself above the "rabble" who must work by their own hands: "What then have I to do in the pursuit of greatness but to procure a gang, and to make the use of this gang centre in myself? This gang shall rob for me only, receiving very moderate rewards for their actions; out of this gang I will prefer to my favour the boldest and most iniquitous (as the vulgar express it); the rest I will, from time to time, as I see occasion, transport and hang at my pleasure; and thus (which I take to be the highest excellence of a *prig*) convert those laws which are made for the benefit and protection of society to my single use" (I xiv 79–80). Wild intends to use what little privilege he has for personal gain, again failing to understand the true nature of privilege. True privilege values the same things that the libertine does: simply enjoying the larger benefits of a superior social position without needing to gain from it, and certainly never desperately. Ironically, it appears that even from this posture of privilege, Fielding's Wild may still be regarded, like the historical Wild, as a servant of the public interest, since his basic function is to arrange for the smooth return of stolen goods, and since he brought so many highwaymen and robbers to justice. Throughout the novel, even when he seems to be in control, Wild is dominated by his own desires (unarticulated and unclear though they may be in his mass of self-deception) and by his Hobbesian fear, which renders him vulnerable to virtually any external attack. Shortly after he announces his plan for control and power, he is defrauded of both the jewels and the money stolen from Heartfree. The truth of his empowerment and privilege is revealed as he goes to the home of LaRuse: "Not the highest-fed footman of the highest-bred woman of quality knocks with more impetuosity than Wild did at the count's door, which was immediately opened by a well-drest liveryman, who answered that his master was not at home" (II iv 95). At what should be the height of his scheming power, Wild is not only compared to a servant, but turned away by one.

He lives in constant fear as he falls more and more into the trap created by his own mask of representation. He becomes increasingly aware, but not more admitting, of his vulnerability and inability to control his prigs or his own life. Less than twenty pages after the nearly triumphant announcement of his plan, Wild makes another suspiciously eloquent speech: "What avail superior abilities, and a noble defiance of those narrow rules and bounds which confine the vulgar, when our best-concerted schemes are liable to be defeated! How unhappy is the state of PRIGGISM!" He mouths the words of noble defiance and social subversion, but he so little considers the evaluative thought which must attend such actions that he immediately despairs of his success, ignorant that it is the considered act of rebellion itself that is significant to the true rebel and the true libertine, not the gains that may come from it. He bemoans the difficulty of defending his own pockets at the same time that he steals from others: "what can be imagined more miserable than a *prig*? How dangerous are his acquisitions! how unsafe, how unquiet his possessions!" His only reward is "the inward glory, the secret consciousness of doing great and wonderful actions" (II iv 96). This solidly individualistic statement, which might even mark Wild as a libertine, is again subverted as he goes on to explain that he is "wise though unsuccessful, [and] a GREAT though an unhappy man" (II iv 97). He has not, of course, been wise, and is not great, even in the context of his upside-down criminal underworld. His fear is also only momentarily assuaged, since even when he seems to be in control of his gang, he is

under a continual alarm of frights, and fears, and jealousies. He thought every man he beheld wore a knife for his throat and a pair of scissors for his purse. As for his own gang particularly, he was thoroughly convinced there was not a single man amongst them who would not, for the value of five shillings, bring him to the gallows. These apprehensions so constantly broke his rest, and kept him so assiduously on his guard to frustrate and circumvent any designs which might be formed against him, that his condition, to any other than the glorious eye of ambition, might seem rather deplorable than the object of envy or desire.   (III xiii 160)

While both Joseph Andrews and Tom Jones are repeatedly mistaken for gentlemen of social position and power whether naked, in livery, or in rags, Wild cannot convince debtors and thieves of his position or power even when dressed in the gentlemanly nightgown, waistcoat, and cap he takes from his predecessor. Significantly, the clothes don't fit: the robe is not warm enough, the waistcoat is infinitely too big for him, and the cap is so heavy that it makes his head ache. Such trappings cannot make a figure out of such a man as Wild, for he lacks from the beginning the good nature and presence that would allow him to wear comfortably the wardrobe of a gentleman of privilege. That he expects to gain power and a confirmation of his egocentric self-perception from the costume stolen from a man who has proved usurpable concretizes the absence of thoughtful consideration in Wild. Roger Johnson's robe is eventually just another of the disguises through which Wild tries unsuccessfully to convince not only those around him of his individualistic power, but himself as well.

Wild continues to strive unsuccessfully for self-determination as he approaches death. He attempts to save himself by gathering false witnesses and controlling the perception of the court, and when that fails he turns to the bottle "by means of which he was enabled to curse, and swear, and bully, and brave his fate" (IV xii 204) until his failed attempt at suicide shows that he cannot manage even his own exit from the world. His egocentricity leaves him with none of the real motivation that might be gained from friendship, love, or loyalty, and so, in the end, Wild's existence is one of lack and negation in which he cannot use even his excessively powerful appetites effectively to serve himself.

Wild's search for those very qualities that determine Fielding's other heroes confirms Fielding's continued interrogation of libertinism as an important part of his culture. The search also incorporates Fielding's political, legal, and moral interests, as he presents a world (even upside-down) that is determined by no single discourse, but informed by many. In any of Fielding's contexts, Jonathan Wild fails as a hero, and in the context examined here, he is also a negative image of the Georgian libertine. The search for a hero then logically turns to Mr Heartfree.

The debate over which character is the hero of *Joseph Andrews* is echoed in discussions of *Jonathan Wild*, with Mr Heartfree, and occasionally both Heartfrees together, often nominated as the true hero of the novel.[5] Those who connect Heartfree to the heroic position often attempt to link him with the sexual potency of Fielding heroes like Tom Jones. Stephanie Barbe Hammer, for example, describes him as "a virile, sexually potent man, as his wife's utter devotion to him and their two children suggests" (69). Mrs Heartfree may be less devoted to her husband, however, than to men who find her attractive and shower her with attention; her vanity undermines Heartfree's heroic qualities.

Even before Heartfree is introduced as a character, Fielding tells us, "I do not conceive my Good Man to be absolutely a Fool or a Coward; but that he often partakes too little of Parts or Courage, to have any Pretensions to Greatness" (*Miscellanies* I 12). Heartfree not only lacks the greatness of ambition essential to a hero, but more importantly, he is so passive that he does not pursue even the defensive actions available to him. Fielding's interest in a shift in both moralism and libertinism back toward the centre and away from extremes is revealed as we realize that neither of the central male characters of *Jonathan Wild* exemplifies an adequate combination of good nature and individuated agency, the combination that is the hallmark of Fielding's unironically great heroes and heroines. Allan Wendt recognizes this as he argues that Heartfree's role in the novel is based on luck and circumstance, since "in his own inability to contribute anything to that [happy] outcome, Heartfree is strikingly unlike the virtuous men in other Fielding novels … Heartfree is limited precisely because he lacks this native energy which Fielding associates with good-nature. All of Fielding's admirable characters are active rather than contemplative" ("Allegory" 309, 315). I would emphasize, however, that the energy Wendt sees in Fielding's good nature comes very often from its connection with the power and intellectual and sexual energy of libertinism.

Still, Heartfree's passivity is not the only thing that separates him from heroism, libertine or otherwise. There is a Pamelian quality to his virtue that reminds the reader at odd uncomfortable moments of Mrs Heartfree's extended self-glorification in the name of virtue and chastity, and of Laetitia, who, between fending off Wild's advances and letting Tom Smirk out of the closet where she has hidden him in order to collect Wild's gift, "proceeded to talk of her virtue" (I ix 65). Throughout his Boethian self-consolation after his wife's sudden departure, Heartfree reminds himself that his reasoned reaction is the response of the virtuous. More unexpected is his self-congratulatory speech after Wild proposes his plan for a robbery (through which he intends to impeach and hang Heartfree). Heartfree outlines the "comfortable expectations" that he gains from his virtue and his intent of "DOING NO OTHER PERSON AN INJURY FROM ANY MOTIVE OR CONSIDERATION WHATEVER. This, sir, is the rule by which I am determined to walk, nor can that man justify disbelieving me who will not own he walks not by it himself … for surely no man can reap a benefit from my pursuing it equal to the comfort I myself enjoy: for what a ravishing thought, how

replete with ecstasy, must the consideration be, that Almighty Goodness is by its own nature engaged to reward me" (III x 151). Only two
chapters later Heartfree violates his own golden rule when he responds
to the "offered" rude handling of his daughter by "catching the fellow
by the collar, [and] dash[ing] his head so violently against the wall, that,
had he any brains he might possibly have lost them by the blow" (III xii
156), an act that renders the suspicion of a dominating pride in his
Pamelian speeches of conscious virtue ever more plausible. Heartfree is
not so much a foil to Wild[6] as simply another example of a mode of life
that is inferior to Fielding's good-natured libertinism. These two characters are the negatives which, overlaid and made positive, might create
the "good-natured libertine" represented by Tom Jones.

The final shadow of inadequacy that Fielding casts over Heartfree
must necessarily shadow Mrs Heartfree as well. In direct opposition to
the conclusion of every other novel, the Heartfrees "are now grown old
in the purest love and friendship, but never had another child" (IV xv
219). The reader wonders immediately why Fielding goes out of his way
to explain that whatever virility and fertility the couple might once
have had is lost after Mr Heartfree's endless gullibility and passivity and
Mrs Heartfree's worldly travels. Mrs Heartfree may no longer need the
affection of her husband to support her self-perception, having had it
confirmed by so many, or she may simply find his passivity unattractive
after her own period of independence and action. Conversely, perhaps
Mr Heartfree's overwhelming delicacy prevents him from anything but
the "purest love," especially if he doubts what Mrs Heartfree has ex-
changed for the jewel with which she returns. Wild believes, and Heartfree can suspect, "[t]hat virtues, like precious stones, were easily
counterfeited; that the counterfeits in both cases adorned the wearer
equally, and that very few had knowledge or discernment sufficient to
distinguish the counterfeit jewel from the real" (IV xv 217). My reading
of Fielding's works, however, suggests that this reference to a final steril-
ity and lifelessness confirms absolutely the incompleteness and lack in
the Heartfrees as heroic figures. The inversion of Fielding's libertine
sexual and cultural values is complete: the reader is unmistakably informed that independence, sexuality and virtue are never successfully
joined in *Jonathan Wild*.

Mrs Heartfree is perhaps as close as Fielding comes in the novel to
offering a straightforward vision of the libertine. During her temporary
presumption of privilege, Mrs Heartfree's character embodies more heroic agency than any other character in the novel, and her tale is particularly suited to the question of Fielding's representations of gendered
agency. Her appropriation of the masculine personae of traveller, ex-

plorer, manipulator, and sexual subject quite specifically upsets eighteenth-century constructions of femininity, even as she is unable to sustain her agency upon her return to London from the cultural, gendered, and geographical margins of her independent experience. Still, she is not entirely successful in meeting the criteria of the hero (as much as we can take them as they appear in *Jonathan Wild* and its prefatory material). She does not function as a combination of the good and great outlined by Fielding in his preface as "A perfect work! the *Iliad* of Nature! ravishing and astonishing, and which at once fills us with love, wonder, and delight" (*Miscellanies* I 12). She does, however, mediate between the anti-libertine characters of Wild and Heartfree to a certain extent. Earla A. Wilputte summarizes eloquently the conflicts that emerge in Mrs Heartfree's brief period of independence and self-reliance: Mrs Heartfree is "learning to use man's reputation of Greatness to her own advantage. In this way, she reverses the power stratum and becomes the dominant figure precisely because she seems the weaker. A new, independent and capable woman emerges here; however, it remains debatable whether she is a self-preserving or self-serving one" ("Heartfree" 232). For Mrs Heartfree to be recognized as a powerful and even libertine figure, though, we must acknowledge that her narrative is one she manipulates, reforms, and almost certainly revises from the reality that her character is assumed to have experienced.[7]

The clearest source of such revision lies in the apparently irresistible attractiveness Mrs Heartfree grants herself in her narrative. No fewer than eight men consider ways to seduce her,[8] and this number encompasses every man of power she encounters, as well as the noble hermit. In Mrs Heartfree's version, men of low status seem too intimidated by her beauty (and the captains who pursue her) to express the desire we are expected to assume they too must feel. She recreates herself as the heroine of a romance, and the fictions of armies of would-be seducers and of her inviolable chastity are parts of that role. The ambiguity of the language used to represent that chastity, however, is unmistakable. The definitive idea of "virtue" has been challenged once again in Fielding's discourse by its association with Laetitia Snap early in the novel. Not only does Laetitia echo Shamela when she "talk[s] of her virtue" (I ix 65), but her virtue is described as "impregnable," suggesting sexual activity in the same phrase. Fielding also makes clear that "the chaste" Laetitia's belief that Theodosia's illegitimate child is "an affront to her [own] virtue" (III xiii 159) is very much the same as the beliefs implied in the advice offered by both Shamela's mother and Sophia's Aunt Western: that which is unacceptable for the unmarried is left unacknowledged once a woman is under the protective veil of marriage. The standard is set, and Laetitia can do "what other married women do" (III viii 144). Mrs Heartfree's inclusion in this "virtuous" group and the comparison implied when the discovery of Laetitia's infidelity interrupts Mrs Heartfree's tale offer her behavioural options not publicly acknowledged, but undeniably present in the collective psychology of the novel.

Such hints of ambiguity are brought back to the reader's mind in later semantically unstable passages. As she describes the man who fashions himself as her protector during their time on the English ship and in Africa, Mrs Heartfree uses phrases that suggest equally the sexual freedoms of the female libertine and a chaste relationship. She explains that from the time of their meeting, "I lived in great familiarity with this man" and that he had "the tenderness of a parent for the preservation of my virtue, for which I was not myself more solicitous than he appeared" (IV vii 186). The negative phrasing in this instance renders her subsequent behaviour unclear at best; neither half of the couple may be particularly solicitous. A storm at sea follows, and although Mrs Heartfree describes the prayer of the atheistic captain and the drinking of the crew, she evades any explanation of her own actions or those of her protector by stating simply, "I need not tell my Tommy what were then my thoughts" (IV viii 188). The reader aware of these ambiguities must wonder too why, after detailing the shipwreck, Mrs Heartfree "cannot help telling you my old friend lay still nearest me on the ground" (IV viii 191). It is Mrs Heartfree who first suggests that her sexual favours could be purchased when she announces to the count that "could [she] be brought to yield to prostitution, he should be the last to enjoy the ruins of [her] honour" (IV ix 192). She protests rather too much as she describes rejecting the jewels he subsequently offers, "till at last casting [her] eye, rather by accident than design, on a diamond necklace," she realizes that they are the very ones stolen from her husband. And closing the lengthy passage of linguistic dalliance is one final reference that must leave the reader dubious: Mrs Heartfree, noting her husband's increasing agitation at her tale, tells him, "My dear, don't you apprehend any harm" (IV ix 193). She may tell her husband not to fear for her safety, but her choice of "apprehend" may also suggest that he should not see, recognize, or understand the harm that may have come to his wife's chastity.

This lengthy encounter with her protector is only the most detailed of the various encounters that Mrs Heartfree represents to be a grave threat so that her tale of preservation will suggest even greater libertine cleverness, intelligence, and power as she uses her sexuality to gain riches and her freedom. She sounds vaguely regretful that the French captain does not take advantage of the fact that she is "totally in his power" (IV vii 184), and she seems to delight in her fortitude in drinking the English captain under the table when he speaks to her like the "most profligate libertines converse with harlots" (IV vii 186). And when the Chief Magistrate of the African community offers her "an immense present" in exchange for her person, she "rejected the present, and never heard any further solicitations; for, as it is no shame for women here to consent at the first proposal, so they never receive a second" (IV xi 202). By having Mrs Heartfree point out the cultural differences in reactions to gifts, Fielding implies that she follows her own cultural system in assuming that she will receive a second offer (a cultural system which again evokes memories of the avaricious Laetitia Snap's demure acceptance of gifts from Wild only on the second offering [I ix 64, II iii 94]). Just as Wild's twelfth maxim, about precious stones and virtue being easily counterfeited, seems structured to bring to mind Mrs Heartfree's tale (and possibly the shadow of Shamela), so does his fourteenth: "That men proclaim their own virtues, as shopkeepers expose their goods, in order to profit by them" (IV xv 217). While telling her tale, Mrs Heartfree relishes her role as an object of desire who maintains control over both her sexuality and the historical representation of that sexuality.

To read Mrs Heartfree's tale with a consistent sense of suspicion is not, however, to suggest that she is a distasteful or unattractive character.[9] Rather, it becomes clear that her sense of libertine privilege and empowerment is simply not strong enough to allow her to represent publicly her desire and her challenges to the strictures of the traditional female role, and to be praised for a series of actions and plots that remove her much more than she will admit from the realm of woman-in-peril into which, in order to suit conventionality, she tries to force the story of her actions. This stumble back into acceptance of and submission to the psychologically ingrained limitations placed by the surrounding masculinist hegemonic structure is what prevents Mrs Heartfree from being a libertine figure effective enough to counter recognizably the libertine negatives of her husband and Jonathan Wild. She herself cannot acknowledge her libertinism, so she cannot be held to challenge social dictates actively. When she states her belief that "PROVIDENCE WILL SOONER OR LATER PROCURE THE FELICITY OF THE VIRTUOUS AND INNOCENT" (IV xi 203), she surrenders the power of self-determination that she might have demonstrated publicly. In the same way that Wild must spend the novel attempting to recreate and disguise himself, Mrs Heartfree's story creates the persona of the individualistically empowered female libertine heroine. By book IV, though, one of her images must be a mask of self-construction: the sexual, creative, and autonomous traveller, or the meek wife who accepts passively her role within the traditional construction of femininity, particularly as represented by the essentially arranged marriage of one daughter and the dedication of the other to her father's service.

Wilputte argues that Mrs Heartfree "aims to construct an egocentric sexual fiction in which she manipulates masculine power, be it the rude English captain's, her husband's, or the listening magistrate's. She discovers through her narrative that she can employ conative language (which tries for an effect) and especially prolepsis (anticipation) to wield power over her male audience" (231). Wilputte is correct in her assessment of the effect of Mrs Heartfree's narrative reconstruction of fictive reality, but I do not believe that Mrs Heartfree "aims" at this power. Instead, the power of such self-determination and control through the libertine use of sexuality, deceit, language and self-creation passes through her grasp as she returns to her old life of "purest love and friendship" with her husband and acceptably passive daughters. Mrs Heartfree is the closest link to the effective Georgian libertinism of the heroes and heroines of Fielding's other novels, but she is an ultimately failed link none the less.

Particularly among those who view *Jonathan Wild* as mere prentice work, it is often suggested that the novel contains basic outlines of the principal characters that recur in Fielding's works (Mr Heartfree as the ancestor of the innocents Adams, Partridge and Harris; Mrs Heartfree as the passive female; and Wild as a diabolical typological precursor of the heroic Tom Jones). Despite the problems of chronology in such readings, there is a certain truth in this recognition of the characters of *Wild* as incomplete manifestations of characteristics that recur throughout Fielding's works of fiction.[10] While *Wild* engages Fielding's political and legal interests more specifically and energetically than any other of his works, the questions about the nature of the hero, of cultural discourses of masculinity, status, power, privilege, and subversion that interest him throughout his career are again present in this notoriously complex novel of irony and inversion. As in so much of Fielding's work, the central aspects of seventeenth- and eighteenth-century discourses of libertinism do not determine the direction of the novel's cultural gaze, but inform the characterization and social representation in subtle but significant ways. It is in *Tom Jones* that Fielding develops the ironic negatives created in *Jonathan Wild* into straightforward images of good-natured sexual freedom, naturalism, individualism and empowered agency.

5 The Road to Archetypal Georgian Libertinism: *Tom Jones*

In *Tom Jones* Fielding brings to life his most successful integration of libertinism and moralism within a single character: Tom Jones is the archetypal Georgian libertine. Throughout the novel, he consciously and actively acts against the socially determined constraints of his society. He negates the value of the letter of the law and of the standard manifestation of institutionalized religion. He actively serves his naturalistic desires despite the impositions of his rationalist contemporaries, and his sexual enthusiasm and freedom certainly reflect that most commonly understood element of libertinism. Beyond this, though, Fielding makes Tom Jones into a true Georgian libertine by giving him good nature and Fielding's redefined virtue: he indulges his own appetites, but, unlike the typical Restoration libertine, he does not glut them, and he does not gain pleasure from comparison with the starvation of others. He strives for and achieves libertine individualism as, through the course of the novel, he absorbs the more stereotypical libertine qualities from various characters around him, but combines them to create a formulation of libertinism that is his own.

Or, rather, it is Fielding's own, as he creates the character who most fully exemplifies his understanding of the function of the libertine in Georgian society. Contemporary audiences recognized the opposing forces of upstanding, honest moralism, and intelligent, independent social subversion within Fielding's hero, and though many accepted the coexistence of the two, others still felt the need to place the work in one of the two traditional moral categories of eighteenth-century prose: immoral or didactic. The first categorization is typified by the pseudonymous 'Arentine,' writing in *Old England*: "That this motely [*sic*] History of Bastardism, Fornication and Adultery, is highly prejudicial to the Cause of Religion, in several Parts of it, is apparent in the gross Ridicule and Abuse which are wantonly thrown on religious Characters. Who reviles the Clergy may be well said to be upon the very Threshold of Immorality and Irreligion" (Paulson and Lockwood 168). The belief that the novel was immoral and a force of corruption was encouraged by others as well, including Samuel Richardson in his extensive correspondence and 'Orbilius' in a book-by-book attack in *An Examen of the History of Tom Jones, A Foundling*. Others, however, chose to read the text as a moral document. Captain Lewis Thomas wrote to Welbore Ellis, "If my design had been to propagate virtue by appearing publickly in its defence, I should rather have been ye Author of Tom Jones than of five Folio Volumes of sermons" (Paulson and Lockwood 162). Many readers, though, regardless of political stripe or position on the moralist-immoralist continuum, recognized Fielding's focus on libertinism. Elie C. Freron's review of LaPlace's French translation of *Tom Jones* is only one of the contemporary sources which notes that Jones's "penchant for libertinage was manifested ever since his infancy" (Paulson and Lockwood 277).

Fielding himself, of course, uses the appellation of libertine for his hero at various points in the novel, despite the heavily moralist claims of the Dedication. The didactic assertions of the Dedication are problematic from the beginning, however, since they make statements that Fielding knows to be false, and use language for which Fielding has established ironic precedents in his earlier works. The Dedication offers useful evidence for Fielding's intention to present the new libertinism in a concrete form, and not just the standard doctrinal lesson he initially appears to introduce:

I hope my Reader will be convinced, at his very Entrance on this Work, that he will find in the whole Course of it nothing prejudicial to the Cause of Religion and Virtue; nothing inconsistent with the strictest Rules of Decency, nor which can offend even the chastest Eye in the Perusal. On the contrary, I declare, that to recommend Goodness and Innocence hath been my sincere Endeavour in this History ... And to say the Truth, it is likeliest to be attained in Books of this Kind; for an Example is a Kind of Picture, in which Virtue becomes as it were an Object of Sight, and strikes us with an Idea of that Loveliness, which *Plato* asserts there is in her naked Charms.   (7)

The passage cries out its ironic intent. The reader's sense that Fielding protests too much to be taken entirely seriously is augmented by phrases like "I hope my reader will be convinced," and "I declare," which throughout the novel, like Fielding's assertions of ignorance, mark out passages to be read closely and critically. Fielding must have known from his theatrical experience that his depictions of Jones's sexuality would certainly "offend even the chastest Eye." Similarly, the word "virtue," considering the unavoidable implied presence of *Shamela* and *Joseph Andrews*, combined with the smug reference to Virtue's "naked Charms," helps to direct the reader away from a straightforward reading and toward an understanding of Fielding's revisionist virtue, as well as the conflation of morality with sexuality, the subversion of normative and linguistic limitations, and the privilege of the author to poke at that "chastest" eye in order to expose its tendency toward affectation and social capitulation.

Such manipulation of readers' assumptions recurs throughout *Tom Jones* as Fielding indulges the same sense of libertine privilege that has been evident in his plays and earlier novels. He asserts that "the Excellence of the mental Entertainment consists less in the Subject, than in the Author's Skill in well dressing it up" (I i 33), and that he "intend[s] to digress, through this whole History, as often as I see Occasion: Of which I am myself a better Judge as any pitiful Critic whatever" (I ii 37). Since he is "in reality, the Founder of a new Province of Writing, so I am at liberty to make what Laws I please therein" (II i 77). Thus the libertine positions himself above even literary norms. For example, Fielding smilingly offers repeated tales of Tom's infatuation with Sophia's muff, Honour's fear that he will "stretch … and spoil it," and her shock that she "hardly ever saw such a Kiss in [her] Life as he gave it" (IV xiv 206–7). That such an explicit, but ultimately deniable, dirty joke runs through the novel reveals Fielding's acceptance of sexual liberty as well a sense of libertine superiority and privilege. He acknowledges these privileges specifically in terms of the libertine discourse in his rebuke to shocked readers after the scene at Upton with Mrs Waters (and another reappearance of Sophia's muff): "I must remind such persons, that I am not writing a System, but a History, and I am not obliged to reconcile every Matter to the received Notions concerning Truth and Nature" (XII viii 651).

Fielding creates a fiction in which privilege is the right of those who function independently of convention. A critical commonplace is to read *Tom Jones* as essentially moralist, with the repentance and reformation of Jones demonstrating the need for prudence and limitation of any natural wildness of the spirit.[1] The novel, however, can equally be held to support not such a bland moralism, but one that requires wildness and subversion in order for the individual to be truly good or good natured. Even critics who recognize this lack of traditional moral judgment, however, generally miss the roles that libertinism and conventional misbehaviour play in Fielding's revisionist Georgian libertine point of view. William B. Guthrie argues that in *Tom Jones*, "Fielding suspends his moral judgment in order to celebrate humanity and affirm the life-spirit. In this sense Tom Jones does teach a moral lesson, but it is the lesson that life itself is sacred" (92). While this perspective does recognize the life force that is so essential to libertinism, such bland readings of exactly the type of morals-of-the-story that Fielding denies needing in his plays result from neglecting Fielding's understanding of social organization and the influences of such forces as the libertinism of Fielding and his social circle. We may not be able to read Jones as the typical eighteenth-century moral hero, but his sexuality and imprudent behaviour are clearly acceptable to Fielding, and the novel's reception suggests that they were also acceptable to most of his audience.

Fielding himself notes that we cannot condemn a character as bad because he is not perfectly good, though it does seem that a character can be bad who appears to be perfectly good. Tom Jones is driven by natural inclinations generally unmediated by the forces of popular constructs of reason and propriety, but he always meets Fielding's standard of good nature. Though John Traugott does not discuss libertinism *per se* in his article on "Heart and Mask and Genre in Sentimental Comedy," he does state eloquently exactly the transition that I see in the libertinism from the Restoration and some of Fielding's early plays (which is the version at which Jonathan Wild fails) to the good-natured version of the Georgians and *Tom Jones*: "Just as his appetite implies neither the incommodities of digestion nor the indecencies of excretion, so it suggests none of the deeper and nastier philosophical problems of appetite that are isolated in Hobbes's egoistic philosophy, nor in the rake figure of Restoration comedy, nor in *Clarissa*'s Lovelace. The brutal and fatal will to satisfy desire of the former and the need for sexual domination of the latter are alike alien to Fielding's outlook on life" (124). It is true that the character of Jones is far removed from the brutality of the Restoration libertine; in response to this, though, other readers have attempted to make him into the opposite extreme, the sentimental hero. In fact, *Tom Jones* is often regarded as a sentimental representation of the need for prudence. Morris Golden, for one, suggests that Fielding does fit the paradigm of sentimentalism. "The word has been used to describe certain kindly assumptions about human nature; an unwillingness to face the existence of evil in man or in society; a wish to exalt the bourgeoisie and its addiction to mediocrity and compromise; a tortuous insistence on happy endings, preferably after agonizing plots; and a reliance on easy devices for eliciting the reader's or audience's emotional involvement. Not surprisingly, Fielding is a sentimentalist by some of these criteria and something else – perhaps a curmudgeon – by others" (*Psychology* 151). I would argue instead that Golden's "something else" is exactly the libertine that Traugott hints at.

In *Tom Jones*, Fielding again reconsiders and redefines the discourses of virtue and libertinism, masculine and feminine. He creates the nominally libertine Tom Jones and then surrounds him with characters who manifest various elements of libertinisms past and present. Fielding thus gives his readers the opportunity to grasp through the fictional world the understanding of libertinism that he considers appropriate for the real society around him. Tom's development as a good-natured libertine is a central paradigm of *Tom Jones*. It is not, of course, the only paradigm, but such a theoretical pattern is suitable here not only for the character of Tom Jones, but because nearly all of the central characters embody at least some elements, some manifested successfully, some not, of the libertinism of the Restoration or the Georgian period. A few of these characters seem specifically connected with libertines or pseudo-libertines in Fielding's other works, and others act as guides for Jones in his continued development as a gentleman and a libertine.

If *Tom Jones* is, at least to some extent, a novel of the road, these various incarnations of libertinism placed along the way provide a comparison to the archetype of the Georgian libertine developing before us in Tom Jones. Jones starts his journey from Paradise Hall, where he has spent much of his youth in the company of Western, who objectifies women, is licentious, and leads a hedonistic and thoughtless lifestyle outside the town. Western is clearly the inheritor of, among other qualities, the sexual exuberance of Old Laroon and the desperate striving for dominance of Sir Positive Trap. He is an old-school libertine, undiluted by doubt or sentimentalism beyond that inherent in his love for his daughter, which lasts only as long as she obeys him.[2] He is not shaken by the news of "a Wench having a Bastard," nor by his belief that Tom is the father, as he asks Parson Supple, "Where is the mighty Matter o't? What, I suppose, dost pretend that thee has never got a Bastard? Pox!" (IV x 189). His understanding of the sexual world is such that he believes that even Allworthy must have bastard children, though, of course, this assessment of the novel's apparent paragon is corrected by the narrator in the next chapter.

As I explained at length in my first chapter, however, a non-traditional conception of sexuality does not a libertine make. Western is not of the court party more traditionally home to the libertine, but he does challenge social norms within his own realm. He will not be directed by what the town or his neighbours think, and he enjoys living in his self-created golden age of indulgence of individual appetite for wine, for the hunt, and for power. It is the last of these, though, that ultimately prevents Western from fitting comfortably into even the Restoration mold of libertinism. In the early part of the novel, he functions easily as a representation of naturalism unimpeded by social constraints. He is a voice of directness and honesty, however brutal. But his desire for the power of self-determination and the concurrent determination of those around him is so strong that as the novel progresses he ceases to consider actively his desires, but simply indulges them blindly. He is no longer a naturalist anti-rationalist, but simply irrational, a character trait derided by libertinism. This irrationalism is, of course, rendered most clearly in his relentless pursuit (aside from one brief burst of appetite again in the impromptu fox chase) of the domination of Sophia from the first time she disobeys him. This aggressive need for control does echo Restoration ideologies, but Western ultimately fails as a libertine of any form as he lacks any actively thoughtful motivation for his actions, socially disruptive though they may be. He certainly fails as a Georgian libertine for this reason, as well as for his inability to offer women self-determination, which is itself symptomatic of the larger flaw of a lack of good nature to mitigate self-absorbed appetite. Western is "good humoured" rather than "good natured" according to Fielding's definitions in "An Essay on the Knowledge of the Characters of Men." Though he certainly does not contemplate abstractly the beauty of virtue or the terrors of religion, instead of feeling the misfortunes and enjoying the happiness of others, Western enjoys only "the triumph of the mind, when reflecting on its own happiness" (*Miscellanies* I 158), which might have been pleasurably appropriate for Wycherley's Horner, Etherege's Dorimant and the other *types* of Restoration libertines, but does not serve adequately the libertine of Fielding's time.

Like Western, Lady Bellaston is another signpost of failed libertinism on Fielding's road toward integrated Georgian libertinism. She represents the urban feminine counterpart to Western's rural masculine embodiment of old-style libertinism. This balance of intended influence is suggested even in the novel's structure, as her appearance in the thirteenth to sixteenth books of the novel effectively parallels the dominance of Western as a pseudo-libertine influence over Jones in the third to sixth books. There are two books at the opening of the novel before Jones is particularly impressionable and two at its close where he is finally beyond the influence of failed libertines. In the four books adjacent to each of these periods, though, Jones is exposed to and affected by the beliefs and grasping dominance of these two opposing representations of weakened old-school libertinism. Even at the end of the novel, it takes four books for Jones to be sufficiently inoculated against Lady Bellaston's able manipulations and examples, and to emerge from his trial the fully formed, fully confident Georgian libertine.

Though manifestation of sexual autonomy and feminized agency may be Lady Bellaston's central role in *Tom Jones*, her categorization as a libertine is not simply dependent on these elements. She challenges social norms not only in her open sexuality, but also in her independent repudiation of the concept of marriage as an institution repressive to women, her use of the libertine topoi of the masquerade and disguise as tools of her liberty, and her effective manipulations and deceptions of others in pursuit of power and her other desires. With such a powerful representation of the complete female libertine, it may seem odd that, if Fielding accepted and even propounded the revised Georgian libertinism, the affair with Lady Bellaston is generally seen as Jones's behavioural nadir before his repentance and redemption in the final books of the novel. In fact, while I can agree that Jones is at his least respectable point here, I challenge the traditional spirit of such assessments. The affair is Jones's weakest moment not because he is a kept man, but because he surrenders all of the power of self-determination that he has gathered through the novel as a good-natured Georgian libertine and surrenders it to Lady Bellaston's more practised, but less perfectly libertine control.

It is Lady Bellaston who brings Jones into the realm of disguise and deceit with her invitation to the masquerade. After their meeting, but still masked, she asks Jones, "And are you so little versed in the Sex, to imagine you can well affront a Lady more, than by entertaining her with your Passion for another Woman? If the Fairy Queen had conceived no better Opinion of your Gallantry, she would scarce have appointed you to meet her at a Masquerade" (XIII vii 715). The intent of the assignation is made clear here, though the identity of the speaker is not revealed until two pages later. The use of the word "gallantry" is especially interesting, since Fielding's readers would recognize that the term carried not only the meanings of nobility and courteousness, but, as the *OED* notes for the period, also those of sexual intrigue and adultery.[3] From the outset, then, Lady Bellaston has intended to possess Jones sexually. After her conquest she advises him to purchase new clothes with the money she offers, placing him in his second disguise of their relationship: that of the well-dressed town figure, something which to this point Jones has neither been nor desired to be. As long as he plays the role of her lover, to which he is obliged, since the ultimately dishonourable "Gallantry to the Ladies" is ironically "among his Principles of Honour" (XIII vi 715), he must wear the public markers of his submission to the power and desires of another.

Despite all of her libertine traits, however, Lady Bellaston ultimately fails as an influence because she cannot maintain the balance between intellectual and emotional awareness in her relationship with Jones. In addition, she embodies quite clearly another of the weaknesses of old-style libertinism. Apparent sexual triumph is often used to mask a deep sense of incompleteness.[4] Lady Bellaston's sexuality is not one of confident joyousness, but one that reflects her need to control some aspect of her life as an aging woman in an era when, libertine or not, older women grow progressively more powerless and more dependent. A weakness or fragility is reflected in her unwillingness to share Jones sexually or emotionally. Her need to possess him entirely, like Western's claim of chattel rights over Sophia, forces her influence to the side because of the lack of good nature in her actions and her inability to accept the independence of her object. She commits the same error of objectification with Jones that earlier male libertines did with women, and this prevents her, even in her role as sexually empowered woman, from effectively demonstrating the necessary equilibrium of sexual power between the genders that denotes Georgian libertines. When she loses Jones she attempts to destroy his other relationships in order to regain his dubious affections. She loses her power, and in bitter retaliation becomes a weakened and vaguely pathetic shadow of her libertine incarnation at its height. She is, simply, a woman whose glory is past; she belongs to a version of libertine ideology that Jones must leave behind.

Other minor characters act as examples of libertinism in transition between the structural bookends of failed libertinism represented by Western and Lady Bellaston. Almost exactly halfway through the novel, Jones encounters the Old Man of the Hill, a reformed libertine of the old school. The Old Man's tale provides Fielding's narrative with the extremes of debauchery, decline, and ecstasy for which Jones does not have time and from which his good nature might not recover. The Old Man's remembered experience is actually set during the Restoration, and it reveals the potential horrors of undeveloped libertinism. From the beginning of his tale he is doomed to failure, as he is unable to maintain his independence; social pressure to conform to publicly defined evils must be negated by the effective libertine just as forcefully as pressure to conform to publicly lauded behaviour. He is passively seduced first by Sir George Gresham, his wealthy school acquaintance.[5] In his youth the Man of the Hill fails to consciously consider his actions or their implications, and his unconventional behaviour is only a futile attempt to mask the same incompleteness that later appears in

Lady Bellaston. He steals from his friend to finance his debauchery (something that Jones's good nature – though it allows him to be bought – would never permit him to do), and abandons reckonings in taverns (stealing from those who can even less afford it). The Old Man's relationship with his unnamed female companion shows what might have happened to Jones with Molly Seagrim. While Jones is ignorant of Molly's promiscuity, the Old Man is aware that his partner "had been the Mistress of half [his] Acquaintance" (VIII xi 457), but both have basically noble intentions toward deceitfully ignoble women, and are at some point willing to marry their fallen lovers. The difference is that Jones considers marrying Molly because he believes that it is his duty to another human being (rather than to society) when he thinks he has fathered a child, while the Old Man lets himself be swept away by his emotional gullibility into a relationship echoing that of Jonathan Wild and Laetitia Snap.

The meeting with the Old Man has other implications as well. We not only realize the near consequences of Tom's encounter with Molly, but also (until we discover the true nature of the Old Man's treacherous lover) experience vicariously with Jones the misery of "love in Distress" (VIII xi 456) which might have been the fate of a Clarissa-like response to the thwarted love of Sophia and Tom. Fielding makes this parallel clear as Jones collapses into a chair crying, "I thank Heaven I have escaped that" (VIII xi 457). The similarities between the paths of these characters and their lives (with different providential interventions yet unseen by Jones) are straightforward in many ways, and the proximity and similar phrasing of the description of Jones's "Flow of Animal Spirits" (IX v 510) and the Old Man's "violent Flow of Animal Spirits" (VIII xi 453) make clear that Fielding expects us to compare the natures of the two and their versions of libertinism, the philosophical and behavioural representation of "animal spirits." The central difference between the two, and that which allows the providential hand of Fielding to differentiate without excessive artifice or hypocrisy, is that of nature. Jones's nature is innately good, promoting the happiness and preventing the misfortunes of others as well as himself, while the Old Man of the Hill is "ambitious" and covetous (evidenced particularly by the collection he has gathered since giving up his dissipated life for travel), and so tends to be entirely self-absorbed. Even when reformed, the Old Man lacks good nature, and since he has sacrificed both worldly pleasure and good nature, the internal quality Fielding sees as fundamental to any complete life, he can never be happy.

More than the interpolated Old Man of the Hill, Mr Square is generally seen as central to the action of the novel, and his influence on the developing Georgian libertinism of Jones is formalized by his role as tutor. Square begins the novel with many of the hallmarks of the old-style libertine, though he would almost certainly deny vehemently any such association. He challenges existing normative values by his very status as a deist who "held human Nature to be the Perfection of all Virtue, and that Vice was a deviation from our Nature in the same Manner as Deformity of the Body is" (III iii 126). Certainly his lessons are not entirely lost on young Tom, whose later actions often echo those of Square in motivation and explanation as he follows his nature sexually, morally, and socially. Square also embodies the idea of freedom of sexuality, and his "Appetite was not of that squeamish Kind which cannot feed on a Dainty because another hath tasted it. In short, he liked [Molly] the better for the Want of that Chastity, which, if she had possessed it, must have been a Bar to his Pleasures" (V v 231). In fact, Square is established early in the novel as a character who parallels the libertine development of Jones. Once Tom reaches adulthood, Square perceives him as a rival in pursuit of the love and fortune of Mrs Blifil, and they turn out actually to be rivals for the affections of Molly Seagrim. Their similarity of character becomes particularly evident when Square is discovered in his absurd posture in Molly's room, where he explains the libertine naturalist understanding that "Fitness is governed by the Nature of Things, and not by Customs, Forms, or municipal Laws. Nothing is, indeed, unfit which is not unnatural" (V v 232). Jones's immediate response is, "Well reasoned, old Boy," and the explanation that, as he sees nothing particularly wrong with Square's actions, the secret will remain between them. Though in strict chronology Square follows Tom in the seductions of Molly, Jones follows developmentally in Square's philosophical footsteps as he manipulates beliefs that have been conveyed, apparently often unintentionally, by his tutor.

Despite these similarities, however, since Square has earlier been described as having "utterly discarded all natural Goodness of Heart" (III iv 129), he is no more an effective model of Georgian libertinism than is Western, Bellaston, or the Old Man of the Hill, at least until his repentance and reformation at the end of the novel. His reformation by the inclusion of religion with his other philosophical beliefs has crucial effects on Jones's history, but, more importantly, parallels Jones's own final achievement of integration of the examples and lessons of those around him and the completion of the true Georgian libertine. Jones emerges still intellectually and socially aware, and not fundamentally changed from his earlier self, but with having accepted fidelity after marriage and the fruitlessness of extremes of behaviour.

This shift is also echoed in Nightingale, who, like Square, manifests libertinism as a discourse in transition. His initial description explicitly acknowledges his role as representative of Restoration libertinism. Nightingale is one of "those young Gentlemen, who, in the last Age were called Men of Wit and Pleasure about Town ... Pleasure may be said to have been the only Business or Profession of those Gentlemen to whom Fortune had made all useful Occupations unnecessary. Play-Houses, Coffee-Houses and Taverns were the Scenes of their Rendez-vous. Wit and Humour were the Entertainment of their looser Hours, and Love was the Business of their more serious Moments. Wine and the Muses conspired to kindle the brightest Flames in their Breasts" (XIII v 700). Fielding then argues that "those young Gentlemen of our Times" should not be given the same title, since they "soar a Step higher than their Predecessors, and may be called Men of Wisdom and *Vertu* (take heed you do not read Virtue)." The libertines of Fielding's day are associated with politics, gaming, the fine arts, and natural philosophy, exactly the interests associated with the new libertinism by Chesterfield, Saint-Evremond, and others.

Nightingale, of course, is also associated with the old-style libertine sexual lexicon as the narrator notes, "In Affairs of Love he was some-what loose in his Morals; not that he was even here as void of Principle as Gentlemen sometimes are, and oftener affect to be; but it is certain he had been guilty of some indefensible Treachery to Women, and had in a certain Mystery called making Love, practiced many Deceits, which if he had used in Trade he would have been counted the greatest Villain upon Earth" (XIV vii 767). At the same time as he makes Nightingale's sexual treachery and deceit of Nancy Miller clear, Fielding also ensures that the reader hears his disapproval of treacherous acts in general, the anti-libertine attitude toward women that permits such be-haviour, and comparisons in which acts of trade are privileged in conse-quence over both the lives of women and the implied acts of patriarchal trade in women. Here, then, is where Nightingale fails as a modern lib-ertine. Like Square, he turns out to be a figure struggling in the para-digmatic shift between the two forms of libertinism, and he has lacked the good nature necessary to fill the new role that Fielding sets out for him at his introduction.

Interestingly, though, Nightingale is perhaps Fielding's best example of that potential limitation of libertinism pointed out by Harold Weber in his discussion of rakes and rogues as manifestations of the Restora-tion libertine. Like Weber's rogues, Nightingale must "recognize a truth that conventional society would avoid: that social identities are arbi-trary creations that possess little power when confronted by economic necessity" ("Misrule" 27). Without the somewhat cunning and deceit-ful assistance that again marks Jones as both good-natured and libertine, Nightingale will be forced to marry his father's moneyed choice. Even Jones himself is forced by economic necessity to surrender his libertine self-determination and power, and to submit for a time to the machinations of Lady Bellaston. Thus, just as Square forecasts some of Tom's philosophical and social development, so does Nightingale echo some of his conflicts and trials. Though Nightingale is farther along the road to Georgian libertinism than are Square or any of the other pseudo-libertine guides who have led Jones to this near-final point of his libertine education, the fallen state of Nightingale and Nancy Miller reveals that Jones has been correct thus far in avoiding causing similar misery to Sophia. The incident also implies that love and desire can be saved through the creative and independent thinking of a well-rounded new libertine, even if the lover he helps still clings to the outmoded discourse where one does not marry a whore, even of one's own making. Since both Jones and Nightingale embody more of the criteria of the good-natured libertine than any other of the male characters depicted, both are eventually left happily in the company of good women, though the slower-developing Nightingale matches with the sexually stumbling Nancy, while the successfully integrated Georgian libertine marries Sophia, the "Idea of Female Perfection" (IV i 154).

These five central exempla of unintegrated goodness and greatness and of incomplete libertinism are ultimately left behind by Jones in favour of Sophia, who represents not only that which her character is usually held to demonstrate – wisdom, grace, and moral strength – but also a feminized version of the ideal good-natured libertinism of the Georgians. Perhaps the most famous comment ever made about the character of Sophia is also the most wrong-headed and prejudicial, and thus a good place from which to begin this re-evaluation. Samuel Richardson's letter to Astrea and Minerva Hill calls Sophia "a Young Creature who was trapsing after [a man], a Fugitive from her Father's House," and asks, "Why did [Fielding] draw his heroine so fond, so foolish, and so insipid? Indeed he has one Excuse – He knows not how to draw a delicate Woman – He has not been accustomed to such company –" (Paulson and Lockwood 174). The irony of the printer Richardson's absurdly paternalistic comments need not be detailed here, but his misreading of Sophia has been answered with a tradition of modern criticism depicting Sophia almost exclusively as a manifestation of prudence and wisdom, untainted and moral, with acceptable reasons for any violations of decorum.[6] Such readings may be necessary to make arguments for Fielding the moralist, but they ignore the many textual hints of social rebelliousness and even libertinism in Sophia herself.

Certainly Sophia is intended to be connected with a moral wisdom, as her name sufficiently demonstrates, but she is wise in other ways as well. One of the adjectives most frequently used for Sophia is "spirited,"[7] and it is significant that in her initial description, Fielding compares her to Hortense Mancini, Duchess Mazarin, a woman reportedly breathtaking in her beauty. Mazarin was also one of the most popularly recognized female libertines of her day.[8] She ran away from her abusive husband in France and sustained herself as the mistress of a series of men across Europe, including Charles II, who established a pension for her that was continued by James II even after his brother's death. Mazarin was also known for her intellectual and philosophical interrogations of social prescription, most notably in the salon she hosted with Saint-Evremond, which was reportedly one of the most influential of the day, attended by political, religious, and social leaders of all stripes including the king. Sophia might have been compared to any number of beauties, but that Fielding chooses the publicly subversive Mazarin, influential and autonomous challenger of religious, social, and sexual regulation, suggests something much more interesting about the heroine's character than traditional constructs of virtuous feminine wisdom.

Allworthy misses the truth about Sophia when he asserts in his final panegyric on her character that she has "no Pretence to Wit, much less to that Kind of Wisdom, which is the Result only of great Learning and Experience" (XVII iii 882). In fact, she has, by that point in the novel, both extensive experience and a clearly demonstrated natural knowledge of humanity and the world. The examples Allworthy cites of her deferential behaviour only show Sophia's adeptness at playing the passive feminine role, and denote both her role in the novel as independent guide for Jones and her true understanding of the ridiculousness of men bound to thoughtless convention:

Whenever I have seen her in the Company of Men, she hath been all Attention, with the Modesty of a Learner, not the Forwardness of a Teacher. You'll pardon me for it, but I once, to try her only, desired her Opinion on a Point which was controverted between Mr *Thwackum* and Mr *Square*, To which she answered with much Sweetness, "You will pardon me, good Mr *Allworthy*, I am sure you cannot in Earnest think me capable of deciding any Point in which two such Gentlemen disagree." *Thwackum* and *Square*, who both alike thought themselves sure of a favourable Decision, seconded my Request. She answered with the same good Humour, "I must absolutely be excused ..."

Indeed, she always shewed the highest Deference to the Understandings of Men; a Quality, absolutely essential to the making a good Wife. I shall only add, that as she is most apparently void of all Affectation, this Deference must be certainly real.   (XVII iii 882–3)

Her deference in this case, of course, is affected, as she sees more clearly than Allworthy the vanity and closed-minded limitations of the two scholars. Her responses are good-humoured, but they are surely knowing, revealing her superior understanding of the world. Her position in the novel is exactly that of teacher of independent understanding, not Allworthy's patronizing ideal construction of woman as learner of social submission.

Knowing as she is, Sophia at no point sacrifices her sexual purity. But this is not to say that she is denied appetites and individualist understandings that must shift the tone of any discussion of her character away from that of the blandly upright heroine. Sophia, for example, is linked to the relationship between appetite and love (which becomes so clear between Jones and Mrs Waters at Upton) as she opens up her roast pullet stuffed with eggs – a delicacy we are told she can never resist regardless of actual physical hunger – to find and devour with her eyes the forbidden note from Jones that Black George has hidden inside. Appetite, the presiding metaphor of the novel from the Bill of Fare to the wedding feast, is at no time seen as a negative force; it is, as in this case with Sophia, a natural one which, as Fielding argued in the *Champion*, true virtue does not preclude us from indulging. Allworthy, for example, is described as having a "Heart that hungers after Goodness" (I iii 41), and Fielding's famous definition of love also allows appetite a role in that truest of good emotions:

That which is commonly called Love, namely the Desire of satisfying a voracious Appetite with a certain Quantity of delicate white human Flesh, is by no means that Passion for which I here contend. This is indeed more properly Hunger … [But true love] though it satisfies itself in a much more delicate Manner, doth nevertheless seek its own Satisfaction as much as the grossest of all our Appetites.

And, Lastly, that this Love when it operates in one of a different Sex, is very apt, towards its complete Gratification, to call in the Aid of that Hunger which I have mentioned above.   (VI i 270)

If Sophia has appetites for adventure, independence, and even love (of both definitions), she is also possessed of both a natural understanding and an understanding of nature. She knows from childhood to admire Jones and to scorn Blifil. As Hatfield eloquently puts it, "Sophia is not without 'art,' but it is the good art of genuine prudence and arises not from her heart, which is pure and innocent, but from her head, which must, in the interests of virtue, sometimes borrow the cunning of the vicious" (24).

Sophia uses her understanding and art to various ends throughout the novel, and her qualities of naturalism and social and intellectual independence connect her to the ideal of the Georgian libertine. She is a role model for Jones not in pushing him away from his libertinism, but in moving him toward a libertinism more appropriate for a husband, rather than a runaway lover. Fielding makes sure that his audience (with the exception of Richardson) feels that Sophia is justified in acting disobediently out of self-defense, and he notes that Sophia herself feels uncomfortable with her series of deceitful actions. She regrets the hurt that she will cause her father, but she still lies to him, and pretends to be a willing participant in the match with Blifil to placate Western the night before she runs away to London and the protection of Lady Bellaston. Later, in what the narrator calls Sophia's "first Practice of Deceit" (though we know it is at least her second), she pretends to Lady Bellaston not to know Jones during and after their accidental meeting in Lady Bellaston's parlour (XIII xii 738). And while she perhaps does not lie outright, Sophia certainly intends to deceive and manipulate her Aunt Western in order to gain her good will in book XVII: she compliments her aunt on all of the suitors she has had and must still have, and on the impressiveness of her presumed exercise of her right of matrimonial refusal. Her confident dissembling earns from the narrator only the note that "*Sophia* by a little well directed Flattery, for which surely none will blame her, obtained a little Ease for herself, and, at least, put off the evil Day" (XVII iv 891). Even more interesting is the way the previous incident of lying to Lady Bellaston is excused. The narrator asserts that "surely there are no Persons who may so properly challenge a Right to this commendable Deviation from Truth, as young Women in the Affair of Love; for which they may plead Precept, Education, and above all, the Sanction, nay, I may say, the Necessity of Custom, by which they are restrained, not from submitting to the honest Impulses of Nature (for that would be a foolish Prohibition) but from owning them" (XIII xii 736). That this rationale contains the central elements of Georgian libertinism is obvious. The use of deceit to achieve one's own happiness is established as a necessary challenge to social mores. Acknowledging the hypocrisy in the social unacceptability of "owning" that which everyone knows to be natural reflects both the naturalism of libertine philosophy and the foolishness of such social injunctions in the first place. Finally, Sophia's last recorded act of dissembling occurs in the closing chapters of the novel as she plays the virtuous innocent

who would wait a year to marry the man she loves, but is clearly
pleased to be commanded by her father to marry the next day (XVIII
xii 974–5).

More than Jones, Sophia feels the constraints of her society, but she
subverts them more often than the casual reader might initially realize,
and thus she is qualified not only by natural understanding, but by experience, to function as Tom's guide in his steps toward his role as the
Georgian libertine.[9]

That Sophia never surrenders her chastity does not imply that she is
devoid of sexual desire, or that she does not recognize the power of un-
ratified sexuality in her society. She expresses desire and exercises her
privileged position of sexual choice in much the same way as Joseph
Andrews does. And in much the same way, the lovers are at no point
left alone long enough to consummate their desire before their eventual
marriage. Fielding walks a fine line here, representing Sophia's unmistakable sexual awareness and desire, but retaining her physical virginity
so that her desire cannot be blameworthy or devalued by prudish readers who still cling to the prescriptive equation of virtue and virginity. In
terms of Fielding's own definition of virtue, Sophia indulges her appetites and desires, but never to self-destructive excess.

The earliest example of her subtle expressions of sexual desire occurs
when Jones carries her off to a stream to resuscitate her after she faints
at the scene of his drunken encounter with Molly Seagrim in the
thicket. As Jones lets her go, he "gave her at the same Instant a tender
Caress, which, had her Senses been then perfectly restored, could not
have escaped her Observation. As she expressed, therefore, no Displeasure at this Freedom, we suppose she was not sufficiently recovered
from her Swoon at the time" (V xii 265). When Fielding's narrator begins to "suppose," he expects the reader to consider alternative explanations. Here we have little choice but to know that Sophia does indeed
feel the caress, and does not object to the freedom which Jones has
taken. In the same scene, Sophia sees the bruises "imprinted on both
his Face and Breast" which "drew from her a Sigh, and a Look of inex-
pressible Tenderness." This passage too offers evidence for a re-evaluation of Sophia's presumed sexual innocence and passivity. First, she is
clearly looking openly at Jones's naked chest without shock or expressions of modesty (in a fictional society where Mrs Wilkins's near faint at
the sight of Allworthy in his shirt is regarded only as a mild overreac-
tion). Second, the sigh and look of tenderness can as easily be attributed to the suggestion of desire that runs under the scene from both
players as to her thankfulness that he has splashed her with water in her
swoon.

As we may have gathered from her ability to deceive (albeit for good reasons) and from the evidence of sexual desire, however adamantly she suppresses its public display, Sophia has a much greater understanding of the ways of the world than is first obvious. She is much less angry at the sexual adventures of Jones than at the reported bandying of her name in kitchens. She is also sufficiently good-natured to attempt to help Molly Seagrim despite her sexual fall and the identity of her partner, and she does nothing to rebuke Mrs Waters or Mrs Fitzpatrick for their traditionally unacceptable sexual behaviour. Most telling is the scene in which Aunt Western advises Sophia that she can pursue any man she wishes as long as she is married and the family name is protected. "I hope, Child, you will always have Prudence enough to act as becomes you; but if you should not, Marriage hath saved many a Woman from Ruin." The narrator then informs us that "*Sophia* well understood what her Aunt meant; but did not think proper to make her an Answer. However, she took a Resolution to see Mr *Blifil,* and to behave to him as civilly as she could" (VI v 290). That Sophia recognizes the meaning of this encoded advice on adultery reveals again her worldly knowledge. The narrator does not deny that she could momentarily consider accepting the idea as much as she may momentarily consider chastising her aunt. In addition, she uses her apparent acquiescence to her aunt's desires as a bribe to control her aunt surreptitiously and to keep her from disclosing to Squire Western Sophia's actual attachment to Jones.

With her inactive libertine sexuality and her active challenging of socially constructed value systems in order to serve her own desires and to preserve her independence, then, Sophia can contribute to the character of Jones much more than the distant example of a paragon of virtue. While it may be true that "Whatever in the Nature of *Jones* had a Tendency to Vice, hath been corrected by continual conversation with [Allworthy], and by his Union with the lovely and virtuous *Sophia*" (VIII xiii 981), the correction is certainly assisted by the fact that Sophia herself seems naturally to understand and use certain tenets of Georgian libertinism herself. She too seeks self-determination and recognizes the potential worth of a changing role for women in the eighteenth century. She too knows the world and has doubts about the worth of the existing hegemonic order, but unlike Tom's other, failed models of libertinism, she also manifests clearly the alternative to the cruel extremes of old-style libertinism that is so essential to the development of Jones.

Having thus examined the various presentations of libertinism in some of the characters who surround and influence Tom Jones, I shall now turn to the character himself. Jones's actions and his triumph dem-

onstrate the libertine understanding that "true liberty [is] an unre-
stricted assertion of the will which can triumph over the straitened
circumstances of [one's] birth" (Weber "Misrule" 18). He acts according
to his own naturalistic standards of good nature to achieve what no one
conceives possible for a bastard (which Tom remains even after the
identity of his mother is revealed), least of all his half-brother Blifil, the
architect of Jones's downfall. Blifil suggests the reappearance of
Jonathan Wild in these respects. He is a would-be old-school libertine,
attempting to manipulate circumstance to get the woman he wants
(though only for revenge and the joy of "rifling her Charms, as it added
Triumph to Lust" [VII vi 346]), and to control the perceptions of those
around him. Like Wild, though, Blifil lacks good nature, and he is ultimately not clever enough to succeed. He emerges not powerful or triumphant, but grasping and cringing in his weakness, depending on the
good nature of his half-brother to defend him to Allworthy and thus to
allow him to live with some dignity after being thrust from Paradise
Hall.[10] His nature does not change, however, and like Wild, Blifil tries
to disguise himself and continue to connive his way into a powerful social position, scheming to purchase a seat in Parliament and turning
Methodist "in hopes of marrying a very rich Widow of that Sect, whose
estate lies in that part of the Kingdom" (XVIII xiii 980). Blifil can
maintain his true nature easily as a Methodist: since it is faith alone,
and not good works which are the source of salvation within Methodism, according to Fielding, if one declares belief in Heaven, one may
still live the life of the devils.

The good nature of Jones and his unwillingness to give Blifil the lie
render him susceptible to the scheming of his half-brother; one of the
lessons Jones must learn in his journey toward the perfection of Fielding's new Georgian libertinism is that of worldly prudence – which Blifil seems to possess as innately as Jones does good nature. In his
germinal work on the idea of prudence, Battestin defines it as "that per-
spicacity of moral *vision* which alone permits us to perceive the truth
behind appearances and to proceed from the known to the obscure; it
implies, furthermore, the power to *choose* between good and evil and to
determine the proper and effective means of achieving the one and
avoiding the other" ("Wisdom" 191). It is useful, however, to note that
prudence is almost invariably associated in the novel with negative
qualities and unsavoury characters. The exception, of course, is Allworthy, but even he is often blind to the "truth behind appearances," and
he is consistently unable to choose effectively between good and evil.
Jones is deceived much less often, at least partly because he does think
actively about the merits and demerits of his actions. For example, be-

fore deciding to pursue a duel with Northerton over his honour and that of Sophia, he asks, "But is not Revenge forbidden by Heaven? – Yes, but it is enjoined by the World. Well, but shall I obey the World in Opposition to the express Commands of Heaven? Shall I incur the divine Displeasure rather than be called – Ha – Coward – Scoundrel? – I'll think no more, I am resolved and must fight him" (VII xiv 387). This is more active thought than is recorded at any time in Allworthy, though his sermons and speeches after he does act go on interminably. Allworthy may be prudent by some standards, but he actually fails to meet all of Battestin's definition. Although he is said to think about his decisions, we realize that he always prefers the side of standard social action and belief based on initial appearances. The libertine Jones contradicts this as he chooses *between* two possible responses to a situation, and he does not always choose the answer most easily accepted by others.

The capitulating prudence of characters like Allworthy, then, does little to affect the behaviour of Jones, even though, as he takes stock of the conditions around him, he suggests the true value of prudence more effectively than those who would be his mentors. Fielding makes this clear as he discusses the assumed necessity of prudence: "Goodness of Heart, and Openness of Temper, tho' these may give them great Comfort within, and administer to an honest Pride in their own Minds, will by no Means, alas! do their business in the World. Prudence and Circumspection are necessary even to the best of Men. They are indeed as it were a Guard to Virtue, without which she can never be safe. It is not enough that your Designs, nay that your Actions are intrinsically good, you must take Care they shall appear so" (III vii 141). Though those who argue for prudence as the central paradigmatic organization of the novel take this passage to be without irony, evidence certainly suggests that Fielding himself has doubts and challenges this generalized assumption about the need to conform even in appearance to the petty moralities and dictates of society. The interjected "alas!" with its exclamation point marker should direct us to query the passage immediately, as should any assertion by Fielding, an individualist if nothing else, that all men require a given set of qualities, particularly ones as ambiguous as prudence and circumspection. In addition, the recurrence of "virtue," especially in combination with prudence and the manipulation of appearances, must bring to mind Shamela, her visions of virtue and prudence, and the redefinition of these terms in *Joseph Andrews* and the *Champion* essays.

Morality is determined in this novel by nature, not by considerations of prudence, and at no point does this paradigm change. One might consider Jones's drunken frolic with Molly and the narrator's explanation thereof as an early example. The narrator explains that "Drink, in reality, doth not reverse Nature, or create Passions in Men, which did not exist in them before. It takes away the Guard of Reason, and consequently forces us to produce those Symptoms, which many, when sober, have Art enough to conceal" (V ix 253). By including the superiority of "nature" over the "art" of "reason," Fielding privileges again the anti-rationalism of libertinism over exactly the type of manipulation and circumspection implied by prudence. He goes on to remind readers that Jones "was not at this Time perfect Master of that wonderful Power of Reason, which so well enables grave and wise Men to subdue their unruly Passions, and to decline any of these prohibited Amusements" (V x 257). By minimizing the repercussions of Jones's sexuality through its association with consensual "amusements" which are "prohibited" only by social convention, Fielding determines the reader's response to his description. He then takes control of the scene further: he excuses Jones from the strictures that social constructs of reason impose on the uncritical individual by ironically allowing the anti-rationalist voice which has just been established to manipulate the significance of "that Wonderful Power of Reason." Tom's drinking does not eliminate rationalism, but emphasizes naturalism; the very privileging of reason allows him to use its loss as a rationalization for his behaviour.

Prudence has no more innate relationship with chastity than with sobriety. As Rawson notes, "in *Tom Jones*, genuine sexual affection, even if mainly carnal, is a form of benevolence, so long as it is a matter of real affection rather than 'Appetite alone' " (*Order* 336). The libertine privilege of both the narrator and Tom Jones himself also comes into play here since the libertine figures are granted a certain level of sexual license as a result of their social and self-positioning.[11] And Tom Jones does position himself sexually as a libertine, though the word is not used specifically until later in the novel. For example, though he states that "to debauch a young Woman, however low her Condition was, appeared to him a very heinous Crime," he does eventually have sex with Molly, and "Jones attributed the Conquest entirely to himself, and considered the young Woman as one who had yielded to the violent Attacks of his Passion" (IV vi 174–5). Wrong though he may be, he believes himself to have been the sexual conqueror, and it is in this frame of mind that he approaches Molly with a common libertine response to accidental pregnancy in a loveless affair: the offer of money. He not only reiterates his power to control the situation (power which he does not realize he has already surrendered intermittently), but he does so by using his social and financial position to purchase both her silence and his freedom to pursue Sophia without guilt. Circumstance, Square, and Will Barnes work together to prevent Jones from actually having to carry out a plan which smacks of the cruel libertinism of the past (which is also narrowly averted by Nightingale), but this self-identification and response establish Jones as a libertine early in the novel and reveal that he still must change and develop his understanding of the libertinism with which he identifies before he can come to represent fully Fielding's ideal.

Despite the potentially damaging connotations of this incident and the one at Upton with Mrs Waters, Jones avoids any affected constructions of modesty which would force him to deny his natural desires. The bared breasts of Mrs Waters "attracted the eyes of her Deliverer, and for a few Moments they stood silent, and gazing at each other" (IX ii 496). While the narrator pretends not to know why Mrs Waters would refuse the coat that Jones offers her to cover herself, it is clear that he is as aware as we are that pretence to modesty or moral prudence is unnecessary between two self-aware and self-determining characters who can so bluntly express their mutual attraction. Jones makes no bones at "stealing a sly Peep or two" and the narrator's pointed assertion that Jones took "all imaginable Care to avoid giving any Offence" (IX ii 500) reveals the more plainly that there is no real risk of offence among two such honest, good-natured libertines. To offer contrast, the narrator follows this representation expression of candid, natural attraction by describing the usual guests of the inn at Upton as "*Irish* Ladies of strict Virtue, and many Northern Lasses of the same Predicament."[12] If the affectation of strict virtue and the maintenance of virginity are something of a predicament in the eyes of the narrator, it is not at all surprising that he shortly goes on to state of Jones and Mrs Waters that "it will be a Mark more of Prudery than Candour to entertain a bad Opinion of her, because she conceived a very good Opinion of him" (IX v 510).

The ridiculousness of limitations on sexual behaviour and on other modes of social challenge is also displayed when Fielding ironically reveals the landlady's perception of virtue as she imagines "that Mr *Jones* and his ragged Companion had certain Purposes in their Intention, which, tho' tolerated in some Christian Countries, connived at in others, and practised in all; are however as expressly forbidden as Murder, or any other horrid Vice, by that Religion which is universally believed in those Countries" (IX iii 500). Though some readers accept this passage as a straightforward statement of Fielding's disdain for sexual misbehaviour,[13] it is, I think, much more plausible to recognize in the exaggerated equation of unmarried intercourse and murder another example of negating social limitations upon the consenting individual. Here also is one of the clearest statements in the novel that religion, when misapplied as in this case or by the ill-natured Thwackum, can be an unnatural force. Certainly attacks on the Church seem to be less essential to the Georgian vision of libertinism than they were to earlier forms, but, like other elements of libertinism that went to extremes of manifestation and then returned toward an open-minded but still socially dubious middle ground, such attacks continue to exist in the revised form that we see here.

Despite the supposed purity of his love for Sophia, who maintains her good-natured virtue without resorting to prudery, Jones clearly and regularly expresses his lust for her. He gives her that inappropriate caress at the stream, but even more explicit is his response to the implication of Sophia's affection in book V around the time of Allworthy's recovery: "While his wanton Fancy roved unbounded over all her Beauties, and his lively Imagination painted the charming Maid in various Ravishing Forms, his warm Heart melted with Tenderness, and at length throwing himself on the Ground by the Side of a gently murmuring Brook, he broke forth into the following Ejaculation" (V x 256). Such a description can hardly be read as anything else but lustful, particularly since after he "ejaculates" his encomiums on Sophia and his love, he slips immediately into the sweaty arms of Molly Seagrim. Tom's lust is expressed externally here, albeit vicariously, but it is psychologically equal to Sophia's sighs at Jones's naked breast which follow in the same book.

As he explains to the less honest Nightingale, though, Jones dallies only with women whom he cannot injure (though, as we have seen above in his first encounter with Molly, this has not always been strictly true). His famous assertion represents the central shift in the libertine sexual paradigm from the Restoration to the Georgian period, a shift which is further emphasized in that the speech comes from the archetypal Georgian to the representative Restoration-style rake in transition: "I am no canting Hypocrite, nor do I pretend to the Gift of Chastity, more than my Neighbours. I have been guilty with Women, I own it; but am not conscious that I have ever injured any – nor would I to procure Pleasure to myself, be knowingly the Cause of Misery to any human Being" (XIV iv 755).[14] Fielding states explicitly the central tenet of the new Georgian libertinism in this speech: pursue your own desires and happiness through any methods, including disguise, deceit, or the subversion of socially determined norms, as long as the independence and freedoms of others – female or male – are not impinged upon.

Those who would deny Fielding's and even Jones's libertinism might argue that such a stance is merely Epicurian rather than libertine. Fielding, however, makes clear that Jones steps beyond mere pleasurable consumption: Allworthy's grand and gloriously pastoral home is described as something of an Epicurian paradise as he "kept a good House, [and] entertained his neighbours with a hearty Welcome at his Table," and each of his many guests "was perfect Master of his own Time: and as [such] he might at his Pleasure satisfy all his appetites within the Restrictions only of Law, Virtue, and Religion" (I iii 38; I x 61). Jones, though, is banished from Paradise Hall because Allworthy believes he has transgressed against even the liberal laws governing the Epicurian life. Allworthy asks angrily, "are you so profligate and abandoned a Libertine, to doubt whether the breaking the Laws of God and Man, the corrupting and ruining a poor Girl, be Guilt? I own, indeed, it doth lie principally upon you, and so heavy it is, that you ought to expect it should crush you" (IV xi 193). For all of his adult life, Jones is termed a libertine, and it is within this discourse that his character evolves.

Because his beliefs and actions are aligned with the developing libertinism that runs through all of Fielding's fictional works, Jones is not punished at any point for his actions except for the fear of incest and the near loss of Sophia, both of which are short-lived. While he is brought to repent for his sexual libertinism, even Jones's apology and explanation to Sophia must raise a few final doubts not of sincerity, but of the need to apologize at all for a necessary part of the libertine process which is quite acceptable even to Sophia. In book XIII, Jones pleads that his "*Heart* was never unfaithful" to Sophia, a noble enough statement until we recollect that, when Jones leaves Molly after the discovery of Square, Molly "vowed" to Square that "tho' [Tom] once had the Possession of her Person, that none but *Square* had ever been Master of her Heart" (V v 234), which we know for an outright lie from three pages previously. Also, in their final reconciliation, Jones tells Sophia that her eyes will keep him constant, and that "They would fix a *Dorimant*, a Lord *Rochester*" (XVIII xii 973). That his first apology and excuse are subtly undermined, and his final assurances have Jones (consciously or not) compare himself to two of the most notorious libertine figures of the past age need not necessarily convince the reader that Jones is insincere or that he will be unfaithful. These things do, however, demonstrate that he never really changes the central touchstones of his motivations or perceptions over the course of the novel, just some of their forms of expression, depending on his own marital and social status. Though much is often made of Tom's repentance, it is really contained in only one line: "'I will learn it,' said *Jones*. 'I have learnt it already'" (XVIII xii 973). "It" here is the difference between love and lust. Since even this line is contained in the same paragraph as the Rochester parallel, and since we know that Jones both loves and lusts after Sophia, and that Fielding has stated in his definition of love that love and lust must both be contained in any true love, the validity of Tom's need for repentance for his libertinism is left largely unsubstantiated.

Jones is consistently supported by circumstances and by the approval of the narrative overvoice in his challenging re-evaluations of individual situations and their places in the larger cultural understanding of his time. Jones's good nature overwhelms generalized prescriptive limitations as he refuses to be dominated by the money culture of his society (though he actively avoids coercing Sophia into choosing the same path). He deceives Nightingale Sr in order to procure the same liberty for his friend and to prevent Nancy from being forever stained not by her appetites, but by society's defensively prudent and ill-natured clinging to conventional definitions of virtue (XIV viii). He rejects the bland didacticism of the new puppet show that he sees (aligning himself with Fielding's own experience as the Great Mogul); Fielding ensures that Jones is supported in this last contravention of publicly expressed opinion as the consensual and good-natured debauchery of the Merry Andrew and a local girl is discovered just as the puppeteer finishes his speech on the traditionally morally educative properties of his shows (XII v–vi). The ridiculousness of attempting to affect public morality through performance – despite what many argue for Fielding's novels – is announced once again here, just as it has been in the plays and in the *Journey from this World to the Next*.

Fielding explains his distrust of fifth-act conversions of character in the first chapter of book VIII, and as we have seen from the evidence of sexual behaviour, motivation and beliefs, and ongoing social challenge, the character of Tom Jones does not undergo one of these artificial transformations. Though he continually develops his understanding of libertinism and its social implications, he remains throughout the novel the well-intentioned, "good natured libertine" (XVIII x 962) that he has been from his adolescence. The problem, then, is often understood to be the question of how to marry Tom and Sophia without the inappropriate coupling of a highly-placed woman with a socially subversive bastard, which Tom remains despite being revealed as the first nephew of Allworthy.[15] The answer, however, is relatively straightforward. Once the matter of the inheritance has been settled, the libertine Tom Jones and the rather greedy iconoclast and would-be libertine Squire Western must feel no compunction to fall in with the rules that govern the rabble and those without the funds to support their philosophical independence. Second, since Sophia has continued to develop her right to self-determination and equality throughout the novel as Jones has developed his libertinism, it is only fitting that she should ultimately snub social convention to marry the man she loves, particularly since she has fulfilled for so long the role of his guide to the golden mean of Georgian libertinism.

Throughout the novel Jones has been on the edge of losing touch with this guide and falling into the trap that affects those who, like Jonathan Wild, are not entirely able to fulfill the role of the libertine; that is, becoming so defined by the libertine role that originality and independence, and thus control, become lost. Both Turner and Reichler note the continual movement of the traditional libertine between two extreme positions: "a fierce individualism that underestimates the power of social forces, and a compliance to social conventions which, though intended to be ironic and self-liberating, eventually traps the self within the mask" (Turner "Paradoxes" 74). Partridge's fiction of the life and mind of Tom Jones becomes truth for those in the kitchens and taverns through which they travel, and when this version reaches Sophia, Jones almost loses his ability to pursue his desires himself. However, unlike Wild and Blifil, who do collapse under their own self-constructions, Jones is clever enough and honest enough, and has surrendered just enough of his need for control to be able to rectify the situation and ultimately to continue on the road to happiness.

In the final chapter of the novel we learn that it is not only Jones who is rewarded for his revised libertine prospect and his defiance of social and sexual codes. Nancy and Nightingale live in happy community with Sophia and Jones. Mrs Waters, for all of her sexual alliances and her disdain for artificial constructions of modesty and traditional patriarchal control of female sexuality, is awarded an annual pension of £60 and married to the generally good-natured (if occasionally grovelling) Parson Supple. Mrs Fitzpatrick is unconventionally but comfortably separated from her brutish husband, controls her own fortune, and continues her illicit relationship with the Irish peer with the apparent consent of his wife. Square is redeemed through his revelation of his early biases against Jones (and the technically purer Thwackum is left unredeemed and ignored for available places). Molly Seagrim receives most of the £500 that Jones returns to Black George's family, and, in an arrangement that is less than perfect but much better than one might expect for a poor, uneducated, and sexually fallen woman in the eighteenth century, is about to be married off by Sophia to the ridiculous but financially stable Partridge. Fielding demonstrates that those who challenge convention and who behave according to natural inclinations and good nature are rewarded, and they are best rewarded who most effectively challenge social mores without moving to extremes or allowing the public character of even the libertine to dominate the private consciousness of the individual.

6   The Mature Faces of Libertinism: *Amelia*

Having developed Tom Jones into a direct representation of the archetypal Georgian libertine, Fielding moves in his final novel *Amelia* to, among other themes, an examination of libertinism in the moral context of mature life. In this approach, *Amelia* is the culmination of Fielding's shift from his early role as a youthful playwright often smugly depicting a somewhat hedonistic libertinism (mediated by a glance ahead to graver moralist concerns in *The Modern Husband*) to a height of joyously licentious but essentially new-virtuous libertinism in *Tom Jones*. In *Amelia* libertinism is used still to express Fielding's desire to challenge existing social constructions and organizations, but the many faces of libertinism in the Hogarthian world he creates demonstrate that this representation is compatible with Fielding's revisionist virtue more than with simply a hedonistic privileging of liberty above all.

In his essay "On the Knowledge of the Characters of Men," Fielding argues that all the world is a whirlwind of disguise and deceit of various types:

Thus while the crafty and designing Part of Mankind, consulting only their own separate Advantage, endeavour to maintain one constant Imposition on others, the whole World becomes a vast Masquerade, where the greatest Part appear disguised under false Vizors and Habits; a very few only shewing their own faces, who become, by so doing, the Astonishment and Ridicule of all the rest.

But however cunning the Disguise be which a Masquerader wears: however foreign to his Age, Degree, or Circumstance, yet if closely attended to, he very rarely escapes the Discovery of an accurate Observer; for Nature, which unwillingly submits to the Imposture, is ever endeavouring to peep forth and shew herself; nor can the Cardinal, the Friar, or the Judge, long conceal the Sot, the Gamester, or the Rake.   (*Miscellanies* I 155)

While the motifs of disguise and deceit appear in Fielding's other fictional works, they do not receive a complete treatment until *Amelia*. The novel raises issues similar to those developed in Fielding's other works – social subversion, worldly and Christian honour, sexual freedom, individualism, and the distribution of power – but it interprets them from a new position. Despite having been set within the confines of a prison, the initial scenes of *Amelia* suggest the Fielding of the other novels: the confident, superior creator of unmistakably satiric portraits of corruption. The morally confident representation of Justice Thrasher, however, is the only entirely categorical characterization in the novel: all of the other characters, including Amelia herself, are morally and motivationally ambiguous, and the situations in which they find themselves suggest Fielding's reconsideration of the often easy choices represented in the more pastoral surroundings of his earlier novels. Disorder and subversion are more complex issues in the static London environment of *Amelia* than in the series of brief interludes in *Joseph Andrews*, *Tom Jones*, and even *Jonathan Wild*. It is not particularly relevant to this study whether this new geographical stasis is the result of Fielding's interest in the sentimentalism of *Clarissa*, of his own declining health and subsequent physical and psychological isolation, or of a shift in his sense of human nature after years as a London justice. It is essential, though, to observe the unmistakable diminution of much of Fielding's heretofore characteristic laissez-faire optimism.

William Booth is clearly an extension of those characters of mixed impulses that Fielding has made his signature, but having mixed impulses creates a very different situation for a married pseudo-hero than for a wandering single youth like Tom Jones or an unmediated rascal like Jonathan Wild. Even Fielding's standard morality of good nature is ambiguous in the enclosed setting of *Amelia*. Fielding establishes in this novel a pattern of introducing characters in their best light of apparently undeniable good nature before demonstrating their weaknesses and evils. Certainly many contemporary readers found that Booth could not be excused for his indiscretions, partly because he must be held to a standard new to Fielding's fiction, and partly because his good nature does not seem to be as consistently his dominant passion as it is in the more forgivable Jones, for example.[1] Catherine Talbot puts this in an epigrammatic nutshell when she writes to Elizabeth Carter in

1752, "Amelia makes an excellent wife, but why did she marry Booth?" (Paulson and Lockwood 350). Sarah Chapone's letter to Carter offers more detail and represents a common series of objections as she expresses her dismay that Carter liked *Amelia*:

Can you forgive his amour with that dreadful, shocking monster, Miss Mathews? Are we to look upon these crimes as the failings of human nature, as Fielding seems to do, who takes his notions of human nature from the most depraved and corrupted part of it, and seems to think no characters natural but such as are a disgrace to the human species? Don't you think Booth's sudden conversion a mere botch to save the author's credit as a moral writer? And is there not a tendency in all his works, to soften the deformity of vice, by placing characters in an amiable light, that are destitute of every virtue except good nature?   (Paulson and Lockwood 318)

Other contemporary readers recognized Fielding's attempts at education and moralism in the novel, but often they found the work instead to be dull and "low."[2] The tendency of modern scholars to read *Amelia* purely as a moralist tract is equally problematic, however, since such a perspective either ignores or denies the moral ambiguity of characters like Colonel James, for example: his complex characterization as perhaps the most typical – albeit challenging – good-natured libertine of the novel is far from the incarnation of unmediated villainy he is often supposed to embody. Among the many significant qualities of *Amelia* is that it continues to place libertinism among the issues for consideration; it does not eliminate the option of good-natured Georgian libertinism as a blueprint for happiness, but, placed in a setting of fictional realism, it allows a more truthful complexity of libertinism to emerge than has yet been seen.

The overarching impetus of libertinism is always that of protest against an existing sociocultural order, and this continues in *Amelia*. So does the paradoxical connection between the social subversion of the libertine and his or her need for those very norms in order to maintain the transgressive libertine identification. The manifest unfairness of Justice Thrasher and Booth's other legal problems obviously demonstrate Fielding's concern with the laws of England and their enforcement, but there are many more subtly subversive implications within the novel, not least those suggested by the acts and thoughts of Amelia herself. For example, Amelia violates social decorum and challenges not only enforced sexual chastity for women, but the necessity of feminine chastity by association, when she actively and publicly maintains her friendship with Mrs Bennet-Atkinson,[3] a woman known to be fallen sexually.[4] Further, as Angela Smallwood demonstrates, the standard Halifaxian ideals of separate spheres for men and women are consciously and conspicuously departed from by Amelia and Booth, as we see Booth present at the birth of his second child and Amelia "intellectually and morally independent and a source of strength to Booth rather than the other way about" (156). The social and moral necessity of honesty is also consistently undermined as deceit and lying are established as ethically complex actions. The paragon Amelia lies, deceives, or dissembles no fewer than eleven times in the novel (with severity ranging from implying to her nurse that Booth is already her husband and the masquerade ruse, to hiding the truth about James, Bagillard, and Atkinson),[5] and it is the white lies of the pawnbroker's pathetic description of Amelia that prompt Robinson's confession.[6] The standard assumption that evil must come of lying is challenged, and the typically libertine deceit and disguise are validated as potentially moral or even providential acts. Thus Fielding explicitly emphasizes the paradoxical moral quality naturally present within intellectually active and challenging libertinism.

The popular definition of honour is also challenged in the novel. Booth is caught between the Cavalier notion of honour that is a major part of Restoration libertinism, and the disdain for senseless violence typical of both Fielding's Georgian libertinism and the Christian moralism exemplified by Dr Harrison. Tom Jones, of course, faces a similar conflict after he is assaulted by Northerton, but where Jones considers both sides of the question and then chooses to privilege his publicly-determined honour over his Christian leanings, Booth vacillates. He reveals himself to be not the self-determining hero who may be imprudent, but a nervous and weak near-hero who cannot decide whether to support his family or "touch" a near-great man. He duels with Colonel Bath (Fielding's emblematic representation of the ultimate fruitlessness of a violently defensive vision of honour) only because he feels he has been "forced"; he has neither the individualism nor the self-empowerment to argue against Bath's fallacious understanding and dubious interpretation of honour. In fact, merit comes not from necessarily choosing one side or the other of the debate on the nature of honour, but from pausing to consider the stakes in an incident and choosing accordingly.

The problematic character of Colonel James exemplifies this: he seems to find his brother-in-law Bath ridiculous throughout the novel, which would place him in the camp of honour without bloodshed, but he still challenges Booth over Mrs Mathews, though the duel itself never takes place because of Amelia's intervention. Interestingly, though, the reader must recognize that if these circumstances place James in an indeterminate position with regard to the accepted version of military and aristocratic honour, they do the same for Amelia. In begging Dr Harrison for advice about James's challenge, she reminds him that her "Husband's Honour is to be preserved as well as his life" (XII iii 503). Even after Harrison's stern lecture on the widely disparate values of "the Opinion of the World opposed to Religion and Virtue," to which she quickly acquiesces, she still cries, "And yet whilst the Opinion of the World is as it is, one would wish to comply as far as possible – especially as my Husband is an Officer of the Army. If it can be done therefore with Safety to his Honour –" (XII iii 505). She cannot abandon the opinion of the world despite being convinced of its fallaciousness and irreligion. It is not Amelia's goodness that the reader is expected to doubt at this moment in the text, but the pointless extremism of both aristocratic honour, and religious honour whose pacifism implies cowardice and shame. Neither of these traditional conceptions of honour, then, serves Fielding's society entirely appropriately, and Fielding's Georgian libertinism moralism begins to show a path between the two. The communicative power of the language of libertines is suggested as Fielding (through Amelia) reterms the idea of honour, "Reputation ... or any other Word you like better – you know my Meaning very well" (XII iii 505). He takes control of a specific cultural discourse and disrupts it linguistically, so that honour becomes a recognition of virtue, agency, or other estimable qualities, a new understanding that finally overcomes the oppositional paradigm of cowardice versus a necessarily bloody satisfaction.

The amended conceptions of honour and deceit that integrate the traditionally moralist and the traditionally libertine are two central examples of *Amelia*'s libertine social revisionism, but Booth falls short of this new libertine social moralism throughout the novel.[7] However, if he seems to be either unaware of or unable to accept the unorthodox approaches to deception and honour that so empower characters like Tom Jones and even Amelia, he remains open to other unorthodoxies, most notably deism. In fact, Booth functions as the novel's primary exemplar of the ubiquitous libertine desire to question the unquestionable, here the assumptions of religion. Subversion of religious dogma and the primacy of the Church has not been a serious focus in Fielding's work before this point, but as even Martin Battestin admits (despite his position as the most consistent of the Fielding-as-latitudinarian proselytes), though *Tom Jones* can be read as a statement of faith in a providential or divine Order, "*Amelia* is the troubled adumbration of an age less certain of the traditional grounds on which the faith was founded" ("Problem" 615). Booth's doctrine of the passions casts back to the religious doubt that was a central tenet of Restoration libertinism; but that tenet shifted in the Georgian paradigm to a desire to reconsider the manifestations of institutionalized religion rather than faith itself.

In *Amelia* the goodness and spiritual leadership of Dr Harrison is clearly the exception to a widespread corruption within institutionalized religion, and this allows even Booth's unorthodoxies to reveal a curious but ultimately highly significant combination of narratorial derision and admiration. Once again, an understanding of the fluidities of eighteenth-century libertinism helps to clarify such apparent inconsistencies. While the narrator accepts Harrison's orthodoxies over Booth's beliefs, what is essential is that the individual has considered and evaluated his or her religious understanding; Booth's doctrine is treated with a certain amount of narratorial respect because, though his eventual conversion brings him into the fold of considered Christianity, his doctrine has always been a conscientious and intelligent one. As he tells Harrison after his conversion, "I never was a rash Disbeliever; my chief Doubt was founded on this, that as Men appeared to me to act entirely from their Passions, their Actions could have neither Merit nor Demerit." Harrison's response is the syntactically complex assertion that "if Men act, as I believe they do, from their Passions, it would be fair to conclude that Religion to be true which applies immediately to the strongest of these Passions, Hope and Fear, chusing rather to rely on its Rewards and Punishments, than on that native Beauty of Virtue which some of the antient Philosophers thought proper to recommend to their Disciples" (XII v 511–12). While this suggestion that true religion must rely on hope and fear to enforce its doctrine may suit Harrison and divines such as Barrow, it is opposite to Fielding's longstanding sense of good nature, that one should do good "without any abstract Contemplation on the Beauty of Virtue, and without the Allurements or Terrors of Religion" (*Miscellanies* I 158). Harrison himself has earlier chided Amelia for her fear that all mankind might be evil. He tells her, "Do not make a Conclusion so much to the Dishonour of the great Creator. The Nature of Man is far from being in itself Evil: It abounds with Benevolence, Charity and Pity, coveting Praise and Honour, and shunning Shame and Disgrace. Bad Education, bad Habits, and bad Customs, debauch our Nature and drive it Headlong as it were into Vice" (IX v 374).

What is significant about the depiction of religious faith in *Amelia*, then, is not any suggestion that Fielding proselytizes a single true path, but that in addition to the latitudinarian stance and the doctrine of the passions, the reader begins to recognize alternative religious and social discourses including stoicism, Mandevillianism, standard conservatism, and even near-atheism, and undergoes experientially the same process that Booth faces – the educated and conscious choosing of a religious discourse, rather than a simple blind faith in a representation of religion proffered by a largely corrupt social institution. The reasons for and fictional viability of Booth's conversion have been discussed at length,[8] but it is entirely plausible that his conversion exists less to foreground one specific and limited doctrine (which at least partially contradicts Fielding's theory of good nature) than to demonstrate a libertine interest in the human potential for individual evaluation and considered choice in something as important as spirituality. Certainly a change in Fielding's stance late in life is possible, but more plausible, I think, considering his consistency in other areas, is the suggestion that Fielding intends through the unironic representations of multiple belief systems to enforce no one path to salvation beyond the broad one of good works and good faith as the individual determines them.[9]

In general, though, contemporary critics seemed to have less difficulty with the apparently contradictory impulses of faith in the novel than with the novel's more specific presumed immorality, particularly its representation of sexuality. In examining the sexuality in *Amelia* and its relation to the libertine sexuality that Fielding has defined and established in his earlier work, it is perhaps useful to begin with a case study of Colonel James, the one character specifically termed a "perfect Libertine with regard to Women" (IV v 174). In Booth's initial description of him, James appears to be nearly identical to the standard of the good-natured libertine established in *Tom Jones*: "The Behaviour of this Man alone is a sufficient Proof of the Truth of my Doctrine, that all Men act entirely from their Passions; for *Bob James* can never be supposed to act from any Motive of Virtue or Religion; since he constantly laughs at both; and yet his Conduct toward me alone demonstrates a Degree of Goodness, which, perhaps, few of the Votaries of either Virtue or Religion can equal" (III v 114). James courts and marries Miss Bath, and then makes her brother a Member of Parliament, a circumstance which the narrator tells us "serves to set forth the Goodness of *James*, who endeavoured to make up in Kindness to the Family, what he wanted in Fondness for his wife." Later in the same chapter, the narrator calls James "the generous Colonel (for generous he really was to the highest Degree)," and states that "scarce one Man in a thousand is capable of tasting the Happiness of others" (IV iv 169–70), implying that James is that one who has true good nature, "a delight in the happiness of mankind, and a concern at their misery, with a desire, as much as possible,

to procure the former, and avert the latter; and this, with a constant regard to desert" (*Champion* 27 March 1740). Even when he is described
as a follower of libertine sexuality, it is not the sexuality itself that is particularly condemned, but the fact that he takes it "to a most unpardon-
able Height" (IV v 174).

The reader's understanding of James's character at this point shifts
away from the Georgian libertinism that the Colonel has apparently
typified, judging from Booth's descriptions, toward a more old-style libertine character, interested in enjoying women "whatever might be the
Consequence" at the same time that he "never think[s] their Minds
worth considering" (IV vi 178). He becomes more and more the cruel,
self-obsessed libertine of old as he suggests to Booth that pimping for
the Noble Lord would forward his career (though it is left unclear
whether he really suggests Amelia or Mrs Mathews for the task), and his
persecution of Booth in order to pursue Amelia seems irreconcilable
with any good nature, libertine or otherwise. James appears to follow
the libertine belief that "true freedom can be found only in surrender to
passion and spontaneity" (Turner "Paradoxes" 82), but is able to disguise his motive effectively, which may "be attributed to that noble Art
which is taught in those excellent Schools called the several Courts of
Europe. By this Men are enabled to dress out their Countenances as
much at their own Pleasure, as they do their Bodies; and to put on
Friendship with as much Ease as they can a laced Coat" (IX ii 361). The
narrator's extended description of James is at this point quite different
from Booth's earlier one: "In Truth, the Colonel, tho' a very generous
Man, had not the least Grain of Tenderness in his Disposition … A
Man of this Temper, who doth not much value Danger, will fight for
the Person he calls his Friend; and the Man that hath but little Value
for his Money will give it him; but such Friendship is never to be absolutely depended on: For whenever the favourite Passion interposes with
it, it is sure to subside and vanish into air" (VIII v 331).

All of this would seem, if *Amelia* is simply the moralist tract many
would have it be, to mark James as a villain, inexcusable and irredeem-
able. But his case is not so simple. Prescriptive moralism is mediated by
an acceptable libertinism in this case as well as many others. The initial
description of James suggests that the ideal of the good-natured libertine still exists in Fielding's world, but that the effort necessary to over-
come the obstacles impeding that ideal is recognizably vast. Even as the
Colonel is struck by his instant passion for Amelia, the narrator excuses
him and uses his case to point out the difficulty of moral eminence:

But indeed such were the Charms now displayed by *Amelia* … that perhaps no
other Beauty could have secured him from their Influence; and here to confess

a Truth in his Favour, however the grave, or rather the hypocritical Part of Mankind may censure it, I am firmly persuaded that to withdraw Admiration from exquisite Beauty, or to feel no Delight in gazing at it, is as impossible as to feel no Warmth from the most scorching Rays of the Sun. To run away is all that is in our Power; and yet in the former Case if it must be allowed we have the Power of running away, it must be allowed also that it requires the strongest Resolution to execute it.   (VI i 232)

Colonel James's attraction is excused as entirely natural, and this allows Fielding to point out the pitfalls inherent in human relationships, as well as the most direct path away from them. In fact, James is depicted as a victim of a natural disorder, and his errors at this point are apparently made out of neglect rather than malignant intent. The emotion James feels is categorized as "love" rather than desire or lust. The description of his entrapment is almost identical to the description of the moment at which Tom Jones and Sophia Western fall in love: "he was taken by Surprize, and his Heart was gone before he suspected himself to be in any Danger" (VI ii 233). His is a noble emotion, but a dangerous one given the circumstances: "Love ... sprouts usually up in the richest and noblest Minds; but there unless nicely watched, pruned, and cultivated, and carefully kept clear of those vicious Weeds which are too apt to surround it, it branches forth into Wildness and Disorder, produces nothing desirable, but choaks up and kills whatever is good and noble in the Mind where it so abounds" (VI i 233). As Fielding's definition of true virtue reminds us, "Virtue is not that coy, nor that cruel mistress she is represented. Nor is she of that morose and rigid nature, which some mistake her to be ... Virtue forbids not the satisfying our appetites, virtue forbids us only to glut and destroy them" (*Champion* 24 January 1739/40). James does not violate Fielding's standard of virtue, but embodies it in the freedom, choice, and independence of Fielding's libertine understanding of virtue. Note particularly that at no point does Colonel James descend to the actively malignant depths of the Noble Peer in plotting the rape of either Amelia or Mrs Mathews. Unlike the Peer's physical and narcotic coercion, James's attempts are all made to secure a potential for seduction. He offers money, shelter, and friendship as bribes, but the women he pursues have always the right of refusal, and even the inconsistently virtuous Mrs Mathews chooses to refuse for an extended period before Booth reveals to James that vanity, rather than generosity, is the route to her heart.

James, then, is closely associated with both new and old traditions of libertinism at various moments in the novel, and in this he demonstrates Richard Braverman's sense of the multiple manifestations of the libertine: "In his various incarnations he is an extravagant, if innocuous, rake, a figure of social, if not sexual, decorum, and ... a cynical aristocrat who has profound doubts about the socio-political order that sustains him" (77). The final and most significant indication that James's libertinism is acceptable – and even essential – to the larger morality of the novel is his presence among the happy community restored to position at the novel's conclusion. Unlike Trent, who is left out of the social circle, unlike the Noble Peer who is left to stink above ground, and unlike Robinson whose redemption is revealed to have been only a temporary one, James and his wife dine "at the Doctor's Insistence" with Amelia and Booth. Much like Tom Jones and Fielding's other libertines, James is rewarded, rather than punished at the novel's close, suggesting that the aggressive actions to which he has been led by passion are balanced by the benevolent actions to which he has been led by friendship and good nature. James is not only as mixed a figure as Tom Jones, he is also almost as attractive to the reader, indicating that the libertine cannot be read as a figure to be despised even in Fielding's apparently most traditionally moralist work.

Castle appears to be the only other critic to take this view of James's attractiveness, though her argument does not include a consideration of the libertine aspects of James's character. She suggests that after his scheme at the masquerade fails, James "lapses into stoic, inoffensive calm ... The frighteningly Machiavellian aspect of his character recedes, or at least becomes indistinguishable from a certain jaded savoir faire, and he becomes merely something of a psychological enigma: a cryptic, intelligent, at times strangely attractive presence in the fictional world. (He is infinitely more witty than the tiresome Booth, and alone among Fielding's characters in *Amelia* possesses a certain indefinable chic.) He retains his ambivalent status as Booth's friend until the end" (*Masquerade* 238). As she notes, James's character never completely ceases to be attractive, and this is at least partly the result of the connection his character has to libertinism. He is witty and passionate, privileged and empowered, and sexually and socially independent of the standardized mores that dominate the world around him. Instead of rendering James a simple villain like the Noble Peer, Fielding uses him at least in part to demonstrate the attractiveness of the libertine even in a moral world. His very subversiveness underlines the necessity of a public morality capable of producing figures like Amelia, Atkinson, and the good justice, both to encourage goodness in those who would pursue it, and to give those who would rebel a standard so good that even acts and figures subversive of all that such a standard signifies are not necessarily repugnant.

The unattractive extremes of libertine sexuality in *Amelia* – which paradoxically deteriorate into specifically unlibertine ideologies – are demonstrated most explicitly by the Noble Peer and Captain Trent. Trent's appearance is brief, and his primary function is to recommend to Booth that Amelia be used as something akin to bait to lure the Peer into giving Booth a regiment: "Let Mrs *Booth*, in whose Virtue I am sure you may be justly confident, go to the public Places; there let her treat my Lord with common Civility only; I am sure he will bite. And thus without suffering him to gain his Purpose, you will gain yours." As much as this plan might be considered merely a scheme typical of Restoration drama, Booth rejects it because "no Man can be too scrupulous in Points which concern his Honour" (X vii 441). When Trent suggests that the proposal is only a part of human nature, Booth replies that it is "Human Nature depraved, stript of all its Worth, and Loveliness and Dignity, and degraded down to a Level with the vilest Brutes" (X vii 440). This continuum of understanding of sexuality again can be linked specifically to libertinism, since, as Turner notes, the libertine appears in "images that run from innocent voluptuousness (Noble) down to bestial violence (Vile)" ("Priapism" 10). James's ambiguity places him somewhere in the middle of the scale, while Trent's fishing metaphor and his flippancy about self-serving and loveless seduction marks his place as vile, bestially appetitive old-style libertine.

This brief scene between Trent and Booth provides another example of Fielding's shifting understanding of the necessary balance between libertinism and standard moralism, as he rejects a ruse that would have been entirely acceptable in his early drama. Part of this rejection, of course, is related to what we later learn of Trent's character: he has deliberately permitted the disguised Peer to pursue Mrs Trent by affecting more than usual negligence with his wife and more than plausible simplicity with the Peer. He does all of this without ever informing his wife of her role in his little drama, despite the fact that the Peer is described as beginning to "prepare all Matters for a Storm" or rape (XI iii 470). When Trent pretends to leave town, the Peer swoops in to seduce Mrs Trent instead, and Trent leaps from his hiding place in the closet, interrupting the action. While Trent does not actually pursue a criminal conversation case, he clearly threatens the Peer with one, and so the outcome is more private, but the same: in exchange for the Peer's temporary possession of Trent's feminine property, Trent receives "a good round Sum, and ... a good Place" (XI iii 471). As an example of the distasteful extremes to which old-style libertinism could go in its desire for control over sexuality, Trent prostitutes his wife (the first of apparently many occasions) and then gains more social power as a result. Unlike

James, who may dislike his wife, but still treats her publicly with respect and privately gives her financial and personal liberty, Trent lacks any semblance of the fundamental respect for women that allows Fielding's vision of libertinism to be compatible with the moral environment represented by the Booths and Dr Harrison.

The Noble Peer is ultimately less interesting even than Trent, since he is merely a one-dimensional type character of the licentious aristocrat. He schemes with Mrs Ellison to rape Mrs Bennet and either to seduce or rape both Mrs Trent and Amelia, but neither his character nor his motivation extends beyond this. That Fielding establishes an apparently widespread knowledge of the Peer's attempts on women (both Mr and Mrs James mention in casual conversation this element of the Peer's character) assures the reader almost from the beginning that Amelia will be safe as long as she avoids his usual traps, and if – unlike the unsuspecting Mrs Trent, objectified as insentient bait by her husband – her husband and friends offer even basic support and shared knowledge. From what little we know of the Peer, he is an old-style libertine to the core, using social position, power, disguise, and clever deceit to fulfill his desires for sexual satisfaction. Unlike the more complex and human characters in the novel, he contributes nothing more to Fielding's assessment of libertinism and morality than an absolute extreme against which to measure the actions of others; he makes James, Booth, and others seem redeemable and balanced, if tenuously, on the libertine moralist continuum.

Booth's affair with Mrs Mathews, his doctrine of the passions, and his doubts about religion invite the reader to associate him with traditional understandings of libertinism. As a "Man of consummate Good-nature," however, he is also explicitly connected to Fielding's mediating doctrine (III xii 150). As he does for Colonel James, Fielding offers an explanation for Booth's infidelity, but the rationalization here is less powerful than that offered for James's love of Amelia, and much weaker than those jovial and undoubting defenses of the unmarried Tom Jones. Fielding positions the reader as judge as he explains how circumstances might have led Booth to stray from the best of wives:

We desire therefore the good-natured and candid Reader will be pleased to weigh attentively the several unlucky Circumstances which concurred so critically, that Fortune seemed to have used her utmost Endeavours to ensnare poor *Booth's* Constancy. Let the Reader set before his Eyes a fine young Woman, in a manner a first Love, conferring Obligations and using every Art to soften, to allure, to win, and to enflame; let him consider the Time and Place; let him remember that Mr *Booth* was a young Fellow, in the highest Vigour of Life; and lastly, let him add one single Circumstance, that the Parties were alone to-gether; and then if he will not acquit the Defendant, he must be convicted; for I have nothing more to say in his Defence.   (IV i 154)

The implication is that Booth himself uses these explanations to justify his actions. Unlike Fielding's archetypal good-natured libertine Tom Jones, who attempts to hide his indiscretions as much out of concern for the reputations of his partners as for his own good, Booth hides his sexual indiscretions primarily because he is aware of the unarguable im-morality of infidelity even for a young fellow in the highest vigour of life, if he is a married man. This distinction is confirmed, for example, in *Town and Country Magazine* in 1778. The opening paragraph of "The Married Libertine" reminds us, "For the unmarried libertine, few apologies can be framed; for the *married* one nothing by way of extenu-ation can be produced." That Fielding's narrator emphasizes the privacy of the circumstance suggests that the sneaking Booth does not expect to be discovered, while the naturalistic descriptions of Jones suggest a cer-tain amount of honour and integrity, even as he romps with Molly in the thicket. A similar comparison is implied in Booth's motivation for continuing his affair after his initial slip, which might by itself have been more forgivable. While Jones continues his affair with Lady Bel-laston out of an honest, if mistaken, sense of honour, Booth finds that "the same Crime which he now repented of, became a Reason for doing that which was to cause his future Repentance; and he continued to sin on, because he had begun" (IV ii 155).

Fielding's moralist vision of Georgian libertinism becomes clear through such suggested comparisons between Booth and Fielding's other heroes, who are implicitly present. Marriage has always been sac-rosanct in Fielding's Georgian libertinism: in the plays, in *Tom Jones*, and in the inverted world of *Jonathan Wild*, the good-natured libertine never harms another individual through his or her sexual intrigue, and this standard is continued in *Amelia*. But, for the first time, Fielding's nominal hero contravenes this standard, and the injury to the most rec-ognizably virtuous character in Fielding's canon confirms the difficulty of maintaining the complex balances of Georgian libertine moralism in a realistic, rather than pastoral world.

Despite the weakness suggested by Booth's sexual lapse and the nar-rator's guiding interpretation of it, later readers have still been willing to excuse Booth, particularly considering his eventual redemption, as merely a typical gentleman of the time. George Sherburn writes that "all of his faults (which are not so many) are those of the eighteenth-century gentleman. No man of his station (except Sir Charles Grandison) could have refused the overtures of Miss Mathews in Newgate. The lady, furthermore, plies him with rack-punch before he yields" (149). Andrew Wright seems to agree: "Will, whose excellence of character and generosity of spirit have landed him in prison, has no wish to play his wife false; and his misadventures, even that of adultery, are extensions of his generous and naive spirit rather than positive evils" (49). Such assessments seem to acknowledge the existence of a socially acceptable libertinism in Georgian England, but do not recognize that Fielding's works, and especially *Amelia*, evaluate and revise that libertinism into a workable balance that permits Jones's abundant sexuality and Sophia's self-determination and independence, but rejects the tearing of a wider social fabric and the devaluation of love and companionate marriage, which are indicated by Booth's weak and unthinking violation of the bonds of marriage, and which Fielding himself finds inviolable.[10]

Certainly Booth's failure to meet Fielding's standard of libertine behaviour after marriage balances Amelia's apparently unending goodness and virtue. But it is useful to note that Amelia herself is not perfectly virtuous, and, more importantly, that her sexual virtue eventually becomes something of an incarnation of libertinism in itself. There are hints throughout the novel that though Amelia never acts in impropriety or out of malignancy, she is not entirely devoid of less than perfect virtue, and her sexuality is one area in which this is particularly notable. Mary Anne Schofield argues that Booth's vision of Amelia as a fortress of virtue sanctifies her, "but by so doing further adds to her imprisonment. No longer free to be a flesh and blood woman, like Mathews, she is shunted aside, trivialized into a sexless, rarefied, angelic guardian presence" (52). Amelia also, however, establishes a clear and individualized opposition to a set of popular socio-sexual mores. In the suffocating society of the novel, there exists the naturalized assumption that Amelia and Booth must eventually surrender to sexual pressure out of financial need and out of the natural human desire to be admired and envied. Booth, of course, does fall sexually himself, but he refuses to market his wife in order to make economic and social ends meet. Amelia, on the other hand, subverts the anti-moralist discourse accepted in her circle and in the society at large that Fielding creates for her, and in so doing inverts earlier manifestations of libertinism which have challenged equally, but differently, limitations on sexuality. By offering a considered and individual challenge to the extreme version of normalized sexual freedom that has become prostitution for place, Amelia uses the tools of libertinism to solidify her moralist stance. Because the social assumptions and mores of Fielding's fictional world have changed, the realm of potential acts of rebellion and subversion has expanded to

include, ironically, sexual constancy. Amelia's sexual virtue, then, en-
trenches Fielding's public role as justice and his belief in the sanctity of
marriage while still encouraging an individualistic, highly conscious
doubt of and challenge to social organizations and hegemonies as they
exist at any given socio-historical moment.

Amelia's successful defenses of her chastity are obvious enough as one
reads the stories of Bagillard, Colonel James, and the Noble Peer. But
the reader must wonder at least briefly about the potential effects on
Amelia's vanity as she listens to the extended battery of compliments offered her by James, a flirtation so obvious that Mrs Atkinson comments
upon it after James's early morning departure. A more interesting trial
of Amelia's virtue (rather than her vanity) is that of her only true temptation, Sergeant Atkinson. Mrs Atkinson has informed Amelia earlier
that the sergeant loves Amelia deeply, but explains that she accepts this
as a good thing, a quality revealing his nobility of spirit. Since the
reader has received hints about Atkinson's regard for Amelia before this
scene, the revelation is no surprise, though it does cast an odd reflection
on the young sergeant's choice of a wife whose physical resemblance to
Amelia is a central plot device. Even when Atkinson confesses his love,
there is little doubt that the temptation will be resisted; these are, after
all, the two most traditionally virtuous characters in *Amelia* (however
unusual that tradition may be in the fictional world of the novel). Amelia gives Atkinson her hand to kiss, crying "Well, nay ... I don't know
what I am doing – well – there –" (XI vii 482), but it is clear that her
forsaking her potential lover as she calls his wife into the room is not a
thoughtless response by a blandly virtuous character. In the bedside
scene, in her agitation and her need for water, Amelia enacts nearly every conventionalized sign of feminine desire, and the narrator finally
makes it plain:

To say the Truth, without any Injury to her Chastity, that Heart which had
stood firm as a Rock to all the Attacks of Title and Equipage, of Finery and
Flattery, and which all the Treasures of the Universe could not have purchased,
was yet a little softened by the plain, honest, modest, involuntary, delicate, heroic Passion of this poor and humble Swain; for whom, in spite of herself, she
felt a momentary Tenderness and Complacence, at which *Booth*, if he had
known it, would perhaps have been displeased ... [She] then left the House
with a Confusion on her Mind that she had never felt before, and which any
Chastity that is not hewn out of Marble must feel on so tender and delicate an
Occasion.   (XI vi 482–3)

Amelia feels a sexual and emotional attraction to Atkinson, but she is
saved from having to face her desire at this moment, since Atkinson is

presumed to be on his deathbed, removing the potential for (or threat of) any type of future relationship, romantic or otherwise. Castle, however, does consider the potential future sexuality of Amelia and Atkinson, and while I find her speculation to be overhypothesized, her observations are nonetheless interesting: "The secret passion between Amelia and the sergeant is simply left unneutralized (the narrator never refers to it again) … Yet as a result of that emotional éclairissement with the sergeant, she is abruptly revealed to us as one likewise responsive to illicit passion, likewise vulnerable to paradoxical depths of emotional experience. However obliquely, the reader is invited to imagine an alternative future for Fielding's heroine, one characterized not by unwavering fidelity to Booth and the ineffable complacency of the paragon, but by the divisive patterns of erotic discovery" (*Masquerade* 242). Castle, I think, goes too far here. Such an "alternative future," which would inevitably bring Amelia into the adulterous morality of the rest of her fictional world, would violate all that Fielding has established as essential to her character; I would suggest instead that Fielding uses Amelia's sexual temptation to show more clearly her neo-libertine inversion of those very social and sexual mores that Castle's comments – and not Fielding's – seem to laud even for the mature and married.

The vision of sexuality that permeates *Amelia* is generally an unpleasant one, very much in contrast to the naturalistic and joyous version in the plays and the other novels. It is a sexuality coloured by power, greed, ambition, and the exchange of feminine flesh between men of equal power and the auctioning of women by men seeking power. As Campbell argues at length, the novel "broods endlessly on the tension between homosocial and heterosexual bonds" (236). Even beyond this, though, by having Amelia (and ultimately Mrs Bennet, Atkinson, and even Booth) subvert the unequal, masculinist incarnation of the power of the individual's sexual presence, Fielding advocates his final alternative re-vision of sexual libertinism: a libertine moralism which transgresses not against an idealized golden-age morality, but against the very failures of society that have become hegemonic.

Fielding the justice seems to have regarded masquerades as one of those failures. In his "Enquiry into the Causes of the Late Increase in Robbers" (1751), Fielding argues that masquerades serve no social function and are a "notorious nuisance," particularly those "inferior" masquerades of the town where the lower social orders gather, and where "men and women of loose reputation meet in disguised habits" (29). In April 1750, Fielding was among a group of Middlesex justices who moved to suppress a masquerade ball to be held at Ranelagh on the grounds that it would encourage gaming, lewdness, all manner of debauchery, and moral corruption of both sexes.

In *Amelia*, however, the masquerade and the ideology of disguise in general are not so morally straightforward or so stable as Fielding's judicial stance would have it. Castle discusses this issue extensively and powerfully in *Masquerade and Civilization*, but as she does not discuss libertinism within the context of masquerade and disguise, I will offer additional clarification of this aspect of disguise in *Amelia*. As early as his "Essay on the Knowledge of the Characters of Men," Fielding links libertinism, disguise, and morality as he quotes the motto of the *Champion* of 11 December 1739: "Quis enim non vicus abundat / Tristibus obscoenic." Amid his discussion of the strengths and weaknesses of physiognomy, Fielding translates this motto as the question, "What Place is not filled with austere Libertines?" (*Miscellanies* I 156). The ability of the libertine to use disguise for individual interest and amusement is recognized, and, as we have seen in the plays and other novels, this is the most common linking of disguise and libertinism. With the social institutionalization of disguise through the masquerade, though, the act of disguising first ceases to encompass the transgression and cleverness that it held previously, particularly once it becomes available to the lower classes in the public masquerades that Fielding opposed. Second, because of this institutionalization, disguise and the licentiousness that was connected to disguise in the communal psychology actually become elements against which one could rebel as a member of the knowing and privileged group. As Lady Bellaston informs Tom Jones, everyone knows everyone at a masquerade (or at least those of the elite), so flirtations and assignations are frequently neither truly anonymous nor entirely accidental.

The contradictions inherent within the masquerade, then, are not unlike those inherent in libertinism; each relies upon the existence of a limited and standardized society in order to maintain its sense of independence and subversion, whether or not the experiential sense of transgression is supported by verifiable evidence of difference. Castle's summary of the significance of Fielding's use of the masquerade topos is useful in pointing out the paradoxical nature of both the masquerade and Fielding's own nature: "The figure of the masquerade, one suspects, gave Fielding a gratifying opportunity to dwell on the tropes of disorder and moral inversion while seeming (even to himself) to preserve his orthodox stance as a satirist and disseminator of official viewpoints and values" (*Masquerade* 249). I agree with Castle's assessment of the duality of the significance of the masquerade, and would argue that the same duality of influence occurs in varying proportions throughout Fielding's career in terms of the libertine discourse as well. I cannot agree, however, with her assessment of Fielding as fundamentally conservative. It is clear from observing Fielding's libertinism and his consistent desire to challenge hegemonic assumption and limitation that he is pulled in multiple directions by his various public roles, but his balance of unorthodox religious and socio-sexual beliefs with his own sense of a larger moralism and need for order as a source for self-differentiation precludes him from being categorized and labelled quite so easily.

In *Amelia* the same devices exemplify both libertinism and idealized morality as manifested in Amelia. The physical and psychological disguises of the Noble Peer as he plays his roles of concerned friend, losing gamester, helper of half-pay officers, unknown man at the oratorio, and lover at the masquerade all mark him as an example of the old-style Restoration libertine: he uses disguise to gain for himself and to injure others. Amelia, though, uses many of the same types of poses in her pursuit of virtue. She disguises herself as the innocent as she pretends not to know things she does know, including significant details like the infidelity of her husband and the plots against her chastity, and, most significantly, she plans and carries out the extended ruse in which Mrs Bennet attends the masquerade in her place, disguised as Amelia in disguise. Because of Amelia's own empowered manipulation of the libertine topoi of disguise and deceit, the malignant characters are robbed of their ability to seduce or rape her by the very fact of the masquerade setting that is designed to lead to conquest. The explicit similarities between the novel's darkest villain and its brightest paragon demonstrate the conflation of traditional libertinism and traditional morality within Fielding's system of Georgian libertine moralism. The two become difficult to separate, and this reveals the fallaciousness of attempting to establish in a real or realistic world binary categorizations of right and wrong, libertine and moralist.

The apparent Amelia's actions at the masquerade and Amelia's dissembling discussion with Booth at home initially provoke the reader to wonder whether Amelia has revealed a true self at the masquerade. Booth worries afterward, "I know not well what I have lost" (X iii 420), and as Fielding notes in his poem "The Masquerade," "Known prudes are there, libertines we find, / Who masque the face, t' unmasque the mind" (73–4); it seems possible that Amelia herself is one of these mixtures of prudery and libertinism. As it turns out, of course, it has been the much less prudish Mrs Atkinson listening to the Noble Peer's proposals, and Amelia's surface polish of virtue is preserved. Even Mrs Atkinson's violation of prudence in her first masquerade experience, her willingness to be party to Amelia's deception, and her apparent surrender of her own and Amelia's reputations at the second masquerade are left morally ambiguous, as her feminine libertine manipulation of opportunity and disguise, through a complex chain of circumstances, results in morally and socially acceptable outcomes, in this case, a happy marriage between Mrs Bennet and the good Sergeant Atkinson.

Amelia too provides an interesting combination of libertinism and morality in her role in what the narrator terms *"Amelia's* Strategem" (X iv 422), despite Harrison's earlier assertion that she is an "Israelite *indeed, in whom there is no Guile"* (IX viii 387). As she answers Booth's questions about "Amelia's" actions at the masquerade, Amelia seems to be lying to her husband, but is in fact technically telling the truth. Amelia imposes a clever inversion of the traditional use of the language of libertines in which conversations depend entirely on the vehicle of metaphor rather than the concrete tenor, and where the butt or observer of the conversation grasps little of the true tenor. The standard libertine practice of witty dissembling is turned to a truthful, virtuous purpose, even as Amelia actively establishes her individualism, agency, and creative power through manipulation and deceit. Booth begins to doubt his wife as they discuss "Amelia's" behaviour, and, as he wishes she had not attended the masquerade, he cries "Nay, you will wish so yourself, if you tell me Truth – What have I said? do I, can I suspect you of not speaking Truth?" It is reasonable doubt, considering Amelia's responses:

'The Gentleman, my Dear,' said *Amelia*, 'what Gentleman?'

'The Gentleman, the Nobleman, when I came up; sure I speak plain.'

'Upon my Word, my Dear, I don't understand you,' answered she; 'I did not know one person at the Masquerade.'

'How!' said he, 'what, spend the whole Evening with a Masque without knowing him?'

'Why, my Dear,' said she, 'you know we were not together.'

'I know we were not?' said he; 'but what is that to the Purpose? Sure you answer me strangely. I know we were not together; and therefore I ask you whom you were with?'

'Nay, but, my Dear,' said she, 'can I tell People in Masques?'

'I say again, Madam,' said he, 'would you converse two Hours or more with a Masque whom you did not know?'

'Indeed, Child,' says she, 'I know nothing of the Methods of a Masquerade; for I never was at one in my Life.'   (X iii 420)

Even this last statement is both true and false, since the phrase could easily mean that she has not attended one before this night. After this brief torment, apparently rather enjoyed by the momentarily witty Amelia, since it was at Booth's insistence that she was supposed to have attended the masquerade, Amelia reveals that she did not in fact attend. Once again, then, actions traditionally associated with the presumed immorality of libertinism are recuperated and reconstructed so that scheming manipulation, deception, wit, and individualistic self-determination different from public expectation become the devices of a good-natured and thoughtful Georgian libertinism.

The contribution of such ambiguity to the realism of *Amelia* is great, and though some readers have commented on the moral instability of other characters, few note the full implications of Amelia's own contradictoriness. Cheryl Wanko, for example, considers the paradox of Amelia as exemplary paragon, but does not note the effort to which the narrator goes to minimize her less traditional acts and understandings when she writes that "Amelia can suspect no evil in others, yet most of the other characters in the novel teach us the necessity of such suspicion. Fielding systematically introduces characters as good, only to reveal hidden evil at a later stage. He presents us with a paragon of virtue to emulate, and yet his deceptive method of characterization simultaneously educates us to reject the innocence essential to his paragon" (505). Wanko's observation is very useful, but I would quibble with her assertion that innocence is essential to Amelia's character. Instead, the *appearance* of innocence may be essential, but a degree of independence and worldliness is even more essential to the nature of her goodness. Amelia has not the thoughtless, ignorant, hyperinnocent goodness of the intellectually cloistered; she is exemplary because she uses her intelligence, individualism, and sexual power to procure good without falling to the influence of the apparently socially dominant immoralism and anti-moralism surrounding her. Even such criticism as Campbell's excellent analysis of the function of gender roles in *Amelia* tends to conclude that Fielding's female characters emerge as fundamentally conservative, ultimately reinforcing the status quo even as male characters challenge popular understandings of masculinity. In acknowledging the underplayed ambiguity and gendered agency of characters like Amelia and Mrs Bennet-Atkinson (with Sophia Western, Mrs Heartfree, Lady Booby and others), we must recognize that such characters do have a significant role in Fielding's redefinition of the social construction of virtue and its determinist power in popular discourses of femininity.

Amelia uses often transgressive libertine devices, then, to establish her moral strength, but Mrs Bennet-Atkinson is perhaps the most interesting example of a character whose circumstances render her both victim and champion in Fielding's representation of the quest for power. She has fallen victim in the novel's past to her society's admiration for power and its methods of bartering for position. She is apparently drugged and raped after the masquerade she attends with Mrs Ellison at the request of the Noble Peer.[11] Her motives are pure as she seeks the Noble Peer's assistance in reclaiming her husband's place in the church, but she is also naive and socially unaware as well as dangerously vain of both her person and her virtue: "I will own the Truth; I was delighted with perceiving a Passion in him, which I was not unwilling to think he had had from the Beginning, and to derive his having concealed it so long, from his Awe of my Virtue, and his Respect to my Understanding" (VII vii 295). It is essential to acknowledge, however, that in these qualities, Mrs Bennet is not at all unlike the paragon Amelia despite the fact that Mrs Bennet considers Amelia a prude (X viii 445). Mrs Bennet admits her vanity and states that she thought the Noble Peer "the handsomest and genteelest Person in the World; tho' such Considerations advanced him not a Step in my Favour" (VII vi 291). Such admissions clearly echo Amelia's own denials of interest in other men and her potential Achilles' heel of vanity, particularly of her own virtue as she exclaims, "Do you really imagine me so weak as to be cheated of my Virtue? Am I to be deceived into an Affection for a Man, before I perceive the least inward Hint of my Danger? No, Mr *Booth*, believe me a Woman must be a Fool indeed, who can have in earnest such an Excuse for her Actions. I have not, I think, any very high Opinion of my Judgment; but so far I shall rely on it, that no Man breathing could have any such Designs as you have apprehended, without my immediately seeing them" (VI vi 252). Like the implied comparison between Booth and Fielding's other heroes, this unmistakable parallel between Amelia and Mrs Bennet again renders ambiguous the apparent paragon status of the heroine and the ostensibly straightforward traditional morality of the novel.

Mrs Bennet chooses to represent herself as a victim in the telling of her own story to the equally vulnerable and endangered Amelia, but she in fact gains power through her exercise in fictionalized self-creation. The narrator informs us that "she was desirous of inculcating a good Opinion of herself, from recounting those Transactions where her Conduct was unexceptionable, before she came to the more dangerous and suspicious Part of her Character" (VII i 268). While Peter Sabor is correct in noting that Mrs Bennet's narrative "raises far more questions about her past than it answers, and her frequent protestations of innocence confirm, instead of removing, our belief in her guilt" (11), it is also necessary to acknowledge that Mrs Bennet is much more successful at maintaining the self-determination gained through her autodiegetic exercise than is Mrs Heartfree of *Jonathan Wild*, the other basically virtuous woman in Fielding offered an opportunity for defensive self-representation.[12] Where Mrs Heartfree tells her husband that she emerges from her tale with her virtue intact, Mrs Bennet must admit her victimization. Interestingly, though, Mrs Heartfree's struggle to maintain her ostensibly essential sexual chastity leads her eventually to fall back into the very cultural limitations that she has so successfully manipulated in her journey. In contrast, Mrs Bennet's failure and its eventual outcome in the death of her husband ultimately empowers her to recreate herself as a good-natured female libertine in the Georgian style, both through her narration and in her own life and remarriage.

The emergent Mrs Bennet-Atkinson is then able to facilitate Amelia's control over the situation of attempted seduction by the Noble Peer. It is not her problematic knowledge of Greek and Latin that enables her to protect her friend in the best tradition of Fielding's good nature, but her knowledge of the world: also traditionally considered inappropriate for women, but recognized and valued in Fielding's world view. Mrs Bennet-Atkinson plays a key role in the subversive manipulation of the accepted understanding of the process of the masquerade through the use of disguise, the language of libertines, and the skills of experienced and empowered sexual and social agency. To borrow Castle's eloquent phrasing, "Mrs Atkinson here revises, so to speak, that dysphoric 'masquerade tale' written for her the first time around by the Noble Peer. She inverts the fictional pattern of manipulation by entrapping him in a 'plot,' a scheme of comic revenge" (*Masquerade* 229). And as the power and self-determination of Amelia and Mrs Atkinson increase, that wielded by figures traditionally granted status decreases. The Peer, grasping at power from the long lost social structure that created Restoration-style libertines, becomes the failed libertine fop whom Fielding has made a stock figure of ridicule from his earliest plays.

Like the Peer, Dr Harrison seems to possess great power, and he is the novel's supposed font of wisdom as well. Like Allworthy before him, however, his position and presumed wisdom are primarily the result of personal wealth and a benevolent nature rather than any specific effort of Fielding's to make him into an entirely exemplary figure. Harrison's overconservatism, mitigated though it is by good nature, denies him the status of paragon that a more morally imperfect figure like Amelia achieves. For example, he seems to deny the prospect of individual self-determination in much the same way that Mrs Heartfree does when she slips into mindless acquiescence to the social constructions of her position. He tells the Booths that their "Sufferings are all at an end; and Providence hath done you the Justice at last, which it will one Day or other render to all Men" (XII vii 522). In addition, and more damaging to his status as fully integrated and contemporary model for Fielding's fictional world, Harrison is still ensconced in a social understanding in which women, however virtuous, are mere chattel. He tells Booth that he has "Priority of Right, even to you yourself. You stole my little Lamb from me" (IX viii 387), and his letter to Colonel James on the folly of adultery argues that to seduce a married woman "includes in it almost every Injury and every Mischief which one Man can do to, or can bring on another. It is robbing him of his Property." The responses of quicklysketched libertines reading the letter aloud at the masquerade reflect what might be Fielding's own reply to Dr Harrison's thoughtlessly patriarchal rhetoric as the text italicizes and repeats ironically: "'Mind that, Ladies,' said the Orator, *'you are all the Property of your Husbands'* " (X ii 414). Harrison is innately good, but he does not evaluate actively enough the social strictures that he takes for granted and holds the power to enforce. This is perhaps most successfully demonstrated as Harrison, upon hearing of the Booths' carriage and finding the child's watch in their home, does not respond to the individual situation of Amelia and Booth, but listens to the voices of the couple's neighbours, the thoughtless masses who construct and entrench generalized social mores and limitations on aspiration and individualism.

This apparent disdain for the ideological and social influence of the rabble is again consistent with the libertine narratorial or directorial presence in Fielding's other works. The narrator's assumed privilege over lesser authors and their low interests is stated explicitly in the prefaces to the plays and prefatory chapters of the other novels. It is still present in *Amelia*, but is integrated into the narrative rather than appended to it. I have already noted the different tone of the narrator's defense of Booth's infidelity; also relevant is the scene of Booth's initial adulterous encounter which closes with a decorous allusion to the events and a suggestion that "over curious Readers" refer to "the Apologies with which certain gay Ladies have lately been pleased to oblige the World, where they will possibly find every thing recorded, that past at this Interval" (IV i 153). The tone of narrative superiority has not changed, but it is more subtly represented. The narrator's power is less directly stated in the more realistic atmosphere of Fielding's last novel, but the effects of his presence are not significantly diminished. The narrative voice, however, balances the novel and its characters on the libertine-moralist continuum more carefully than would be necessary in the different surroundings in many of the earlier works. While demonstrating his superior knowledge of human nature by describing a woman he has seen at a bagnio, the narrator is careful to explain, "remember, Critic, it was in my Youth" (I vi 47); he again implies the different criteria by which unmarried youth and married maturity must be judged, and thus the necessity of a merging of the values of libertine youth and moral maturity. Booth's moral slippage and his challenges to traditional mores are emphasized while Amelia's are minimized throughout the novel, and this control over representation forces the reader to evaluate individuals and systems of belief and organization rather than simply to accept the version of events proffered by the narrator. Fielding's narrator challenges the reader to engage in thoughtful consideration and personal re-evaluation of assumptions and appearances of moral and social rights and wrongs, confidently refusing the didactic role which he himself has established as standard in his earlier narrative works.

Amelia may be "an embodiment of moral courage" (Sherburn 149), but her character and her world are more complex than many critics recognize. Her pattern of deceit falls into the category of what Fraser terms the "virtuous secret" (194), and this is a part of the heretofore unrecognized pattern that is slowly but unmistakably established in *Amelia*. The narrator forces readers not to accept characters or events at face value, and Amelia is thus revealed to be much more cognisant of the ways of the world than her status as virtuous paragon usually allows her. It is Mrs Bennet's violation of socially determined limitations on her intellect, and her determination of her own future after she is rendered a fallen woman that eventually give her the power and skill to share with Amelia the capacity to avoid the manipulation and victimization that dominate her society. The sexual machinations of the otherwise good-natured Colonel James are not sufficiently damaging to bar him from the community established at the end of the novel, and Booth's challenge to religious convention merely establishes him as a man who will not be led by thoughtless blind faith. The divisions between that which is accepted as moral and that which is transgressive of moral and social norms are blurred in *Amelia*, and the existence of a moralist understanding of qualities and acts traditionally associated with libertinism is confirmed. Fielding's final novel is certainly different in its focus from the earlier works that redefine Georgian libertinism as a valuable social, political, and sexual philosophy, but his interest in libertinism as a cultural force remains consistent. He offers in his favorite fictional work a system of morality that values goodness, good nature, and generosity at the same time that it encourages constant evaluation of the qualities and understandings that traditionally define these terms.

Conclusion

It is a critical commonplace that Fielding's novels and plays offer a panoramic view of life in eighteenth-century England; in so doing, these works examine many different elements of Georgian society from religion and the hegemonic social order to sexuality and the empowerment of the individual. For decades critics have argued which of these interests is most essential to the understanding of Fielding as artist and as social critic, with Battestin's latitudinarian moralist consideration rising to critical prominence. Modern criticism, however, has thus far overlooked the socio-philosophical discourse of libertinism, a tradition that encompasses so many elements of eighteenth-century culture in different ways.

It is clear that neither Fielding's fiction nor his own life was ruled consistently by a single static approach to his society and its implications for the individual, but his active participation in the discourse of libertinism is clearly one of the philosophical involvements that mediate his work, and this participation must be considered in any attempt to develop a complete image of the man and the writer. Fielding does not proselytize libertinism; to do so would violate the ironic distance and privilege of the libertine position itself. As we recognized in this book's first chapter, though, libertinism continued to be a prominent social force in the early and middle parts of the eighteenth century, particularly among men of Fielding's status, and it could hardly avoid becoming a prominent figure in the carpet of Fielding's fictional world.

Libertinism was by its nature a discourse in transition, and Fielding's work is not only affected by the ideology of social, religious, and sexual challenge and subversion, but it also contributes to the connected understandings of libertinism, virtue, and morality undergoing often tumultuous revision in the eighteenth century. The consistent presence of aspects of libertinism in both the heroes and villains of the plays and the novels demonstrates Fielding's continuing consideration of the role that libertinism might play in eighteenth-century society. His ideal seems to have manifested itself in the 'good-natured libertine,' named explicitly in *Tom Jones*, but it is also present in versions masculine and feminine and in various stages of integrated completion throughout the plays and novels. The good-natured Georgian libertine acts independently of the limitations on thought and behaviour constructed by his or her society, self-positioning above the rabble for whom such strictures are designed. The libertine challenges received truth and religious doctrine not necessarily to the extreme form of atheism typified by old-style Restoration libertinism, but in a way that the individual consciously examines that which others thoughtlessly take for granted in following the dogma of institutionalized religion. In a further manifestation of the desire to establish originality and to challenge artificial constructs of virtue that limit the natural desires of both sexes, Fielding's Georgian libertine pursues consensual sexual relationships between men and women which are empowering for both the individuals involved and the discourses of sexuality and gender relations they represent.

The plays offer our first opportunity to see the public representations of Fielding's libertine challenges to literary and social form. They reveal, among other things, interests in hypocrisy, the natures of love, sexuality, and marriage, and the implications of the existing social order for the privileged individual. With the publication of *Shamela* and the *Champion* essays, Fielding continued to develop these interests by subverting the widespread Richardsonian definition of virtue as the feminine quality of sexual virginity, thus clearing the way for the explicit re-vision of the concept as independent and autonomous libertinism in *Joseph Andrews*. In *Jonathan Wild*, Fielding's ironic allusion to everything and nothing, the political and social allegory is augmented by the presence of libertine and anti-libertine qualities of character and narration that add an individualist element to the questions of liberty, power, and independence in realms intellectual, legal, political, and sexual. In *Tom Jones* Fielding finally creates his archetypal Georgian libertine, self-empowered, actively questioning the constructions of morality, power, and libertinism that surround him until his models – good and bad – direct him toward the balances necessary to embody Fielding's ongoing investigation of the capacity for good nature in the presumed egocentric world of the libertine. Then, having seen Fielding's ideal of the youthful and unencumbered libertine, the reader finds in *Amelia* an acknowledgment of the difficulty of achieving such a balance in marriage, maturity, and a more realistic London setting as Fielding's final novel presents a series of characters who manifest more problematically and less pastorally the paradoxes of even the best attempts at good-natured libertinism.

Fielding's conceptualization of libertinism thus changes over his career: he emphasizes the more joyous, privileged, and licentious elements of the philosophy in his earliest works, then develops the effects of libertinism on the social constructs of virtue and morality amidst the pastoral naturalist surroundings of his middle works, and finally evaluates the complexities of manifesting any given philosophical system in the real world he saw every day as a justice. Throughout this process Fielding positions himself as a libertine, demonstrating his privilege through shocking settings or characterizations, by withholding or manipulating information, and by guiding the critical reader through an experiential evaluation of the strengths and weaknesses of any number of cultural discourses, including Restoration and Georgian versions of libertinism. Readers, like Fielding's characters, discover for themselves the validity of Georgian libertinism as a social and philosophical approach to life in eighteenth-century England.

Recognition of the influence of the cultural presence of the revised Georgian libertinism on Fielding's works implies recognition of the corollary influence of Fielding's essays, drama, and fiction on the popular recognition and acceptance of new standards of faith, philosophy, and sexuality. This dual recognition is essential to understandings of eighteenth-century culture and the perspective on human behaviour that Fielding adds to it. With this new sense of Fielding's engagement with the debates on human nature, the reader becomes aware that Fielding presents much more than just the clichéd panorama of Georgian society. He represents not only his own culture from a Georgian libertine perspective, but the philosophical underpinnings of that culture, simultaneously substantiating it and subverting it in the best paradoxical libertine form.

Georgian libertinism informed Fielding's work throughout his career, and fostered often unrecognized reconsiderations of his society's perceptions of gender and sexuality, autonomy and hegemony, stricture and liberty. For almost three decades, Fielding engaged and challenged what became the popularly entrenched cultural history of gender, religion, and philosophy; at the end of this time, his own intellectual challenge of integrating the libertinism he respected with the overarching morality whose necessity he acknowledged was finally met through *Tom Jones* and *Amelia,* and their successful combination of ostensibly contradictory values into the Georgian libertinism he had been addressing for most of his literary career.

Notes

1 See Turner's "The Culture of Priapism," "'Illustrious Depravity' and the Erotic Sublime," "The Libertine Sublime: Love and Death in Restoration England," "Lovelace and the Paradoxes of Libertinism," "Pope's Libertine Self-Fashioning," "Properties of Libertinism," and "Sex and Consequence."

2 A common quality of poorly-defined libertinism is an intense focus on the attention-getting element of sexuality to the neglect of other interesting elements of the philosophy. The most extreme case of this is David Foxon's promisingly-titled 1964 work *Libertine Literature in England 1660–1745* which is primarily a history of pornography with a brief nod to Underwood in its conclusion. David Coward's "The Sublimations of a Fetishist" is another example of a study that uses the word "libertinism" but discusses only sexual deviance, in describing Restif de la Bretonne's shoe fetishes and incestuous behaviour. A final example is surprising given that it comes from Maximillian Novak, who discusses libertinism regularly: his analysis of "Margery Pinchwife's 'London Disease': Restoration Comedy and the Libertine Offensive of the 1670's," never clearly defines libertinism, but instead refers to the differences between city and country mores as exemplified by the simple illicit sexuality that he represents with the word "libertine." Novak elsewhere offers a broader but still problematic definition of libertinism as "not merely for sexual freedom and for a life of sensations rather than of thoughts; it also argued for a life free from the conventions of society" ("Freedom, Libertinism, and the Picaresque" 43–4). The suggestion

that libertines lived without thought eliminates much of the intellectual and social value of the libertine challenge to social convention, and again leaves a complex social and philosophical perspective in the realm of mere bad behaviour.

3 Claude Rawson and Janet Todd also offer space for something other than a binary relationship between sentimentalism and libertinism. Rawson explains that "[s]entimentalism included more than a cult of refined emotion: it embraced also the broad benevolence of *Tom Jones* and the intense passion of Mary Wollestonecraft's *The Wrongs of Woman: or, Maria* (1798)" (*Order* 349). Though her introduction to sensibility does not address libertinism specifically, Todd notes in a similar vein that "La Mettrie associated sexuality and sensibility, seeing the mind and body as different forms of the same substance, and many less systematic thinkers, considering sensibility as moral and physical susceptibility, inevitably found sexuality a component: Tom Jones's robust and Yorick's whimsical sexuality feed into and derive from their sensibility" (8).

4 In *Epicurus in England (1650–1725)*, Thomas Franklin Mayo explains that while declining in popular significance, Epicurianism did not cease to exist after 1700; in fact, "so far as mere number is concerned, Epicurian publications between 1700 and 1725 are rather formidable." Such publications, however, faced "a hostile atmosphere" and tended to be the products of lesser known philosophers and writers (185).

5 Shearer West discusses the role of anti-Church rhetoric and its connection to other forms of undefinedly libertine thought and behaviour in the Society of Dilettanti (with expansion into other groups including the Medmenham Monks) in "Libertinism and the Ideology of Friendship in Portraits of the Society of Dilettanti."

6 Daniel Statt's "The Case of the Mohocks: Rake Violence in Augustan London" provides a useful summary of the contrasts between court documents and popular reports on the events of the Mohock Crisis of 1712. One of his conclusions echoes my own, that the Mohocks represent a secondary line of libertinism which continued alongside the more cultured and philosophical version that is so much more prominent, particularly in eighteenth-century fiction: his Mohock is a "type, better designated by the term rake, whose sexuality found expression not in promiscuous 'gallantry,' but in violence and misogyny" (199), a figure "typically bereft of wit, refinement, style, and sense" (181). For additional historical documentation, see Neil Guthrie's "'No truth or very little in the whole story'? – A Reassessment of the Mohock Scare of 1712," in which he concludes that "the Mohocks were merely one of a series of similar nine days' wonders that caught the attention of the eighteenth-century public, among them the reports of blasphemous hellfire clubs in the early 1720s and the prurient in-

terest in the activities of Sir Francis Dashwood and the so-called 'Monks of Medmenham' in the 1760s" (49).

7 A useful analogy in the understanding of Free-thinking is offered by Henry St. John, Viscount Bolingbroke, in the philosophical work circulated among his friends in the 1720s and 30s, but not published until after his death in 1751. Bolingbroke uses the famous clock metaphor to explain that those who argue that God is active in His own creation are like the overly clever residents of the Cape of Good Hope, likely to believe that the "workman is concealed in the clock, and there conducts invisibly all the motions of it" (III 355).

8 Turner notes of Lovelace what is equally true of all libertines: "he comes to realize that to reform, to breach the libertine character expected by his 'confraternity,' would be the *real* act of individuality. Consequently, it is misleading to present the rake-hero as a radical figure and to label objecters such as Blackmore as 'conservative.' Historically, the moralists represent a new Whiggish order, and the rake, despite his modishness, is a throwback, a boudoir version of the old absolutism" ("Priapism" 15).

9 Other articles by Trumbach useful in the discussion of libertinism include "Erotic Fantasy and Male Libertinism in Enlightenment England" in *The Invention of Pornography: Obscenity and the Origins of Modernity, 1500–1800*, and "Modern Prostitution and Gender in *Fanny Hill*: Libertine and Domesticated Fantasy" in *Sexual Underworlds of the Enlightenment*. Other valuable resources for the consideration of the changing relationship between sodomy and libertinism include Michael Kimmel's "'Greedy Kisses' and 'Melting Extasy': Notes on the Homosexual World of Early Eighteenth Century England as Found in *Love Letters Between a Certain Late Nobleman and the Famous Mr. Wilson*"; G.S. Rousseau's "An Introduction to the *Love Letters*: Circumstances of Publication, Context, and Cultural Commentary"; and David F. Greenberg's "The Socio-Sexual Milieu of the *Love Letters*," all in *Love Letters*. For an excellent overview of the presence of homosexuality throughout eighteenth-century Europe, see the more than twenty essays included in Kent Gerard and Gert Hekma's *The Pursuit of Sodomy: Male Homosexuality in Renaissance and Enlightenment Europe*.

10 In his article on "The Socio-Sexual Milieu of the *Love Letters*," Greenberg disputes Trumbach's sense of the disappearance of age-asymmetric male homosexuality, arguing that such activity did not disappear, but simply attracted less notice compared to the more effeminate mollies.

11 See my essay, "The Female Libertine" in *TransAtlantic Crossings: Sexuality & Textuality in the Eighteenth Century*.

12 Turner's "Paradoxes of Libertinism" offers another approach to the libertinism of gender as demonstrated in *Clarissa*. He suggests that Clarissa herself is a libertine (because of the part of his definition of libertinism which

refers to an aesthetic element of "improvistory freedom of style" and Clarissa's spirit and wit), though of a different branch from Lovelace.

13   The concept of "traffic in women" as a mode of social organization which has existed as long as the patriarchal hegemony is articulated (from various sources) in Eve Kosofsky Sedgwick's *Between Men: English Literature and Male Homosocial Desire.* Briefly, it is "the use of women as exchangeable, perhaps symbolic, property for the primary purpose of cementing the bonds of men with men. For example, Levi-Strauss writes, 'The total relationship of exchange which constitutes marriage is not established between a man and a woman, but between two groups of men, and the woman figures only as one of the objects in the exchange, not as one of the partners' " (25–6).

14   See, for example, "The Female Libertine" (*Town and Country Magazine,* June 1772), a morality tale that concludes with the madness and death (though not the regret or apology) of the heroine, as well as the deaths from grief of her father and mother, and "the sudden death of Miss Hornby [her fellow libertine], who fell a blooming sacrifice to her voluptuousness." Such cautionary publications seem tacitly to confirm the existence and sense of community of female libertines of various stripes, as well as the concern that such an autonomous discourse for women evoked in more conservative circles.

15   In reviewing Castle's article Turner offers evidence from other diaries and correspondence of the period to argue that it seems more likely that "masquerades functioned as a containment rather than a release of erotic simulacra, a Foucaultian control-by-proliferation, a guarantee that no real 'assault' would take place and that the 'polymorphous subject' remained only a fantasy" ("Sex and Consequence" 152).

16   Consider, for example, Fielding's Tom Jones and his friend Nightingale, the narrator of *A Journey from this World to the Next,* Richardson's Belford and Colonel Morden, Sterne's Tristram Shandy, and the sentimental but rakish heroes of much of eighteenth-century drama, including Steele's Charles Myrtle and Bevil Junior (the latter of whom is guided by a principle of "honest dissimulation"), many of Fielding's dramatic heroes, and Sheridan's Charles Surface.

17   While I find much of Stone's commentary convincing, the necessity (rather than the fact) of a patriarchal power structure is somewhat problematic, particularly when considered in light of the frequently open-minded libertine understanding of the role of women.

18   Battestin, of course, argues in *Moral Basis* that good nature is an offshoot of latitudinarianism, and H.K. Miller includes in his introduction to the *Miscellanies* a theory that the Benevolist school of moralists from the late seventeenth century serves as the origin for the concept.

19 See John K. Sheriff, *The Good-Natured Man* for a very useful assessment of the historical and philosophical roots of the discourse from which Fielding develops his own understanding of good nature. Sheriff quotes Hume's summary on p. 16.

CHAPTER TWO

1 Kristina Straub's *Sexual Suspects* offers a well researched and highly interesting analysis of figures like that of the feminized macaroni in terms of the theatrical community of the eighteenth century. Straub traces developments of homosexuality and masculinity in the period by assessing individual actors and critics, particularly the Cibber family.

2 See *Henry Fielding: A Life*, where Battestin summarizes this period of Fielding's life under the subtitle "Playwright and Libertine (1727–39)." Battestin notes that Fielding "freely indulged his own powerful sexual appetites" (129), and includes religious and political Free-thinker James Ralph, rakish deist Thomas Cooke, notoriously dissolute libertine Anthony Henley, "madcap priest" Leonard Howard (160), and pleasure seeker Henry Hatsell among "a circle of clever libertines and free-thinkers whose company in these early years Fielding found congenial" (81).

3 In the *Grub-street Journal* of 20 July 1732, 'Publicus' writes, "But to come to particulars, (and yet I'm ashamed to come to them too) observe the following speech of LOVEGIRLO, Page 13.

> *Oh! I am all on fire, thou lovely wench;*
> *Torrents of joy my burning soul must quench,*
> *Reiterated joys!*
> *Thus, burning from the fire, the washer lifts*
> *The red hot iron to make smooth her shifts;*
> *With arm impetuous rubs her shift amain,*
> *And rubs, and rubs, and rubs it o'er again;*
> *Nor sooner does her rubbing arm withold,*
> *'Till she grows warm, and the hot iron cold.*

Abominable! sure a man must wrest with all his might to make any thing else of this but the most gross obscenity" (Paulson and Lockwood 56–7).

4 Fielding's inversion of his own typical epilogue is itself libertine in its need to be original and inimitable and to defy public expectation. The opening reads:

> The play once done, the Epilogue, by rule,
> Should come and turn it all to ridicule;
> Should tell the ladies that the tragic bards,
> Who prate of virtue and her vast rewards,
> Are all in jest, and only fools should heed 'em;

> For all wise women flock to Mother Needham.
> This is the method Epilogues pursue,
> But we to-night in everything are new.

5 Fielding's use of St Francis throughout this play is significant to his libertinism as well. Francis of Assisi was a man of pleasure and debauchery who
challenged many aspects of the social organization of his day before he was
led by a series of events to found the order of Friars Minor in 1209, an order dedicated to the "loving, joyous worship of the Sacred Humanity of
Christ" (Benedictine Monks 288). Biographers have described Francis as
having "walked the streets of Babylon, wallowed in his sins, and wantonly
stirred up trouble" (Nigg 13).

6 Again, for excellent analysis of the implications of such speeches and characterizations for actresses' offstage lives, see Straub, especially 89–108. Very
briefly, Straub argues that public women (and particularly actresses) faced
attempts to recuperate their sexuality (and femininity more generally) by
containing it within established discourses of domesticity. Such women
were often represented to be of lower class origins (and thus subject to
spectatorial scrutiny without real subversive potential); to be toys or pets of
the upper classes (and thus without the status for real influence); or to be
appropriately domestic at their roots (thus actresses' memoirs and biogra-
phies with an otherwise surprising focus on motherhood and familial
roles).

7 On Charke's cross-dressing, see her autobiography, *A Narrative of the Life of
Mrs Charlotte Charke* (1755) and Straub's chapter on Charke and female
theatrical transvestism. Despite the challenges offered to hegemonic constructions of gender by such appropriation of masculine dress on and off
stage, both Charke and Fielding elsewhere decline links to a positive representation of homosexuality. Fielding's *The Female Husband* (1746) is a sala-
cious representation of the case of Mary Hamilton, a woman who passed as
a man even in sexually active marriages. Fielding's telling panders to public
voyeurism, and despite moments of apparent sympathy, ultimately rejects
woman-woman sexual desire. Similarly, in spite of Charke's own life of
gendered transgression, she too takes a public stance against homosexuality
in *The History of Henry Dumont, Esq.*, her representation of male-male desire and its (rightly, she implies) violent consequences. Such public dis-
tancing from this particular alternative sexual expression initially seems
contradictory, but is actually reasonably predictable considering the extremely marginal position of homosexuality in eighteenth-century culture.
As I discussed in chapter 1, even the libertine moved away from this most
extreme of challenges to sexual norms, leaving behind the Rochesterian image of bisexuality as hypersexuality as the effeminate and passive image of
the mollies became the dominant construction. Both Charke and Fielding

had the status to disrupt normative values from their privileged familial and social positions in London society; in another example of the central libertine paradox outlined by Turner, Fielding and Charke were unwilling to take their public subversion so far as to risk actual change that would weaken the source of their own capacity to remain both subversive and powerful.

8 From Stormandra's line of reconciliation with Bilkum, "Nor modesty, nor pride, nor fear, nor rep, / Shall now forbid this tender chaste embrace" (II xiii).

9 Similarities between *The Modern Husband* and *Amelia* are easily spotted. These include the unfashionable closeness and love of the Bellamants and the Booths, the similarities in the behaviour of Mr Bellamant and Mr Booth, the reaction of their wives to their infidelity, and the suggestion (and truth) in both cases that blessings are in store for the virtuous. Incidentally, these parallels seem to confute the frequent critical suggestion that *Amelia* is semi-autobiographical, since Fielding created nearly identical issues and actions in a play written four years before he married Charlotte Cradock.

10 See Hume's *Henry Fielding and the London Theatre* 74–5.

11 For a parallel expression of the unacceptability of adultery within later constructions of libertinism, see *Town and Country Magazine*'s "The Married Libertine" (10 August 1778), which opens with this distinction: "For the unmarried libertine few apologies can be framed; for a *married* one nothing by way of extenuation can be produced."

12 The play ran only six performances, and is generally considered to have been a failure. Fielding's wife Charlotte was gravely ill at the time of the planned revisions, and the playwright later claimed these circumstances precluded him from completing all of the revisions he had planned. He was unable to put off staging this imperfect work, Battestin notes, because of a pressing need for income (*Life* 363).

CHAPTER THREE

1 Turner offers a fascinating discussion of the role of letter writing and reporting in the discourse of libertinism in *Clarissa* in "Lovelace and the Paradoxes of Libertinism."

2 This type of redefinition of semantically unstable terms is not new to Fielding. In addition to the redefinition of virtue in *The Champion*, Fielding also reassesses "reason" (5 January 1739/40), "turncoats" (12 January 1739/40) and "authority" (15 January 1739/40). Neil Rhodes presents an interpretation similar to my own as he asserts in his discussion of "The Innocence of *Joseph Andrews*" that Fielding's goal was "to put forward an ideal

of virtue which could resist a variety of charges: in particular, those of sanc-
timoniousness, faint-heartedness and mere gullibility ... Innocence as distinct from 'purity' is the basis for a sexual ethic rather more humane than
Richardson's" (104–5). In contrast, Earla Wilputte argues in "Ambiguous
Language and Ambiguous Gender" that Fielding, even in his redefinitions
of such concepts as virtue and libertinism, is ultimately conservative:
"Fielding, however, is concerned not only about the irresponsible employment of words for the purpose of deceiving but about the intentional mis-
application of ethical terms and the consequent propagation of immorality
... Fielding [has a] strategy of introducing mannish women, womanish
men, and sexually ambiguous creatures to represent perversions of language ... Fielding emerges as both sexist and homophobic" (510–11).

3 In "'Silenc'd by Authority' in *Joseph Andrews*," Raymond Stephanson concurs with my sense of Adams's consistently thoughtless capitulation to traditional authorities as he analyses power and authority in the interpolated
tale 'The History of Two Friends.' "Adams is a 'hungry,' 'insatiable' reader
whose passive need for narrative titillation outweighs any critical participation or active intellectual response" (4). Adams also responds to Wilson's
apology for the length of his mention of his discovery of Harriet Hearty's
love for the young Wilson with "'So far otherwise,' said *Adams*, licking his
Lips, 'that I could willingly hear it over again'" (III iii 223).

4 For an original view of Adams's nature as self-serving, see James Cruise
"Fielding, Authority, and the New Commercialism."

5 Fielding's own defense of the clergy appeared in *The Champion* of
29 March and 5, 12, and 19 April 1740. The essays outline the legal and
moral status of the clergy, as well as the fundamental place of true charity:
"By this virtue, which is generally called charity itself (and perhaps it is the
chiefest part of it), is not meant the ostentatious giving a penny to a beggar
in the street (an ostentation of which I do not accuse the clergy, having to
my knowledge never seen one guilty of it), as if charity was change for six-
pence, but the relieving the wants and sufferings of one another to the utmost of our abilities. It is to be limited by our power, I say, only" (5 April).

6 For outlines of the connections between "fanny" as a name and as a common term for the female genitalia, see Campbell in *Natural Masques* (25),
and Rothstein in "The Framework of *Shamela*." The possible link to discourses of homosexuality is made by Carl Kropf in "A Certain Absence:
Joseph Andrews as Affirmation of Heterosexuality."

7 See Battestin's *The Moral Basis of Fielding's Art* and Howard Weinbrot's
"Chastity and Interpolation."

8 See, for example, Kropf's article on the implied discourse of homoerotism
in *Joseph Andrews*.

9   I have cited above critical works that accept Joseph's virginity as a straightforward statement of Christian morality. The other popular approach is
typified by Arthur Sherbo's argument that Fielding's comments on chastity
are intended to be ironic, since all actions of the novel are mediated by the
implied presence of Pamela and Shamela in the background (114–16).
Hunter agrees, and offers the interesting suggestion that the sentence
"Male Chastity [is] doubtless as desirable and becoming in one Part of the
human species, as in the other" functions in the same way as the opening
sentence of *Pride and Prejudice*, a statement consonant with the grander
hegemonic assumptions, but open to reconsideration from many different
approaches (96).

CHAPTER FOUR

1   See Rawson, "The Hero as Clown: Jonathan Wild, Felix Krull, and Others."
2   Battestin bases his dating of the composition process on the arguments of
T. Keightley's "On the Life and Writings of Henry Fielding," Austin
Dobson's *Henry Fielding*, A. Digeon's *Les Romans de Fielding*, F.H.
Dudden's *Henry Fielding: His Life, Works and Times*, and Thomas
Cleary's *Henry Fielding: Political Writer*.
3   David L. Evans discusses Fielding's understanding of the idea of liberty at
length in "The Theme of Liberty in *Jonathan Wild*."
4   Doshy Snap, one of the few female characters in the novel whom Jonathan
Wild does not pursue, suggests a sense of feminine sexuality consistent
with that expressed in the other novels and the plays. True to the form of
the novel, though, this direct representation of the libertine understanding
of sexuality is mentioned only briefly before the reader is sent back to
Wild's inverted values. Doshy is the only character of Wild's world who is
not hanged or broken on the wheel at the end of the novel. Instead, the
good-natured woman whose chastity is surrendered to a man who deceived
her is rewarded with a happy life in the Americas after her transportation.
Fielding notes briefly amid the fuss over Doshy's pregnancy that she "was
sufficiently punished for a fault which, with submission to the chaste Laetitia and all other strictly virtuous ladies, it should be either less criminal in
a woman or more so in a man to solicit her to it" (III xiii 159). This assessment of the situation is closely aligned with similar occasions in *Joseph Andrews* and *Tom Jones*.
5   See Stephanie Barbe Hammer *The Sublime Crime* (72) and Claude Rawson's discussion of the work of William R. Irwin in "Fielding's 'Good' Merchant" (306).

6 Rawson assesses Heartfree's character as significant primarily as a foil to Wild ("Fielding's 'Good' Merchant" 310), and Wendt concurs in his sense that "as such a foil, Heartfree is carefully subordinated to Wild" ("Allegory" 308). Hammer, though, writes, "Of course, the opposite is true; Wild is the foil for Heartfree, whose sterling qualities should shine out all the more brilliantly" (69).

7 In "Fielding's 'Good' Merchant," Rawson argues that after the burlesque chapter was eliminated in the second edition, the "other travel chapters are largely sober narrative, especially by the standards of what they are alleged to be parodying, and not at all difficult to take straight" (307n). He is supported in his reading by Angela Smallwood's *Fielding and the Woman Question*, Frank Felsenstein's "'Newgate with the Mask on': A View of *Jonathan Wild*," Murial Williams's *Marriage: Fielding's Mirror of Morality*, and Ruml's "*Jonathan Wild* and the Epistemological Gulf between Virtue and Vice." The view of Mrs Heartfree's tales as constructs to serve her own needs for both power and the self-positioning of her choice without harming any other party is most effectively argued in Michael McKeon's *Origins of the English Novel* and Wilputte's "The Autodiegetic Power of Mrs Heartfree in Henry Fielding's *Jonathan Wild*: The Moderately Good Wife."

8 This count includes Jonathan Wild, the French captain, the English captain, Count LaRuse, the hermit, the sailors walking her from the hermit's cave to the African village, the Chief Magistrate, and the captain of the final English ship.

9 Wilputte notes that "Fielding employs Mrs Heartfree, in an environment of extremes, as an inflated example of human good-nature or more pointedly, *female* good-nature, being no better than it ought to be" ("Heartfree" 229). However, Wilputte develops this reading in a different direction from my own, particularly in her extensive psychoanalytical analysis of the deleted chapter of the travel narrative.

10 See Andrew Wright, *Henry Fielding: Mask and Feast* (167–8), for example. This assertion is problematic in that though a portion of *Jonathan Wild* was composed before *Joseph Andrews*, the Heartfree sections were probably not part of the initial drafts. Thus arguments suggesting chronological development of typical characterizations, rather than thematic ones like that of the paradigm of libertinism, are left with a central contradiction.

CHAPTER FIVE

1 See, for example, Morris Golden's *Fielding's Moral Psychology*, Bernard Harrison's *Henry Fielding's* Tom Jones: *The Novelist as Moral Philosopher*, Battestin's "Fielding's Definition of Wisdom: Some Functions of Ambiguity and Emblem in *Tom Jones*," William Empson's "*Tom Jones*," and Glenn W. Hatfield's "The Serpent and the Dove: Fielding's Irony and the Pru-

dence Theme of *Tom Jones*." For an opposing perspective, see Mark Kinkead-Weekes's "Out of the Thicket in *Tom Jones*."

2   Angela Smallwood makes much of this desire for control in *Fielding and the Woman Question*, as she argues that Western is a misogynist abuser of women who is attacked by Fielding for his stance. While I find this reading interesting, I cannot find sufficient evidence in the text for anything but an indulgently patronizing tone rather than the outright disdain that Smallwood hypothesizes in Fielding's depiction of Western.

3   Lawrence Stone asserts in his study of *The Family, Sex, and Marriage* that the word "adultery" was replaced during the Restoration by the word "gallantry" (530).

4   For additional discussion of this link, see Turner, "Priapism" (3).

5   In one of many explicit parallels between Jones and the Old Man, both first stray from the expected path in the company of a man named George, the Old Man with George Gresham, and Jones with Black George.

6   See Battestin's "Fielding's Definition of Wisdom" and his discussion of *Tom Jones* in *Henry Fielding: A Life* for the highest profile examples.

7   In *Natural Masques*, Campbell lists examples of assertions of Sophia's "spirit" on pp. 167, 559, 579, 797, and 903 of the Wesleyan edition (171).

8   See my essay "The Female Libertine" in *TransAtlantic Crossings: Sexuality & Textuality in the Eighteenth Century*.

9   The discussion of *Tom Jones* in Jill Campbell's valuable book on Fielding and gender focuses almost exclusively on locating the significance of Fielding's representation of gender difference in a political point on Jacobitism. Campbell's central thesis is essentially that "Tom and Sophia cannot be located within a single period's paradigms of ideal male and female character, but instead combine elements of paradigms from the two political cultures at issue in the Jacobite revolt" (173). It seems essential also to note that Sophia's violations of codes of femininity are just as significant to Fielding's representation of his culture and its flaws as is Jones's fragmentation of codes of cultural authority.

10 In this failure, Blifil becomes a concrete version of Fielding's definition of the hypocrite from "On the Knowledge of the Characters of Men": "Now in destroying the Reputation of a virtuous and good Man, the Hypocrite imagines he hath disarmed his Enemy of all Weapons to hurt him; and therefore this sanctified Hypocrisy is not more industrious to conceal its own Vices, than to obscure and contaminate the Virtues of others" (*Miscellanies* I 170).

11 J. Paul Hunter also notes Fielding's tendency toward moral exemptions for things like "masculine sexual license" in *Occasional Form*.

12 In "Sex and the Foundling Boy," John Valdimir Price pays particular attention to this passage and suggests that "If nothing else, the novel at this point implies that chastity is, to use a word Fielding might have chosen, unnatural – even in females" (47).

13 See Empson 237, for example.

14 Note similar speeches from Fielding's plays discussed in chapter 2, particularly that from *The Wedding Day* in which the Heartfort explains to Millamour, "My practice, perhaps, is not equal to my theory; but I pretend to sin with as little mischief as I can to others: and this I can lay my hand on my heart and affirm, that I never seduced a young woman to her own ruin, nor a married one to the misery of her husband" (V iii).

15 For an example of this critical interest in the role of class and marriage in Fielding's plot, see Ian Watt's *The Rise of the Novel* (306–8).

CHAPTER SIX

1   As Cynthia Griffin Wolff points out, "It is significant that Tom Jones's sexual transgressions would be classified as fornication, a private sin. Booth's error is the more serious offense of adultery which violates not only his private morality but the public institution of marriage" (54n).

2   For examples, see Paulson and Lockwood's *Critical Heritage* (286, 321–4, and 335).

3   I will follow what appears to be the most reasonable established convention in referring to Mrs Bennet (who becomes Mrs Atkinson) by referring to her by the name she is given by Fielding in the scene of the novel to which I refer. In this case, she is actually Mrs Atkinson, but since the wedding has not yet been revealed, the narrator still calls her Mrs Bennet; hence the hyphenation.

4   Smallwood proves that Fielding is not ignorant of this convention but invokes it intentionally, since he depicts Leonora's abandonment by her peers after her perceived fall in the interpolated tale of *Joseph Andrews*, and Sophia's conscientious departure from Mrs Fitzpatrick's lodgings after the true arrangement with the Irish Peer is made clear in *Tom Jones*.

5   For this count I include Amelia's implying to her nurse that Booth is already her husband (II vi 85); hiding from Booth Bagillard's attempts on her chastity (III ix 133); hiding from Booth Mrs Bennet's story and Mrs Ellison's character and past (VIII iv 320); giving "a little into the Deceit" to allow Booth to believe that she avoids James because of Mrs James (IX ii 362); dissembling to Booth in an extended discussion of James (IX vi 382); perpetrating the masquerade deceit and the dissembling discussion with Booth before her revelation of the plot (X iii); her dissembling response to Booth's plan to see the great man ("With this comfortable News he acquainted his Wife, who either was, or seemed to be extremely well pleased with it") (XI iv 475); hiding from Booth her near love scene with Atkinson (XI vi 490); hiding from Booth the letter she receives from Mrs Mathews and her knowledge of his inconstancy (XII ii 498); apparently creating a

"dream" as the reason she does not want Booth to see James in jail (XII ii 500); and hiding from Booth (apparently permanently) James's challenge (XII viii 530).

6 For an extensive listing of examples of the moral ambiguity of deceit, see Donald Fraser's "Lying and Concealment in *Amelia.*"

7 Booth's inability to understand his circumstances accurately and to react appropriately is discussed by Jill Campbell in *Natural Masques.*

8 In *Imagining a Self,* Patricia Meyer Spacks suggests that Booth has little conversion to undergo: "Although Booth is said to shift from the beliefs of a social nonconformist to the views that his society nominally upholds, only his state of mind really seems to alter; he has never had truly operative convictions" (281). Terry Castle argues that "the allegorical antithesis between virtue and vice has itself by now been so severely undermined … the masquerade and its ambiguous consequences have thrown entirely into question those logical dichotomies on which the notion of conversion is founded" (*Masquerade* 243). Castle's point on the undermining of the ideas of virtue and vice is somewhat analogous to my own reading, though I find the emphasis on the masquerade here (while obviously essential to her reading) somewhat overstated, since such an epistemological gap has existed from the beginning of the novel. In *Natural Masques* Campbell writes, "Battestin assumes that Booth, in embracing a real faith in Christianity at the end of this novel, turns to an old system of belief from his flirtation with a new religious skepticism and psychology of the passions; I have made the apparently more peculiar assumption that, with his conversion, Booth moves forward to a *new* social position into which his wife has already proleptically advanced" (228).

9 The importance of an individualistic determination of good or evil for Fielding is demonstrated particularly interestingly by the paragon Amelia (with an approving nod from the narrator), who perhaps unconsciously teaches her children that the good or evil of another can be determined by the way that person treats William Booth, rather than by a generalized set of criteria. Amelia tells her children that Booth "'is the best Man in the World, and therefore they [those who ruin him] hate him.' Upon which the Boy, who was extremely sensible at his Years, answered, 'Nay, Mamma, how can that be? Have not you often told me, that if I was good, every body would love me?' 'All good People will,' answered she. 'Why don't they love Papa then?' replied the Child, 'for I am sure he is very good.' 'So they do, my dear,' said the Mother, 'but there are more bad People in the World, and they will hate you for your Goodness.'"

10 Fielding's concern about adultery and the inviolable nature of marriage is summarized by Battestin in the notes to *Amelia.* Battestin notes that Fielding dedicated two leaders from *The Covent-Garden Journal* (21 and 28 Oc-

tober 1752) to the discussion of "'this atrocious *Vice*' and regretting the levity with which his own countrymen regarded it." Further, on at least one occasion, "Fielding publicly deplored the fact that, as a magistrate, he was powerless to see justice done, 'ADULTERY BEING NO CRIME BY THE LAWS OF ENGLAND' (*Covent-Garden Journal* 5 May 1752)" (*Amelia* 375n).

11 Susan Staves's "Fielding and the Comedy of Attempted Rape" offers a fascinating discussion of the difficulties of legal prosecution for rape in the eighteenth century. She points out, "that rape could occur challenged patriarchal ideology, according to which men were the protectors of women, especially good women" (105). Rapes were difficult to prosecute partly because of this social assumption that rape was implausible, and partly because a conviction required proof of penetration, testimony to which effect would blacken a woman's reputation irreparably, since a woman giving such testimony would have been accused of indecency, and thus often accused of having consented to intercourse.

12 I distinguish Mrs Mathews, obviously the third female character who creates herself through self-narrative, from Mrs Heartfree and Mrs Bennet in this discussion because of the differing circumstances of their autodiegetic exercises. Both Mrs Bennet and Mrs Heartfree tell quite traditional Pamelian tales of women in peril, defensive of their virtue, and seduced or nearly so by force or by deceit. Mrs Mathews's story is one of personal weakness and of full surrender to sensuality as she chooses to run off with Hebbers and live with him out of wedlock. All three tales are told to present the teller in the most positive possible light, but Mrs Mathews's goal is the seduction of Booth, while the others attempt to salvage their reputations and allow a return to respectability.

Bibliography

Alter, Robert. "On the Critical Dismissal of Fielding: Post-Puritanism in Literary Criticism." *Salmagundi* 1 (1966): 11-28.

– *Fielding and the Nature of the Novel*. Cambridge: Harvard University Press, 1968.

Amory, Hugh. "Magistrate or Censor? The Problem of Authority in Fielding's Later Writings." *Studies in English Literature* 12 (1972): 503–18.

Armstrong, Nancy. *Desire and Domestic Fiction: A Political History of the Novel*. New York: Oxford UP, 1987.

Baird, John D. "Criminal Elements: Fielding's *Jonathan Wild*." *Rough Justice: Essays on Crime in Literature*. Ed. M.L. Friedland. Toronto: University of Toronto Press, 1991: 76–94.

Barker-Benfield, G.J. *The Culture of Sensibility: Sex and Society in Eighteenth-Century Britain*. Chicago: University of Chicago Press, 1992.

Battestin, Martin C. "Fielding's Definition of Wisdom: Some Functions of Ambiguity and Emblem in *Tom Jones*." *ELH* 35 (1968): 188–217.

– *The Moral Basis of Fielding's Art: A Study of Joseph Andrews*. Middletown, CT: Wesleyan UP, 1959.

– "The Problem of *Amelia*: Hume, Barrow, and the Conversion of Captain Booth." *ELH* 41 (1974): 613-48.

Battestin, Martin C. with Ruthe R. Battestin. *Henry Fielding: A Life*. London: Routledge, 1989.

Bell, Ian A. *Henry Fielding: Authorship and Authority*. New York: Longman, 1994.

Bender, John. *Imagining the Penitentiary: Fiction and the Architecture of the Mind in Eighteenth-Century England*. Chicago: University of Chicago Press, 1987.

Benedict, Barbara M. *Framing Feeling: Sentiment and Style in English Prose Fiction 1745–1800*. New York: AMS Press, 1994.

Benedictine Monks of St Augustine's Abbey, Ramsgate. *The Book of Saints*. Fifth ed. London: Adam and Charles Black, 1966.

Berglund, Lisa. "The Language of Libertines: Subversive Morality in *The Man of Mode*." *Studies in English Literature 1500–1900* 30.3 (1990): 369–86.

Berland, K.J.H. "Satire and the *Via Media*: Anglican Dialogue in *Joseph Andrews*." *Satire in the 18th Century*. Ed. J.D. Browning. Garland: New York, 1983: 83–99.

Blackmore, Sir William. *Prince Arthur: An Heroick Poem*. London, 1695.

Bloch, Tuvia. "*Amelia* and Booth's Doctrine of The Passions." *Studies in English Literature* 13 (1973): 461–73.

Boucé, Paul-Gabriel. "Aspects of Sexual Tolerance and Intolerance in XVIIIth-Century England." *British Journal of Eighteenth-Century Studies* 3.3 (1980): 173–91.

– "Sex, Amours and Love in *Tom Jones*." *Studies on Voltaire and the Eighteenth Century* 228 (1984): 25–38.

– "Some Sexual Beliefs and Myths in Eighteenth-Century Britain." *Sexuality in Eighteenth-Century Britain*. Ed. Paul-Gabriel Boucé. Manchester: Manchester UP, 1982: 28–46.

Bowers, Toni O'Shaughnessy. "Sex, Lies, and Invisibility: Amatory Fiction from the Restoration to Mid-Century." *Columbia History of the British Novel*. Ed. John Richetti. New York: Columbia UP, 1994: 50–71.

Braudy, Leo. *Narrative Form in History and Fiction*. Princeton: Princeton UP, 1970.

Braverman, Richard. "Libertines and Parasites." *Restoration: Studies in English Literary Culture, 1660–1700* 11.2 (1987): 73–86.

Brissenden, R.F. *Virtue in Distress: Studies in the Novel of Sentiment from Richardson to Sade*. London: Macmillan, 1974.

Brophy, Elizabeth Bergen. *Women's Lives and the 18th-Century English Novel*. Tampa: University of South Florida Press, 1991.

Burns, Bryan. "The Story-telling in *Joseph Andrews*." *Henry Fielding: Justice Observed*. Ed. K.G. Simpson. London: Vision, 1985: 119–36.

Butler, Judith. *Gender Trouble: Feminism and the Subversion of Identity*. New York: Routledge Chapman & Hall, 1990.

Campbell, Jill. *Natural Masques: Gender and Identity in Fielding's Plays and Novels*. Stanford: Stanford UP, 1995.

Castle, Terry. "The Culture of Travesty: Sexuality and Masquerade in Eighteenth-Century England." *Sexual Underworlds of the Enlightenment*. Ed. G.S. Rousseau and Roy Porter. Chapel Hill: University of North Carolina Press, 1988: 156–80.

– *Masquerade and Civilization: The Carnivalesque in Eighteenth-Century English Culture and Fiction.* Stanford: Stanford UP, 1986.

– "Matters not Fit to be Mentioned: Fielding's *The Female Husband.*" *ELH* 49 (1982): 602–22.

Cazenobe, Colette. "Le Système du libertinage de Crébillon à Laclos." *Studies on Voltaire and the Eighteenth Century* 282. Oxford: The Voltaire Foundation, 1991.

Cecil, C.D. "Libertine and *Précieux* Elements in Restoration Comedy." *Essays in Criticism* 9 (1959): 239–53.

Charke, Charlotte. *A Narrative of the Life of Mrs Charlotte Charke* 1755. Ed. Leonard R.N. Ashley. Gainesville, FL: Scholars' Facsimiles and Reprints, 1969.

– *The Trials of Henry Dumont, Esq; and Miss Charlotte Evelyn.* London, 1756.

Cleary, Thomas R. *Henry Fielding: Political Writer.* Waterloo: Wilfrid Laurier UP, 1984.

Collins, Anthony. *A Discourse of Free-Thinking, occasioned by the Rise and Growth of a Sect call'd Free-Thinkers.* London, 1713.

Conrad, Peter. "The Libertine's Progress." *The Don Giovanni Book: Myths of Seduction and Betrayal.* Ed. Jonathan Miller. Boston: Faber and Faber, 1990: 81–92.

Cooper, Anthony Ashley, Third Earl of Shaftesbury. *Characteristicks of Men, Manners, Opinions, Times, etc.* 2 vols. Ed. John M. Robertson. Gloucester, MA: Peter Smith, 1900.

Costa, Astrid Masetti Lobo. "Up and Down Stairways: Escher, Bakhtin, and *Joseph Andrews.*" *Studies in English Literature* 31 (1991): 553–68.

Coward, David. "The Sublimations of a Fetishist: Restif de la Bretonne (1734–1806)." *'Tis Nature's Fault: Unauthorized Sexuality during the Enlightenment.* Ed. Robert Purks Maccubbin. Cambridge: Cambridge UP, 1987: 98–108.

Cross, Wilbur L. *The History of Henry Fielding.* 3 vols. New Haven: Yale University Press, 1918.

Cruise, James. "Fielding, Authority, and the New Commercialism in *Joseph Andrews.*" *ELH* 54.2 (1987): 253–76.

Digeon, A. *Les Romans de Fielding.* Paris, 1923.

Dircks, Richard J. "The Perils of Heartfree: A Sociological Review of Fielding's Adaptation of Dramatic Convention." *Texas Studies in Language and Literature* 8 (1966): 5–13.

Dobson, Austin. *Henry Fielding.* London, 1907.

Donaldson, Ian. *The World Upside-Down: Comedy from Jonson to Fielding.* Oxford: Clarendon, 1970.

Donovan, Robert Alan. "*Joseph Andrews* as Parody." *Henry Fielding: A Critical Anthology.* Ed. Claude Rawson. Harmondsworth: Penguin, 1973: 472–91.

Dudden, F.H. *Henry Fielding: His Life, Works, and Times.* 2 vols. Oxford: Clarendon, 1952.

Eaves, T.C. Duncan. "Amelia and Clarissa." *A Provision of Human Nature: Essays on Fielding and Others in Honor of Miriam Austin Locke.* Ed. Donald Kay. University: University of Alabama Press, 1977: 95–110.

Ehrenpreis, Irwin. "Fielding's Use of Fiction: The Autonomy of *Joseph Andrews.*" *Henry Fielding und der Englische Roman des 18. Jahrunderts.* Ed. Wolfgang Iser. Darmstadt: Wissenschaftliche Buchgesellschaft, 1972: 236–50.

Ellis, Markman. *The Politics of Sensibility: Race, Gender and Commerce in the Sentimental Novel.* Cambridge: Cambridge UP, 1996.

Empson, William. " *Tom Jones.*" *Kenyon Review* 20 (1958): 217–49.

Evans, David L. "The Theme of Liberty in *Jonathan Wild.*" *Papers on Language and Literature* 3 (1967): 302–13.

Evans, James E. "Fielding, *The Whole Duty of Man, Shamela* and *Joseph Andrews.*" *Philological Quarterly* 61.1 (1982): 212–19.

Farrell, William J. "The Mock-Heroic Form of *Jonathan Wild.*" *Modern Philology* 63 (1966): 216–26.

Felsenstein, Frank. "'Newgate with the Mask on': A View of *Jonathan Wild.*" *Zeitschrift fur Anglistik un Amerikanistik* 28: 3 (1980): 211–18.

"The Female Libertine: A Moral Tale." *Town and Country Magazine* 4 (June 1772): 305–9.

Fielding, Henry. *Amelia.* (1752) Ed. Martin C. Battestin. Middletown, CT: Wesleyan UP, 1983.

– "Articles in the Champion." 1739–40. *The Complete Works of Henry Fielding, Esq.* Vol. 15. Ed. William E. Henley. 1902. New York: Barnes and Noble, 1967.

– "The Coffee-House Politician." 1730. *The Complete Works of Henry Fielding, Esq.* Vol. 9. Ed. William E. Henley. 1902. New York: Barnes and Noble, 1967.

– "The Covent Garden Tragedy." 1732. *The Complete Works of Henry Fielding, Esq.* Vol. 10. Ed. William E. Henley. 1902. New York: Barnes and Noble, 1967.

– "An Enquiry into the Causes of the Late Increase of Robbers." 1751. *The Complete Works of Henry Fielding, Esq.* Vol. 13. Ed. William E. Henley. 1902. New York: Barnes and Noble, 1967.

– *The Female Husband: or, the Surprising History of Mrs Mary, Alias Mr George Hamilton.* London, 1746.

– "The Grub Street Opera." 1731. *The Complete Works of Henry Fielding, Esq.* Vol. 9. Ed. William E. Henley. 1902. New York: Barnes and Noble, 1967.

– *The History of Tom Jones: A Foundling.* 1749. Ed. Fredson Bowers. Middletown, CT: Wesleyan UP, 1975.

- *Joseph Andrews.* 1742. Ed. Martin C. Battestin. Middletown, CT: Wesleyan UP, 1967.
- Joseph Andrews *with* Shamela *and Related Writings.* Ed. Homer Goldberg. New York: Norton, 1987.
- "A Journey from this World to the Next." *Miscellanies by Henry Fielding Volume Two.* 1743. Ed. Hugh Amory and Bertrand Goldgar. Oxford: Clarendon, 1993.
- *The Life of Mr. Jonathan Wild the Great.* 1743. Ed. David Nokes. Harmondsworth: Penguin, 1982.
- "Love in Several Masques." 1728. *The Complete Works of Henry Fielding, Esq.* Vol. 8. Ed. William E. Henley. 1902. New York: Barnes and Noble, 1967.
- *Miscellanies by Henry Fielding Volume One.* 1743. Ed. Henry Knight Miller. Oxford: Clarendon, 1972.
- *Miscellanies by Henry Fielding Volume Two.* 1743. Ed. Hugh Amory and Bertrand Goldgar. Oxford: Clarendon, 1993.
- "Miss Lucy in Town; A Sequel to the Virgin Unmasked." 1742. *The Complete Works of Henry Fielding, Esq.* Vol. 12. Ed. William E. Henley. 1902. New York: Barnes and Noble, 1967.
- "The Modern Husband." 1732. *The Complete Works of Henry Fielding, Esq.* Vol. 10. Ed. William E. Henley. 1902. New York: Barnes and Noble, 1967.
- "The Old Debauchees." 1732. Ed. Connie Thorson. Los Angeles: Augustan Reprint Society, 1989.
- "An Old Man Taught Wisdom; or, The Virgin Unmasked." 1735. *The Complete Works of Henry Fielding, Esq.* Vol. 11. Ed. William E. Henley. 1902. New York: Barnes and Noble, 1967.
- "Pasquin." 1736. *The Complete Works of Henry Fielding, Esq.* Vol. 11. Ed. William E. Henley. 1902. New York: Barnes and Noble, 1967.
- "The Wedding Day." 1743. *The Complete Works of Henry Fielding, Esq.* Vol. 12. Ed. William E. Henley. 1902. New York: Barnes and Noble, 1967.
Finke, Laurie. "Aphra Behn and the Ideological Construction of Restoration Literary Theory." *Rereading Aphra Behn: History, Theory, and Criticism.* Ed. Heidi Hutner. Charlottesville: UP of Virginia, 1993: 17–43.
Folkenflik, Robert. "Tom Jones, the Gypsies, and the Masquerade." *University of Toronto Quarterly* 44.3 (1975): 224–37.
Foxon, David. *Libertine Literature in England 1660–1745.* London: Book Collector, 1964.
Frank, Judith. "Literacy, Desire, and the Novel: From *Shamela* to *Joseph Andrews.*" *Yale Journal of Criticism* 6.2 (1994): 157–74.
Fraser, Donald. "Lying and Concealment in *Amelia.*" *Henry Fielding: Justice Observed.* Ed. K.G. Simpson. London: Vision, 1985: 174–98.
Frye, Northrop. *Anatomy of Criticism.* Princeton: Princeton UP, 1957.

"The Generous Libertine: A Tale." *Town and Country Magazine* 1 (September 1769): 465–9.

Gerard, Kent and Gert Hekma, eds. *The Pursuit of Sodomy: Male Homosexuality in Renaissance and Enlightenment Europe.* New York: Harrington Park, 1989.

Golden, Morris. *Fielding's Moral Psychology.* N.p.: University of Massachusetts Press, 1966.

– "Public Context and Imagining Self in *Amelia*." *University of Toronto Quarterly* 56.3 (1987): 377–91.

– "Public Context and Imagining Self in *Joseph Andrews* and *Jonathan Wild*." *Journal of English and Germanic Philology* 88.4 (1989): 487–509.

– "Public Context and Imagining Self in *Pamela* and *Shamela*." *ELH* 53 (1986): 311–29.

Green, Julien. *God's Fool: The Life and Times of Francis of Assisi.* Trans. Peter Heinegg. San Francisco: Harper and Row, 1985.

Greenberg, David F. "The Socio-Sexual Milieu of the *Love Letters*." *Love Letters Between a Certain Late Nobleman and the Famous Mr. Wilson.* Ed. Michael S. Kimmel. London: Haworth, 1990: 93–103.

Guicciardi, Jean-Pierre. "Between the Licit and the Illicit: The Sexuality of the King." Trans. Michael Murray. *'Tis Nature's Fault: Unauthorized Sexuality during the Enlightenment.* Ed. Robert Purks Maccubbin. Cambridge: Cambridge UP, 1987: 88–97.

Guthrie, Neil. "'No truth or very little in the whole story'? A Reassessment of the Mohock Scare of 1712." *Eighteenth-Century Life* 20.2 (1996): 33–56.

Guthrie, William B. "The Comic Celebrant of Life in *Tom Jones*." *Tennessee Studies in Literature* 19 (1974): 91–105.

Hagstrum, Jean H. *Eros and Vision: The Restoration to Romanticism.* Evanston, IL: Northwestern UP, 1989.

Hammer, Stephanie Barbe. *The Sublime Crime: Fascination, Failure and Form in Literature of the Enlightenment.* Carbondale: University of Illinois Press, 1994.

Harrison, Bernard. *Henry Fielding's* Tom Jones*: The Novelist as Moral Philosopher.* London: Sussex UP, 1975.

Hassall, Anthony J. "Fielding's *Amelia*: Dramatic and Authorial Narration." *Novel* 5 (1972): 225–33.

– "Women in Richardson and Fielding." *Novel* 14 (1981): 168–74.

Hatfield, Glenn W. "The Serpent and the Dove: Fielding's Irony and the Prudence Theme of *Tom Jones*." *Modern Philology* 65 (1967): 17–32.

Hope, Quentin M. *Saint-Evremond: The Honnête Homme as Critic.* Bloomington: Indiana UP, 1962.

Hopkins, Robert H. "Language and Comic Play in Fielding's 'Jonathan Wild.'" *Criticism* 8 (1966): 213–28.

Hughes, Peter. "Wars within Doors: Erotic Heroism in Eighteenth-Century Literature." *The English Hero, 1660–1800.* Ed. Robert Folkenflik. Newark: University of Delaware Press, 1982.

Hume, Robert D. *Henry Fielding and the London Theatre 1728–1737.* Oxford: Clarendon, 1988.

– "The Myth of the Rake in 'Restoration' Comedy." *Studies in the Literary Imagination* 10 (1977): 25–55.

Hunter, J. Paul. "Fielding and the Disappearance of Heroes." *The English Hero, 1660–1800.* Ed. Robert Folkenflik. Newark: University of Delaware Press, 1982: 116–42.

– *Occasional Form: Henry Fielding and the Chains of Circumstance.* Baltimore: Johns Hopkins UP, 1975.

Hutchens, Eleanor H. "O Attic Shape! The Cornering of Square." *A Provision of Human Nature: Essays on Fielding and Others in Honor of Miriam Austin Locke.* Ed. Donald Kay. University: University of Alabama Press, 1977: 37–44.

Irwin, Michael. *Henry Fielding: The Tentative Realist.* Oxford: Clarendon, 1967.

Ivker, Barry. "Towards a Definition of Libertinism in 18th-Century French Fiction." *Studies on Voltaire and the Eighteenth Century* 73 (1970): 221–40.

Johnson, James William. "England, 1660–1800: An Age without a Hero?" *The English Hero, 1660–1800.* Ed. Robert Folkenflik. Newark: University of Delaware Press, 1982.

Jordan, Robert. "The Extravagant Rake in Restoration Comedy." *Restoration Literature: Critical Approaches.* Ed. Harold Love. London: Methuen, 1972: 69–90.

Keightley, T. "On the Life and Writings of Henry Fielding." *Fraser's Magazine* 57 (June 1858).

Kelly, Hugh. *The Babler.* XII (30 April 1766).

– *The Babler.* XLII (3 December 1767).

Kemp, Betty. *Sir Francis Dashwood: An Eighteenth-Century Independent.* London: Macmillan, 1967.

Kimmel, Michael S. "'Greedy Kisses' and 'Melting Extasy': Notes on the Homosexual World of Early Eighteenth-Century England as Found in the *Love Letters Between a Certain Late Nobleman and the Famous Mr. Wilson.*" *Love Letters Between a Certain Late Nobleman and the Famous Mr. Wilson.* Ed. Michael S. Kimmel. London: Haworth, 1990: 1–9.

Kinkead-Weekes, M. "Out of the Thicket in *Tom Jones.*" *British Journal of Eighteenth-Century Studies* 3.1 (1980): 1–19.

Knight, Charles A. "*Joseph Andrews* and the Failure of Authority." *Eighteenth-Century Fiction* 4.2 (1992): 109–24.

Kropf, Carl R. "A Certain Absence: *Joseph Andrews* as Affirmation of Heterosexuality." *Studies in the Novel* 20.1 (1988): 16–26.

Lamb, Jonathan. "Exemplarity and Excess in Fielding's Fiction." *Eighteenth-Century Fiction* 1.3 (1989): 187–207.

Lewis, Peter. *Fielding's Burlesque Drama: Its Place in the Tradition*. Edinburgh: Edinburgh UP, 1987.

London, April. "Controlling the Text: Women in *Tom Jones*." *Studies in the Novel* 19.3 (1987): 323–33.

Longmire, Samuel E. "*Amelia* as a Comic Action." *Tennessee Studies in Literature* 17 (1972): 69–79.

Lynch, James J. "Moral Sense and the Narrator of *Tom Jones*." *Studies in English Literature* 25 (1985): 599–614.

Mack, Edward C. "Pamela's Stepdaughters: The Heroines of Smollett and Fielding." *Henry Fielding und der Englische Roman des 18. Jahrunderts*. Ed. Wolfgang Iser. Darmstadt: Wissenschaftliche Buchgesellschaft, 1972: 348–60.

Madelin, Hervé. "Henry Fielding and Jacques Esprit." *REAL* 1 (1982): 27–74.

"The Married Libertine: A Moral Tale." *Town and Country Magazine* 10 (August 1778): 409–13.

Mayo, Thomas Franklin. *Epicurus in England, 1650–1725*. Dallas: Southwest Press, 1934.

McCrea, Brian. *Henry Fielding and the Politics of Mid-Eighteenth Century England*. Athens: University of Georgia Press, 1981.

– "Rewriting *Pamela*: Social Change and Religious Faith in *Joseph Andrews*." *Studies in the Novel* 16.2 (1984): 137–49.

McKenzie, Alan T. "The Physiology of Deceit in Fielding's Works." *Dalhousie Review* 62.1 (1982): 140–52.

McKeon, Michael. *The Origins of the English Novel 1600–1740*. Baltimore: Johns Hopkins UP, 1987.

Merrett, Robert. "The Principles of Fielding's Legal Satire and Social Reform." *Dalhousie Review* 62.2 (1982): 238–53.

Miller, Henry K. "Some Relationships between Humor and Religion in Eighteenth-Century Britain." *Thalia: Studies in Literary Humor* 6.1 (1983): 48–59.

Miller, Jane. "The Seductions of Women." *The Don Giovanni Book: Myths of Seduction and Betrayal*. Ed. Jonathan Miller. Boston: Faber and Faber, 1990: 48–61.

Moore, Robert Etheridge. *Hogarth's Literary Relationships*. Minneapolis: University of Minnesota Press, 1948.

Montagu, Lady Mary Wortley. *The Complete Letters of Lady Mary Wortley Montagu*. 3 Vols. Ed. Robert Halsband. Oxford: Oxford UP, 1966.

Mulford, Carla. "Booth's Progress and the Resolution of *Amelia*." *Studies in the Novel* 16.1 (1984): 20–31.

Murphy, Arthur. *The Works of Henry Fielding, Esq; With the Life of the Author*. London, 1762.

Neill, Michael. "Heroic Heads and Humble Tails: Sex, Politics, and the Restoration Comic Rake." *The Eighteenth Century: Theory and Interpretation* 24.2 (1983): 115–39.

Nickel, Terri. "Pamela as Fetish: Masculine Anxiety in Henry Fielding's *Shamela* and James Parry's *The True Anti-Pamela.*" *Studies in Eighteenth-Century Culture* 22 (1992): 37–49.

Nigg, Walter. *Francis of Assisi*. Trans. William Neil. London: Mowbrays, 1975.

Novak, Maximillian E. "Congreve as the Eighteenth-Century's Archetypal Libertine." *Restoration and Eighteenth-Century Theatre Research* 15.2 (1976): 35–39, 60.

– "Freedom, Libertinism, and the Picaresque." *Studies in Eighteenth-Century Culture* 3 (1973): 35–48.

– "Margery Pinchwife's 'London Disease': Restoration Comedy and the Libertine Offensive of the 1670's." *Studies in the Literary Imagination* 10 (1977): 1–23.

– *William Congreve*. New York: Twayne, 1971.

Orange, Michael. "Prudes, Lusciousness and *Joseph Andrews.*" *Sydney Studies in English* 17 (1991–2): 46–66.

Paulson, Ronald. *Satire and the Novel in Eighteenth-Century England*. New Haven: Yale UP, 1967.

Paulson, Ronald and Thomas Lockwood. *Henry Fielding: The Critical Heritage*. London: Routledge and Kegan Paul, 1969.

Pettit, Alexander. "What the Drama Does in Fielding's *Jonathan Wild.*" *Eighteenth-Century Fiction* 6: 2 (1994): 153–68.

Porter, Roy. "Libertinism and Promiscuity." *The Don Giovanni Book: Myths of Seduction and Betrayal*. Ed. Jonathan Miller. Boston: Faber and Faber, 1990: 1–19.

– "Mixed Feelings: The Enlightenment and Sexuality in Eighteenth-Century Britain." *Sexuality in Eighteenth-Century Britain*. Ed. Paul-Gabriel Boucé. Manchester: Manchester UP, 1982: 1–27.

– "A Touch of Danger: The Man-Midwife as Sexual Predator." *Sexual Underworlds of the Enlightenment*. Ed. G.S. Rousseau and Roy Porter. Chapel Hill: University of North Carolina Press, 1988: 206–32.

Potter, Tiffany. "The Female Libertine." *TransAtlantic Crossings: Sexuality & Textuality in the Eighteenth Century*. Ed. Don Nichol. St. John's: Memorial UP, 1998: 75-88.

– "Honest Sins: Henry Fielding's *The Old Debauchees* as Libertine Moralist Drama." *Text and Presentation* 14 (1994): 75–80.

Price, John Valdimir. "Patterns of Sexual Behaviour in Some Eighteenth-Century Novels." *Sexuality in Eighteenth-Century Britain*. Ed. Paul-Gabriel Boucé. Manchester: Manchester UP, 1982: 159–75.

– "Sex and the Foundling Boy: The Problem in *Tom Jones.*" *Review of English Literature* 8.4 (1967): 42–52.

The Rake of Taste, or The Elegant Debauchee: A True Story. London, 1760.

Rawson, C.J. "Fielding's 'Good' Merchant: The Problem of Heartfree in *Jonathan Wild* (with Comments on Other 'Good' Characters in Fielding)." *Modern Philology* 69 (1972): 292–313.

– *Henry Fielding.* London: Routledge and Kegan Paul, 1968.

– "The Hero as Clown: Jonathan Wild, Felix Krull and Others." *Studies in the Eighteenth Century 2.* Ed. R.F. Brissenden. Toronto: University of Toronto Press, 1973: 17–52.

– *Order from Confusion Sprung: Studies in Eighteenth-Century Literature from Swift to Cowper.* London: George Allen & Unwin, 1985.

– *Satire and Sentiment 1660–1830.* Cambridge: Cambridge UP, 1994.

Rhodes, Neil. "The Innocence of *Joseph Andrews.*" *Henry Fielding: Justice Observed.* Ed. K.G. Simpson. London: Vision, 1985: 101–18.

Richardson, Samuel. *Pamela; or, Virtue Rewarded.* 1740. Ed. Peter Sabor. Harmondsworth: Penguin, 1980.

Richmond, Hugh M. *Puritans and Libertines: Anglo-French Literary Relations in the Reformation.* Berkeley: University of California Press, 1981.

Rivero, Albert J. *The Plays of Henry Fielding: A Critical Study of His Dramatic Career.* Charlottesville: UP of Virginia, 1989.

Rogers, Katharine M. *Feminism in Eighteenth-Century England.* Chicago: University of Illinois Press, 1982.

– "Sensitive Feminism vs. Conventional Sympathy: Richardson and Fielding on Women." *Novel* 9 (1976): 256–70.

Rogers, Pat. *Henry Fielding: A Biography.* New York: Scribner's, 1979.

Rothstein, Eric. "The Framework of *Shamela.*" *ELH* 35 (1968): 381–402.

Rousseau, G.S. "An Introduction to the *Love Letters*: Circumstances of Publication, Context, and Cultural Commentary." *Love Letters Between a Certain Late Nobleman and the Famous Mr. Wilson.* Ed. Michael S. Kimmel. London: Haworth, 1990: 47–91.

Ruml, Treadwell, II. "*Jonathan Wild* and the Epistemological Gulf Between Virtue and Vice." *Studies in the Novel* 21: 2 (1989): 117–27.

– "*Joseph Andrews* as Exemplary Gentleman." *Studies in Eighteenth-Century Culture* 22 (1992): 195–207.

Sabor, Peter. "Joseph Andrews and Pamela." *British Journal for Eighteenth-Century Studies* 1 (1978): 169–81.

Saint-Evremond, Seigneur de. *Miscellanea: or Various Discourses ... Together With Epicurus his Morals.* Trans. Ferrand Spence. London: Samuel Holford, 1686.

St. John, Henry, Viscount Bolingbroke. *Philosophical Works.* London, 1754.

Scheuermann, Mona. *Her Bread to Earn: Women, Money, and Society from Defoe to Austen.* Lexington: UP of Kentucky, 1993.

– "Man Not Providence: Fielding's *Amelia* as a Novel of Social Criticism." *Forum for Modern Language Studies* 20.2 (1984): 106–23.

– *Social Protest in the Eighteenth-Century English Novel.* Columbus: Ohio State UP, 1985.

Schneider, Aaron. "Hearts and Minds in *Joseph Andrews*: Parson Adams and a War of Ideas." *Philological Quarterly* 66.3 (1987): 367–89.

Schofield, Mary Anne. "Exploring the Woman Question: A Reading of Henry Fielding's *Amelia.*" *Ariel* 16.1 (1985): 45–57.

Sedgwick, Eve Kosofsky. *Between Men: English Literature and Male Homosocial Desire.* New York: Columbia UP, 1985.

Sherbo, Arthur. *Studies in the Eighteenth-Century English Novel.* East Lansing: Michigan State UP, 1969.

Sherburn, George. "Fielding's *Amelia*: An Interpretation." *Fielding: A Collection of Critical Essays.* Ed. Ronald Paulson. Englewood Cliffs NJ: Prentice-Hall, 1962: 146–57.

Sheriff, John K. *The Good-Natured Man: The Evolution of a Moral Ideal, 1660–1800.* University: University of Alabama Press, 1982.

Smallwood, Angela J. *Fielding and the Woman Question.* Hemel Hempstead: Harvester Wheatsheaf, 1989.

Snider, Alvin. "Professing a Libertine in *The Way of the World.*" *Papers on Language and Literature* 25.4 (1989): 376–97.

Spacks, Patricia Meyer. *Desire and Truth: Functions of Plot in Eighteenth-Century English Novels.* Chicago: University of Chicago Press, 1990.

– "Female Changelessness; or, What do Women Want?" *Studies in the Novel* 19.3 (1987): 273–83.

– *Imagining a Self: Autobiography and Novel in Eighteenth-Century England.* Cambridge: Harvard UP, 1976.

– "Some Reflections on Satire." *Genre* 1 (1968): 13–30.

Spilka, Mark. "Comic Resolution in Fielding's *Joseph Andrews.*" *Fielding: A Collection of Critical Essays.* Ed. Ronald Paulson. Englewood Cliffs NJ: Prentice-Hall, 1962: 59–68.

Stanhope, Philip Dormer, Fourth Earl of Chesterfield. *The Letters of the Earl of Chesterfield to his Son.* 2 vols. Ed. Charles Strechey. London: Methuen, 1901.

Statt, Daniel. "The Case of the Mohocks: Rake Violence in Augustan London." *Social History* 20 (1995): 179–99.

Staves, Susan. "Fielding and the Comedy of Attempted Rape." *History, Gender, and Eighteenth-Century Literature.* Ed. Beth Fowkes Tobin. Athens: University of Georgia Press, 1994: 86–112.

Stephanson, Raymond. "The Education of the Reader in Fielding's *Joseph Andrews.*" *Philological Quarterly* 61.3 (1982): 243–58.

– "'Silenc'd by Authority' in *Joseph Andrews*: Power, Submission, and Mutuality in 'The History of Two Friends.'" *Studies in the Novel* 24.2 (1992): 1–12.

Stone, Lawrence. *The Family, Sex and Marriage In England 1500-1800.* London: Weidenfeld and Nicolson, 1977.

Stratmann, Gerd. "Undermining Public Opinion. The Function of Narrative in Fielding's *Tom Jones.*" *Telling Stories: Studies in Honour of Ulrich Broich on the Occasion of his 60th Birthday.* Ed. Elmar Lehmann and Bernd Lenz. Amsterdam: John Benjamins, 1992: 84–96.

Straub, Kristina. *Sexual Suspects: Eighteenth-Century Players and Sexual Ideology.* Princeton: Princeton UP, 1992.

Taylor, Dick, Jr. "Joseph as Hero in *Joseph Andrews.*" *Tulane Studies in English* 7 (1957): 91–109.

Thomas, Donald. *Henry Fielding: A Life.* New York: St. Martin's, 1990.

Todd, Janet. *Sensibility: An Introduction.* London and New York: Methuen, 1986.

Traugott, John. "Heart and Mask and Genre in Sentimental Comedy." *Eighteenth-Century Life* 10.3 (1986): 122–44.

– "The Rake's Progress from Court to Comedy: A Study in Comic Form." *Studies in English Literature* 6 (1966): 381–407.

Trumbach, Randolph. "Erotic Fantasy and Male Libertinism in Enlightenment England." *The Invention of Pornography: Obscenity and the Origins of Modernity, 1500–1800.* Ed. Lynn Hunt. New York: Zone, 1993: 253–82.

– "Modern Prostitution and Gender in *Fanny Hill*: Libertine and Domesticated Fantasy." *Sexual Underworlds of the Enlightenment.* Ed. G.S. Rousseau and Roy Porter. Chapel Hill: University of North Carolina Press, 1988: 69–85.

– "Sodomy Transformed: Aristocratic Libertinage, Public Reputation and the Gender Revolution of the Eighteenth Century." *Love Letters Between a Certain Late Nobleman and the Famous Mr. Wilson.* Ed. Michael S. Kimmel. London: Haworth, 1990: 105–24.

Turner, James Grantham. "The Culture of Priapism." *Review* 10 (1988): 1–34.

– "'Illustrious Depravity' and the Erotic Sublime." *The Age of Johnson* 2 (1989): 1–38.

– "The Libertine Sublime: Love and Death in Restoration England." *Studies in Eighteenth-Century Culture* 19 (1989): 99–115.

– "Lovelace and the Paradoxes of Libertinism." *Samuel Richardson: Tercentenary Essays.* Ed. Margaret Anne Doody and Peter Sabor. Cambridge: Cambridge UP, 1989: 70–88.

– "Pope's Libertine Self-Fashioning." *The Eighteenth Century: Theory and Interpretation* 29.2 (1988): 123–44.

– "Properties of Libertinism." *Eighteenth-Century Life* 9.3 (May 1985): 75–87.

– "Sex and Consequence." *Review* 11 (1989): 133–77.

Underwood, Dale. *Etherege and the Seventeenth-Century Comedy of Manners.* Cambridge: Yale UP, 1957.

Wagner, Peter. *Eros Revived: Erotica of the Enlightenment in England and America.* London: Secker and Warburg, 1988.

Wanko, Cheryl. "Characterization and the Reader's Quandary in Fielding's *Amelia*." *Journal of English and Germanic Philology* 90.4 (1991): 505–23.

Ward, Ned. *A Compleat and Humorous Account of all the Remarkable Clubs and Societies in the Cities of London and Westminster.* Sixth edition. London: M. Cooper, 1746.

Watt, Ian. *The Rise of the Novel: Studies in Defoe, Richardson and Fielding.* Harmondsworth: Penguin, 1957.

Weber, Harold. "The Rake-Hero in Wycherley and Congreve." *Philological Quarterly* 61.2 (1982): 143–60.

– "Rakes, Rogues, and the Empire of Misrule." *Huntington Library Quarterly* 47.1 (1984): 13–32.

– *The Restoration Rake-Hero: Transformations in Sexual Understanding in Seventeenth-Century England.* Madison: University of Wisconsin Press, 1986.

Weinbrot, Howard D. "Chastity and Interpolation: Two Aspects of *Joseph Andrews*." *Journal of English and Germanic Philology* 69 (1970): 14–31.

Weinstein, Arnold. *Fictions of the Self: 1550–1800.* Princeton: Princeton UP, 1981.

Wendt, Allan. "The Moral Allegory of *Jonathan Wild*." *ELH* 24 (1957): 306–20.

– "The Naked Virtue of Amelia." *ELH* 27 (1960): 131–48.

West, Shearer. "Libertinism and the Ideology of Male Friendship in the Portraits of the Society of Dilettanti." *Eighteenth-Century Life* 16 (1992): 76–104.

Williams, Carolyn D. "Fielding and Half-Learned Ladies." *Essays in Criticism* 38 (1988): 22–34.

Williams, Murial Brittain. *Marriage: Fielding's Mirror of Morality.* University: University of Alabama Press, 1973.

Wilner, Arlene Fish. "Henry Fielding and the Knowledge of Character." *Modern Language Studies* 18.1 (1988): 181–94.

Wilputte, Earla A. "Ambiguous Language and Ambiguous Gender: The 'Bisexual' Text of *Shamela*." *Modern Language Review* 89 (1994): 561–71.

– "The Autodiegetic Power of Mrs Heartfree in Henry Fielding's *Jonathan Wild*: The Moderately Good Wife." *Durham University Journal* 53:2 (1992): 229–34.

– "'A Friendly Conspiracy': Sexual Power-Plays in Fielding's Early Comedies." *Wascana Review* 24.2 (1989): 17–32.

Wintle, Sarah. "Libertinism and Sexual Politics." *Spirit of Wit.* Ed. Jeremy Treglown. Oxford: Basil Blackwell, 1982: 133–65.

Wolfe, George H. "Lessons in Evil: Fielding's Ethics in *The Champion* Essays." *A Provision of Human Nature: Essays on Fielding and Others in Honor of Miriam Austin Locke.* Ed. Donald Kay. University: University of Alabama Press, 1977: 65–82.

Wolff, Cynthia Griffin. "Fielding's *Amelia*: Private Virtue and Public Good." *Texas Studies in Literature and Language* 10 (1968): 37–55.

Wright, Andrew. *Henry Fielding: Mask and Feast.* London: Chatto & Windus, 1965.

Wycherley, William. *The Country Wife.* Ed. Gamini Salgado. Harmondsworth: Penguin, 1968.

Index

adultery, 66, 69–70, 78–9, 91, 135–6, 156–8, 167, 185n10

Amelia, 64, 145–68, 171; Sergeant Atkinson, 159–60; Mrs Bennet-Atkinson, 162, 164–6, 168; Amelia Booth, *see* Booth, Amelia; William Booth, *see* Booth, William; change of cultural context in, 146–7; doctrine of the passions in, 150, 152; Dr Harrison, 150, 166–7; honour in, 148–50; Colonel James, 147, 148–9, 151–4, 168; Noble Peer, 64, 154, 155–6, 162; religion, investigation of, 149–51; sexuality in, 151–8, 159–60; Captain Trent, 154, 155–6

Andrews, Joseph (in *Joseph Andrews*), 88–9, 97–100, 112; on authority, 99; on religion, 98; sexuality of, 97

anti-vice societies, 19–20

Armstrong, Nancy, 25

atheism, 12, 16, 70

Barker-Benfield, G.J., 8–9, 23

Battestin, Martin, 31, 45, 52–3, 136–7, 149

Behn, Aphra, 24

Bell, Ian, 82

Bentham, Jeremy, 17

Berglund, Lisa, 28–9

Blackmore, Sir Richard, 15

Booth, Amelia (in *Amelia*), 152–3, 156–60, 168; on honour vs religion, 149; use of libertine devices, 147–8, 158–9, 162–4; as paragon, 164; sexuality of, 158–60

Booth, William (in *Amelia*), 146, 149–51, 156–8, 168, 185n8; compared to Tom Jones, 156–7

Bowers, Toni O'Shaughnessy, 24

Braverman, Richard, 26–7

Brissenden, R.F., 8

Butler, Judith, 20–2, 38–9

Campbell, Jill, 164, 183n9, 185n8

Castle, Terry, 27, 160–1, 185n8

The Champion: essays in, 76, 77, 87, 152, 161, 179n2, 180n5

Charke, Charlotte, 58, 178n7

Chesterfield, Philip Dormer Stanhope, Lord, 12–13

The Coffee-House Politician, 83

Cooke, Thomas, 62, 177n2

The Covent Garden Tragedy, 34, 43, 45–7, 50–1, 55–7, 59–60, 102

criminal conversation, 66, 91, 109–10, 155–6

Dashwood, Sir Francis, 16, 30

disguise, 27–9, 41–3, 105–6, 145–6, 161–2. *See also* masquerade

Epicurianism, 12–13, 141, 174n4

The Fathers; or The Good Natured Man, 40

female characters, 5; in novels, 78–82, 92–7, 114–18, 124–5, 130–5, 155–6, 158–60, 162–6; in plays, 39–41, 50–1, 53–9, 65–6, 68–70. *See also individual works by title*; women

The Female Husband, 178n7
"The Female Libertine," 8, 176n14
female libertines, 8, 23–5, 95–6, 125, 166, 176n14;
femininity, constructioned nature of, 25, 38–9, 42, 53–5, 69, 95–6, 114–15, 131–2, 164
Fielding, Henry, 14, 31–172 *passim*; life of, 3–4, 31; contemporary comments on, 44–5, 59, 62, 83, 119–20, 130, 146–7; on didacticism in literature, 35–6, 55, 120–1, 142; and libertinism, 4–5, 169 and *passim*; moral flexibility of 35, 45, 167; on religion, 14, 31–2, 35, 150; on virtue, 75–7, 84, 119, 153, 164. *See also individual works by title*: novels, *Amelia, Jonathan Wild, Joseph Andrews, Shamela, Tom Jones*; plays, *The Coffee-House Politician, The Covent Garden Tragedy, The Fathers, Love in Several Masques, The Modern Husband, The Old Debauchees, Pasquin, The Virgin Unmasked, The Wedding Day*; other works, *The Champion, The Female Husband*, "Of Good Nature," "To John Hayes, Esq," *A Journey from this World to the Next*, "On the Knowledge of the Characters of Men"
Finke, Laurie, 24
Free-thinking, 16–17, 175n7

gender, 20–2, 38–9, 114–15
"The Generous Libertine," 9–10
Georgian libertinism, 3–31 *passim*, 170; brief definition 11; evolution in Fielding's work, 71, 170–1; and good nature, 9, 14, 142, 170; history of, 5, 7–31; morality in, 43–4, 54, 140, 155, 158–9; and "reformations," 68, 71–3, 141–2. *See also* libertinism; Restoration libertinism
Golden, Morris, 122–3
good nature: Fielding on, 14, 32–3, 87, 104, 124, 151–2, 170; and libertinism, 9, 14, 142, 170; in plays, 40, 51–2, 64, 71–2; in novels, 86–8, 104, 113–14, 122, 124, 146–7, 151–2, 154, 156, 182n9
Great Mogul, the, 64–5, 142
The Grub-street Journal, 43, 57, 59, 61, 62

homosexuality, 20, 178n7
honour, 148–50; religion, 137, 149
Hume, David, 16, 32
Hume, Robert, 6–7, 35, 71

Johnson, Samuel, 3

Jonathan Wild, 101–18, 170; irony in, 102–3; Mr Heartfree, 112–14; Mrs Heartfree, 113, 114–18, 166; liberty in, 106; as precursor to major works, 118; Jonathan Wild, 103–12, 127
Jones, Tom (in *Tom Jones*), 9, 112, 135–43, 148, 154, 156–7; as Epicure, 141; good nature of, 72; libertine sexuality of, 125–6, 138–40; "reformation" of, 141–2; on religion vs honour, 137
Jordan, Robert, 6
Joseph Andrews, 34, 83–100, 137, 170; Abraham Adams, 86–90; Joseph Andrews, *see* Andrews, Joseph; Lady Booby, 94–7; libertinism in, 83–4, and 83–100 *passim*; religion, investigation of, 88, 98–9; virtue in, *see* virtue; Mr Wilson, 90–2
A Journey from this World to the Next, 31, 35–6

Kelly, Hugh, 18–19
"On the Knowledge of the Characters of Men," 14, 33, 86, 124, 145, 183n10

libertinism, *passim*; brief definition 10–11; class and, 14–15; female, *see* female libertines; Free-thinking and, 16–17, 175n7; gender and, 20–2; homosexuality and, 20–1; language and, 28–9, 56–7, 81, 106–8, 162–4; marriage and, 60–2, 78–9, 91, 157–8, 167–8; naturalism and, *see* naturalism; paradoxical nature of, 14–15, 21–2, 28, 161; privilege and, *see* privilege; religion and, *see* religion; sexuality and, *see* sexuality; taxonomic definitions, 6–7, 173n2; women and, *see* women. *See also* Georgian libertinism; Restoration libertinism
Love in Several Masques, 34, 36–43; representation of women in, 37–41

McCrea, Brian, 87, 89
Mandeville, Bernard, 32, 91
Manley, Delariviere, 24
marriage: and libertinism, 60–1, 66–7, 156–8, 179n11; in novels, 78–9, 91, 97–8, 155–8, 167–8; in plays, 60–1, 66–7, 69–70
"The Married Libertine," 157, 179n11
masculinity, constructions of, 38–9, 122–3
masquerade, 27–8, 125–6, 145–6, 160–4. *See also* disguise
masturbation, 46, 140, 177n3
Mazarin, Hortense Mancini, Duchess of, 131

Medmenham Monks, 16
Miller, Jane, 25–6
Miss Lucy in Town, 83
The Modern Husband, 34, 42, 60–7, 145; and *Amelia*, 60, 179n9
Mohocks, 16, 174n6
Montagu, Lady Mary Wortley, 23, 38
morals-of-the-story, 45–6, 47–8, 50–1, 71, 121–2

naturalism: and libertinism, 16, 17, 29–30; in novels, 93–4, 128, 138–9, 153; in plays, 48, 49–50, 56, 64–5

"Of Good Nature," 32–3
"On the Knowedge of the Characters of Men," 14, 33, 86, 124, 145, 183n10
The Old Debauchees, 31, 34, 43–5, 48–52, 53–5; religion in, 43, 48–50, 53

Pasquin, 34, 43, 47–8, 52–3, 57–9
Porter, Roy, 16, 17
Price, John Valdimir, 26
privilege: Fielding's sense of, 45–6, 51, 57–60, 63–5, 68, 75, 102, 120–2; and libertinism, 14–15, 24–5, 110–11; and narrators, 84–6, 167–8; in novels, 84–6, 99, 102, 110–11, 120–22, 167–8; in plays, 57–9, 63–5

"The Rake of Taste, or The Elegant Debauchee," 13–14
rape, 88, 108, 155–6, 162, 186n11
Rawson, Claude, 75, 81
Reichler, Claude, 104–5
religion: Fielding on, 14, 35, 150; libertinism and, 15–17; in novels, 70, 75, 77–8, 82, 88–9, 98–9, 149–51; in plays, 43, 48–50, 52–3
Restoration libertinism: compared to Georgian, 5, 7, 10–11, 13, 16, 17, 18, 20; in novels, 90, 103–4, 124, 126–8, 129, 151–4; in plays, 46, 51, 65–6
Richardson, Samuel, 74–5, 130; *Pamela*, 8, 74; *Clarissa*, 26, 146
Rochester, John Wilmot, Earl of, 46, 86, 141
Rogers, Pat, 35

Sabor, Peter, 165
Saint-Evremond, Seigneur de, 11–12, 131
Schofield, Mary Anne, 158
Sedgwick, Eve Kosofsky, 176n13. *See also* women, homosocial exchange of
sentimentalism, 5, 8, 32; libertinism and, 8–10, 122–3, 174n3; women and, 9; sexuality and, 23

sexuality: female, 22–3, 132, 134–5; gender and, *see* gender; homosexuality, 20–1; libertinism and, 17–20, 22–3, 80, 140, 160
Shaftesbury, Anthony Ashley Cooper, Earl of, 17, 32, 91
Shamela, 74–82, 170; Shamela as victim, 78–80; Shamela as libertine, 80–2, 137; Parson Williams, 75, 77–9
Smallwood, Angela, 92
Spacks, Patricia Meyer, 185n8
Stone, Lawrence, 30
Straub, Kristina, 177n1, 178n6

"To John Hayes, Esq," 3
Tom Jones, 9, 32, 119–44, 145, 170; accusation of irreligion, 120; Allworthy, 136–7; Blifil, 136; Lady Bellaston, 124–6, 161; didacticism in, 120–1, 142; Tom Jones, *see* Jones, Tom; Nightingale, 128–30, 140, 143; Old Man of the Hill, 126–7; prudence in, 121–3, 136–8; Square, 127–8, 143; Mr Waters, 139–40, 143; Sophia Western, *see* Western, Sophia; Squire Western, 123–4
Town and Country Magazine, 8, 9–10, 157, 176n14, 179n11
Trumbach, Randolph, 20
Turner, James Grantham, 5, 7, 14–15, 22, 80

Underwood, Dale, 6, 29–30

The Virgin Unmasked, 83
virtue, 31–2, 55–6, 74, 75–7, 120–1, 153, 164; Fielding's redefinition of, 75–7, 84, 119; as posture, 31, 74, 79–81, 113–14, 115–16, 139–40; vice and, 3–4, 32, 35–6, 128, 185n8; as virginity, 37–8, 74, 76, 78, 92–3, 97, 134

Ward, Edward (Ned), 15
Weber, Harold, 6, 28
The Wedding Day, 34, 67–73, 184n14
Western, Sophia (in *Tom Jones*), 130–5, 141; artifice of, 131–4; sexuality of, 132, 134–5; worldly knowledge of, 132–3, 135
Wilkes, John, 16, 30
Wilputte, Earla, 115, 118
women: autodiegetic representations of, 81–2, 115–18, 165–6; homosocial exchange of, 37–8, 40, 68–9, 109, 155–6, 160, 176n13; and libertinism, 22–7, 54–5. *See also*: female characters; femininity; Sedgwick, Eve Kosofsky; sentimentalism; sexuality; virtue